PLAY
THE
SCENE

Also by Michael Schulman and Eva Mekler

Great Scenes and Monologues for Actors

PLAY THE SCENE

SCENE

The Ultimate Collection of Contemporary
and Classic Scenes and Monologues

Michael Schulman
and
Eva Mekler

 **ST. MARTIN'S GRIFFIN**  **NEW YORK**

PLAY THE SCENE. Copyright © 2004 by Michael Schulman and Eva Mekler. All rights reserved. Printed in the United States of America. For information, address St. Martin's Press, 175 Fifth Avenue, New York, N.Y. 10010.

www.stmartins.com

Design by Phil Mazzone

Library of Congress Cataloging-in-Publication Data

Play the scene : the ultimate collection of contemporary and classic scenes and monologues / [compiled by] Michael Schulman and Eva Mekler.— 1st ed.
    p. cm.
  ISBN 0-312-31879-0
  EAN 978-0312-31879-6
  1. Acting. 2. American drama—20th century. 3. English drama—20th century. 4. Monologues. I. Schulman, Michael, 1941– II. Mekler, Eva.

PN2080.P59 2004
812'.508—dc22

2004050859

10 9 8 7 6 5 4

Contents

Scenes for Two Women

Scenes for Two Men

Monologues for Women

MONOLOGUES FOR MEN

Acknowledgments

Thanks to Al Zuckerman.
   And love to all the actors who will tap into their hearts and souls
to bring the characters in these scenes to life.

Introduction:
On Audition Readings

BY MICHAEL SCHULMAN

In many auditions, the director or casting director will give you a scene or monologue from a script (called a "side") and ask you to present it. Sometimes you'll have a few days to prepare (and then you might be given the whole script to read); sometimes you'll have only a few minutes. Customarily, you are not expected to memorize the lines but to make your presentation reading from the script.

At your audition the director will be looking for three things: 1) Can you act? 2) Do you fulfill his vision of the role? 3) Are you someone he wants to work with? Obviously, no director ever gave someone a part simply because the person knew how to read. Some teachers instruct actors to just "read simply" and "stay relaxed." This is not good advice. If you were a director, would you give someone a part because they could read simply and stay relaxed? Not likely.

Some actors have a knack for such "cold" readings. By intuition or craft, they quickly imagine themselves into the part and their actor's juices start to flow—even though they barely know what comes next and have to keep turning the pages of the script as they go along. Other actors find the process daunting. Indeed, some very good actors are very bad at cold readings. These actors do fine when they have time to construct a role and uncover their character's relationships to the other characters in the play. Cold readings don't give you that time.

So the key to cold readings is in engaging your craft and making your choices quickly. But first let's talk about attitude and style.

ATTITUDE AND STYLE

Whether you are auditioning for a movie, a Broadway show, or a showcase in a cellar, there is a lot at stake for the director. *You're only as good as your last show* is an old theater truism. Every director feels her career is riding on the results of the current production. After a flop it's hard to get work, so directors want to cast people who are not only good actors, but who they believe they can count on—people who handle themselves *professionally*. Actors who are not poised, who seem confused or embarrassed, who are fawning or apologize too much, who are condescending as if they are doing a director a favor by auditioning for her meager production, or who seem angry about the whole "stupid" audition process do not inspire confidence. Whether the production costs a few hundred dollars or many millions of dollars, the people who are putting it together want it to be a success. You may believe they don't have a shred of talent, but never doubt the sincerity of their hopes.

You need to treat them with respect and come across to them as someone who respects yourself and your talent. If you are not sure about something in the script, don't be afraid to ask. The director wants you to be good. She is going through this audition process in the hopes of finding actors who can make her look good. On occasions in which you find the director (or stage manager or anyone else running the audition) less than respectful to you—she is inattentive, or rushes you, or dismisses your question—take it as a sign that she doesn't really know what she's doing or has little confidence in her ability. Still, I advise that you stay in control and stay polite. Just do the best you can, or if you decide you don't want to go through with the audition, it is better to say something like "I don't think this is for me" than to tell the director what you really think of her. The director may be an ass, but you need to take care of your reputation as a professional.

When you begin your audition, it will take you a moment to get focused and feel your way into the character. Inexperienced actors frequently worry that they are taking too much time. My advice is to take the time a star would take. In other words, if you know what you need to do to get yourself into the role, take the time to do it—and feel free to tell the director, "I need a moment." On the other hand, don't just stall in the hopes that something will stir in you. It will be obvious that you are floundering. And don't use your audition time for your personal concentration and relaxation exercises. Do these privately before you get up to perform—just as you will have to do if you get the part. It is hard to have confidence in an actor who is visibly engaging in relaxation tactics while performing.

Great acting takes a boldness and a generosity of spirit (not arrogance or salesmanship). When you aspire to great acting, you are inviting others to witness your passion and sensitivity to human truth, and you are saying, "Look at what I can do. Pay close attention and you will be rewarded." This is the attitude you need to bring with you to an audition.

READING TACTICS

As you read during the audition, keep the script up near eye level. Some actors read a block of text, move the script down to their side, speak the words they've read, then bring the script back up and start all over again. This will interfere with your developing any sense of continuity, and the auditor will find it distracting. Accept that your timing in a reading will be slower and chunkier than if you were speaking memorized lines. By holding the script at eye level it will be easier for you to stay in the moment as you look at the page for the next block of words.

The director may provide you with another actor to read with. This will allow you to engage in a give and take with someone who, like you, is trying to bring a character to life. More often, you'll be asked to read with the stage manager or an assistant, and this person may feed you the other character's lines in an expressionless manner. If your reading consists of a monologue that is spoken to another character, the director may ask you to read to him, or he may ask you to imagine the character to whom the speech is addressed. The latter is often preferable, since you can have your imaginary partner react to what you are saying in ways that will help stimulate your emotions (for example, you can "see" your imaginary partner mock something you say). When you read to the director, he is likely to just give you a neutral stare. If the director doesn't give you any instructions or gives you a choice, I recommend creating an imaginary partner—but place that partner in the direction of the director so your face will be visible to him.

If the speech you are reading is a soliloquy addressed to the audience, you can use the director and anyone else watching the audition as the audience (unless you are asked not to), or you may prefer to imagine the audience. Either way, remember that when a character speaks to an audience, she wants something from that audience (such as understanding, sympathy, admiration). That is, your character has a relationship with the members of the audience—or she wouldn't be talking to them (so forget your grade school teacher's instructions to look at the exit sign when talking to an audience—unless your character has a thing for exit signs).

Try to make as much contact as possible with whomever you are reading to, whether it is to one person or an audience, whether it is to someone real or someone imagined. Do as little reading with your face down into the script as you can. That means you will have to learn to read and keep in mind chunks of words at a time. With practice it isn't hard to do. And don't worry if you leave out or change a word here and there. No one is judging you on the perfection of your reading skills (although if your basic reading skills are poor, spend a lot of time practicing reading aloud).

If you are reading with a real person, listen to her, just as you would if you were actually in a performance with her. Let yourself react to everything she does, every nuance in her voice and body. And, when appropriate, allow yourself time to think about what you are hearing before you do your next line. Frequently, one's best acting is in the pauses. If the other person is expressionless, do your best to bring her into the scene by really being there with her and speaking *to* her, not just toward her. If you are really alive with her, she will feel uncomfortable just reading blankly and you may very well pull her into the scene with you.

And don't worry about picking up your cues quickly. When the other person stops reading, you'll know it is time for you to look at the script for your next line. Remember, allow yourself the time a star would take. If a director is going to have confidence in you, she needs to see that you have confidence in yourself.

While a reading is not an improvisation (since you aren't making up the lines as you go along), it is helpful to have an improvisational attitude so that you allow yourself to go where the scene takes you on a moment to moment basis. Don't preplan how you will say a line, and if you have an impulse to move, sit, stand up, laugh, or cry, do it. These kinds of *in-the-moment* impulses are more likely to occur if you really speak and listen to the other person, and if you've done the proper preparation—which gets us to the "choices" I referred to earlier. Here's where your craft comes in.

MAKING CHOICES

We've established that you need to *act* in a cold reading—and act well. So you need to provide yourself with the ingredients that will put you inside the life of the character, and you need to do it quickly. On your first read-through of the script, simply allow the playwright's words to draw you into the story and the lives of the characters. Try not to prejudge anything, but do incorporate anything the director has said about the story or characters into your vision of the events as you read them.

On your second read-through, start making choices.

1. Choose an objective and obstacle for your character. You need to decide what your character wants and what is in the way of getting what he or she wants. Acting requires *action*, and all action emerges out of pursuing something one wants. Actions can be physical, vocal, or mental. If you are playing a detective, a scene may have you rummaging through a drawer in search of evidence (a physical action), questioning a suspect (a vocal action), and trying to figure out whether you have enough evidence to make an arrest (a mental action). Mental actions, if played fully, will be visible to those watching the scene. If you really try to figure something out, really evaluate the pros and cons that go into making a decision, it will register on your face and in your body.

The deeper the objective the better. In the scene, your character may be trying to con someone out of money. Wanting money is a shallow objective. Pursuing money to buy a car to impress a girl is a deeper objective. Deeper objectives will spontaneously spark an inner life for your character, such as thoughts about how impressed that girl will be when she sees you drive by in your shiny new car, and what it will be like to make love to her in the back seat of that car—if you get the money.

The script might provide a deep objective, but sometimes it won't, especially in film scripts where there are many characters who enter and exit the story in one short scene. Make your objectives as strong as possible. For example, your pursuit of the money will be more intense if you have a girl in mind who truly excites you and if you establish for yourself that this is your last chance with her since she is going away to school soon.

To play a scene well you'll need to give your character one or more obstacles that get in the way of reaching his or her objective. An obstacle can be *external,* as when your character wants to make love to someone who is resistant. Or it can be *internal,* as when a priest is torn between his desire to make love to someone and fulfilling his vow of chastity. All good dramas require conflict, and conflict is nothing more than the interplay of an objective and an obstacle.

As you read through the scene, quickly choose at least one objective and obstacle to play. Look for both an external and an internal obstacle for your character. Acting is generally most interesting when the character must confront both kinds of impediments. Also see if there is a place where your character's objective changes. Objectives and obstacles aren't static. The priest may start out obsessed with pursuing the object of his desire, but then when he gets close to achieving his goal he may pull back out of shame and fear. (He might, for example, picture the disappointed look on the face of his mentor or imagine being shunned and denounced by parishioners.) Acting is interesting when the relative strengths of objectives and obstacles seesaw back and forth; if they are equally strong at the same time, they tend to cancel each other out, leaving the actor devitalized and immobile.

If you aren't sure what the character's objectives and obstacles are, and if you can't get any clarification from the director, pick something anyway. It is better to play the wrong thing than to play nothing. If the director likes your acting, but feels you are playing the wrong storyline, she'll usually give you some direction and a chance to try again.

2. Place your character in an environment. If the scene takes place in a garden, picture some trees, bushes, and flowers, and decide where they are. Decide if you are walking on grass or on patio tiles. Again, don't worry about whether your choices are right. Just give yourself some specific aspects of the physical setting so you will feel that you are in the character's world. It will help you avoid feeling self-conscious and awkward in your body, and it will keep you from nervously wandering around the audition space as you read. But even if you are doing the reading sitting in an old sofa in a cramped casting director's office, create a sense of place for yourself.

If there is something special about what your character is wearing, try to incorporate that into your sense of your character's physical world.

3. Your character not only takes actions, but also *reacts* to stimuli. Some of the stimuli are physically present in the current moment of the scene, such as someone insulting her, or pulling a knife on her, or offering her some food that she hates. Other stimuli are in her mind, such as remembering her deceased father or a great pasta dish at a posh restaurant on her birthday, or planning what she will say to her boss when she gets to work. As you go through the script, note the important stimuli that your character responds to, including any physical objects she comes in contact with or handles (such as a fragile vase or a sentimental photograph), and make sure you have images for all of them.

For example, you need to know who you will think about when your character reminisces about her father. It may be your own father, or someone else you've known, or a fantasy father you've made up—or each of these at different moments. In life, if you were to tell someone about your father or even about what you ate for dinner last night, you'd get flooded with images, and they would most definitely affect how you speak. If your character is talking about her father or a meal she ate, she won't come alive unless she has similar images.

Your first stimulus is the most important because it impels you into your first line. For example, if your first line is "I love you," you need to know why you are saying it, and why *now*. We tell people we love them only at particular moments, so if your character is saying it now, something is going on. Perhaps the person has become increasingly distant from you, or perhaps something has disappointed her, or perhaps you're feeling guilty about the way you've been treating her. You want to define what you will think about so that the line "I love you" will, essentially, come out on its own and in its own way.

When you work with images that stir you, you are less likely to *push* or force an emotion. Acting in an audition, like any acting, is good when it is true. You need to trust that the truth is interesting. Actors who don't trust the truth often add a breathlessness to their delivery, and they sit on the edge of a chair rather than in the chair, and they widen their eyes and sometimes even flare their nostrils, ultimately resembling silent film performers.

4. Try to get a sense of what your character is like. Think about who you know in your life who is like that character. Then imagine that person taking over your being as you play the scene. You will find that this process, which I call *getting possessed by a character*, affects how you speak, how your body behaves, and even your emotions. Acting is about playing a life, a particular life—not about playing lines. By getting possessed by a character you will *feel* that life as you do the scene, and your behavior will become more expressive, distinctive, and authentic.

In selecting the person who will inhabit your being, don't pick an actor you've seen in films or on stage. Because what you've observed is that actor playing a character, you are more likely to feel that you are doing a bad impersonation of him than bringing an authentic character to life.

Selecting a character is especially useful in comedies, Shakespeare, and period plays, where it is easy to slide into caricature and bland generalities.

5. Note if there are big emotional moments in the scene—moments, for example, where it is clear that the character is in a rage or is breaking down in tears. If the play calls for these kinds of moments, a smart director will want to make sure you are up to them before casting you. If the writing is good and you identify with the character, such emotional outpourings might happen to you spontaneously as you present the scene. But in case they don't, you should be prepared with personal stimuli that you can summon to achieve these big emotions.

Big emotions ride on your autonomic nervous system, so you need stimuli that you can rely on to arouse that system. If you need an angry outburst, you should be prepared to think about someone or something that reliably rouses you to anger. If you need to cry (as when another character says of your character, "Look, she's crying"), you should be prepared to think about something that you can count on to make you cry. If the part calls for these emotions and you don't have the craft to produce them, then you are not the right person for the part.

Actors feel great when big emotions pour out by simply living the life of the character, but most actors find that there are many times when they need to add personal stimuli to kick that sluggish autonomic nervous system into gear.

6. Your scene is about a moment in your character's life. But your character had a life that preceded the first moments in the scene and led right into them. You can't possibly understand what the first lines and actions of the scene are really about unless you know what was going on in your character's life before the scene began. Without that knowledge, you won't know what your character has come into this scene to do.

Acting feels good when you have a sense that your character is grounded in an ongoing life. To achieve this, decide what your character was doing and thinking just prior to the scene and begin your acting with that prior moment. You don't need to actually play it out physically, but you should play it out in your mind.

7. You need to define your character's relationships to other characters in the scene. If your character is telling a friend about a girl he has fallen for, how you speak the words will depend on your relationship to the friend. Has he been sensitive to your feelings in the past or has he used things you've shared with him against you? Is your relationship a competitive one? Do you want his approval? Might he get nervous that you are going to abandon him for the girl?

How you play the scene will depend on your answers to such questions. Different answers will give you a totally different inner monologue and will affect many subtle aspects of your behavior, such as how you look at the friend and how much of your feelings you're willing to display to him.

Making choices in the seven areas I've described will improve your audition readings. But you might be thinking that this seems like a lot of work and would require a lot of time. Actually, if you are ready to go out and audition, these should be things you are already practiced in. If you work with objectives, obstacles, character elements, and stimuli, making quick choices in these areas should not be that difficult for you.

As you make your choices, note them in your script. Write in the margins, in large print, a word or two to remind you of the images and other stimuli you plan to use at different moments in the scene. These reminders will be especially useful if you get nervous and lose your concentration during the audition.

With regard to concentration, you'll find it helpful to have a "confidence stimulus" in your kit of techniques. A confidence stimulus is something you can think about quickly and briefly that makes you feel good about yourself. It might be the thought of your grandmother, or your dog, or a phrase in a song, or the smell of suntan lotion at the beach. If you start to feel nervous, you flash on that stimulus (such as your grandmother's merry eyes) for a brief private moment. Your confidence stimulus should help ground you and allow you to reenter the scene.

TAKING DIRECTION

If the director likes your acting and thinks you have the right qualities for the role, she might give you some direction and have you do the scene again. She might do this to see if you can get closer to her vision of the character, or she might do it to find out whether you have the skills to make quick adjustments, or she might be trying to determine whether she will like working with you.

Try to follow her directions and don't get into a debate about interpretations of the script. If she asks you how you see the character, describe your vision as best you can, but convey that you are not locked into any particular interpretation. She might be the kind of director who gives actors lots of room to define their characters, or she might feel that each character must fit like pieces in a puzzle into her overall conception of the play. There are good and bad directors of both types, and if you want the role, try to be sensitive to the kind of director you are working with.

If you do a good audition, it may lead the director to see the role in a new way. For example, a director may feel that a character needs to be menacing, but may not have defined his vision beyond that general quality. Dracula and a Mafia wiseguy are both menacing, but in very different ways. You might create a character, based perhaps on someone you have known, who is menacing in a way the director never imagined, and she might recognize that your particular kind of menacing would not only work for the play but be especially interesting.

You usually won't know why a director didn't choose you for a role. You might have been too good-looking, or not good-looking enough. He might have thought you were too tall or too short, given other actors he had already cast. It's not worth agonizing over. All you can hope for is to feel good about the performance you gave at the audition. What the poet T. S. Eliot wrote about the struggles of writers applies equally well to actors: "For us there is only the trying. The rest is not our business."

Scenes for One Man
and One Woman

Picasso at the Lapin Agile

BY STEVE MARTIN

Germaine is a thirty-five-year-old waitress at the bar Lapin Agile in Paris in 1904. The bartender, Freddy, is her boyfriend, but she is having an affair with Pablo Picasso, an intense, hypersexual, egocentric, twenty-three-year-old painter. Freddy has gone off on an errand and Picasso, wanting to be alone with Germaine, has gotten rid of an older patron by reminding him that he has to pee.

....

(PICASSO walks over to GERMAINE and they kiss . . . you can tell it's not the first time. They break.)

PICASSO: Tasty. Quite tasty.
GERMAINE: What was I? Dessert?
PICASSO: What do you mean?
GERMAINE: I mean how many meals have you had today?
PICASSO: Why be nasty? We're not so different . . .
GERMAINE: Oh yes, we slept together but there's a difference. Women are your world. For me, you are the thing that never happened. You and Freddy exist in separate universes. What I do in one has nothing to do with the other.
PICASSO: How convenient.
GERMAINE: Oh, don't get me wrong. I'm not being nasty. I like you. It's just that I know about men like you.

PICASSO: Men like me? Where are there men like me?

GERMAINE: Have a drink. You don't want me to go on.

PICASSO: No, tell me about men like me.

GERMAINE: *(settles in)* A steady woman is important to you because then you know for sure you have someone to go home to in case you can't find someone else. You notice every woman, don't you?

PICASSO: *(pause)* Many.

GERMAINE: I mean every woman. Waitresses, wives, weavers, laundresses, ushers, actresses, women in wheelchairs. You notice them, don't you?

PICASSO: Yes.

GERMAINE: And when you see a woman you think, "I wonder what she would be like." You could be bouncing your baby on your knee and if a woman walks by you wonder what she would be like.

PICASSO: Go on.

GERMAINE: You have two in one night when the lies work out, and you feel it's your right. The rules don't apply to you, because the rules were made up by women, and they have to be if there's going to be any society at all. You cancel one when someone better comes along. They find you funny, bohemian, irresistible. You like them young because you can bamboozle them and they think you're great. You want them when *you* want them, never when they want you. Afterwards you can't wait to leave, or if you're unlucky enough to have her at your place you can't wait for *her* to leave because the truth is we don't exist afterwards, and all conversation becomes meaningless because it's not going to get you anywhere because it already got you there. You're unreachable. Your whole act is a camouflage. But you are lucky, because you have a true talent that you are too wise to abuse. And because of that you will always be desirable. So when you wear out one woman, there will be another who wants to taste it, who wants to be next to someone like you. So you'll never have to earn a woman and you'll never appreciate one.

PICASSO: But I appreciate women: I draw them, don't I?

GERMAINE: Well, that's because we're so goddamn beautiful isn't it?

PICASSO: Germaine, men want, and women are wanted. That's the way it is and that's the way it will always be.

GERMAINE: That may be true, but why be greedy? By the way, I knew you were using me, but I was using you back.

PICASSO: How?

GERMAINE: Now I know what a painter is like, tomorrow night a street paver maybe, or a news agent, or maybe a bookseller. A street paver may not have anything to talk about to a girl like me, but I can write my romantic scenarios in my head and pull them down like a screen in front of me to project my fantasies onto. Like you project your fantasies onto a piece of paper.

PICASSO: How does Freddy fit in? Why are you with him?

GERMAINE: *His* faults I can live with. And occasionally, occasionally, he says something so stunning I'm just glad to have been there. But really? What I wouldn't give for a country boy.

The Graduate

ADAPTED BY TERRY JOHNSON, BASED ON
THE NOVEL BY CHARLES WEBB AND THE
MOTION PICTURE SCREENPLAY BY CALDER
WILLINGHAM & BUCK HENRY

ACT II, SCENE I

The year is 1964 and Benjamin has returned to his upper-middle-class California home for the summer after completing a very successful four years of college. He tied for first in academics, was captain of the cross-country team, editor of the school newspaper, and head of the debating club. And he's been accepted to some top graduate schools. But Benjamin is confused about what to do next in his life. He is not very worldly, has no interests or ambitions, and feels alienated from his family and their lifestyle.

During the summer he gets seduced by Mrs. Robinson, a close friend of his parents. Although Benjamin feels ashamed and disgusted with himself for having gotten involved with what he considers a sordid relationship, he meets Mrs. Robinson in a hotel on a number of occasions throughout the summer. Unfortunately, during this same summer, Benjamin falls in love with Mrs. Robinson's sincere, vivacious, and beautiful daughter Elaine, who also falls for him. When Mrs. Robinson forbids Benjamin to date Elaine and threatens to tell her about their liaison if he tries, Benjamin takes up her challenge and tells Elaine himself. Elaine, shocked and revolted, orders Benjamin out of her house and soon goes back to college at Berkeley.

Unable to get her off his mind, Benjamin announces to his parents that he is going to Berkeley to marry her—even though she hates him. As the scene opens, Elaine is standing in the doorway of Benjamin's room at the Berkeley Boarding Home.

....

(Attic room, Berkeley Boarding House. Evening. BENJAMIN stands holding the door open for ELAINE.)

ELAINE: Benjamin, why are you here?

BENJAMIN: Would you like to come in?

ELAINE: I want to know what you're doing here in Berkeley.

BENJAMIN: Would you like some tea? I have tea.

ELAINE: I want to know why you're stalking me.

BENJAMIN: I'm not.

ELAINE: I see you on campus. You duck behind doorways. On the bus you hid behind a magazine.

BENJAMIN: I've been meaning to speak to you.

ELAINE: You've been following me around for days.

BENJAMIN: Would you like to come in?

ELAINE: No!

BENJAMIN: Why not?

ELAINE: I don't want to be in a room with you. Now why are you up here?

BENJAMIN: I'm just living here temporarily. I thought I might be bumping into you. I thought I remembered you were going to school up here.

ELAINE: Did you move up here because of me?

BENJAMIN: No.

ELAINE: Did you?

BENJAMIN: I don't know.

ELAINE: Well, did you?

BENJAMIN: Well, what do you think?

ELAINE: I think you did.

BENJAMIN: I'm just living in Berkeley. Having grown somewhat weary of family life, I've been meaning to stop by and pay my respects but have not been entirely certain how you felt about me after the incident with your mother which was certainly a serious mistake on my part but not serious enough I hope to permanently alter your feelings about me.

(ELAINE comes in, slamming the door.)

ELAINE: Benjamin, you are the one person in the entire world I never want to see again. I want you nowhere near me. I want you to leave here and never come back. *(He hangs his head.)* Promise me you'll go.
BENJAMIN: Elaine . . .
ELAINE: Promise me.

(He stares at her for a moment.)

BENJAMIN: Alright.
ELAINE: Pack your bags and go tonight.
BENJAMIN: Alright!
ELAINE: So promise me.
BENJAMIN: Alright!

(He flops down, his head in his arms.)

ELAINE: Goodbye, Benjamin.
BENJAMIN: I love you.
ELAINE: You what?
BENJAMIN: I love you. I love you and I can't help myself and I'm begging you to forgive me for what I did. I love you so much I'm terrified of seeing you every time I step outside the door. I feel helpless and hopeless and lost and miserable, please forget what I did please Elaine O God Elaine I love you please forget what I did? Please forget what I did Elaine, I love you.
ELAINE: Yeah, well, I don't think so.
BENJAMIN: I do.
ELAINE: You do not.
BENJAMIN: Honestly, I. . . .

ELAINE: How can you love me Benjamin when you're so full of hate?

BENJAMIN: Of hate?

ELAINE: How else could you have done that?

BENJAMIN: Done what?

ELAINE: How could you have raped my mother?

BENJAMIN: What?

ELAINE: You must have so much hate inside you.

BENJAMIN: Raped her? (*ELAINE* starts to cry.) Did you say raped her?

ELAINE: Virtually raped her.

BENJAMIN: Did she say that?

ELAINE: I want you out of here by the morning.

BENJAMIN: No!

(*He runs between* ELAINE *and the door.*)

ELAINE: Don't you touch me.

BENJAMIN: I'm not.

ELAINE: Then get away from the door.

BENJAMIN: What did she say? What did she say?

ELAINE: Why?

BENJAMIN: Because it isn't true.

ELAINE: She said you virtually raped her.

BENJAMIN: Which isn't true.

ELAINE: Is it true you slept with her?

BENJAMIN: Yes.

ELAINE: Alright then, get away from the door.

BENJAMIN: What did she say? What did she say?

ELAINE: She said you dragged her up to the hotel room . . .

BENJAMIN: I dragged her!?

ELAINE: . . . and you made her pass out and you raped her.

BENJAMIN: I what . . . I drugged her? I dragged her up five floors and I drugged her? I *raped* her?

ELAINE: You *virtually*, yes.

BENJAMIN: I *what*?

ELAINE: Could I leave now please?

BENJAMIN: That is not what happened.

ELAINE: I have to leave.

BENJAMIN: My parents gave me a party when I got home from college. Your mother came up to my room.

ELAINE: I don't want to hear this.

BENJAMIN: She asked me to unzip her dress.

ELAINE: May I go now?

BENJAMIN: She took off all her clothes. She stood there entirely naked and she said. . . .

(ELAINE screams, long and hysterical. BENJAMIN frozen. She calms down. He brings her a chair. He brings her a glass of water. She drinks it.)

ELAINE: What did you think would happen?

BENJAMIN: What?

ELAINE: When you came up here?

BENJAMIN: I don't know.

ELAINE: You just came up here?

BENJAMIN: I drove up. I made reservations at a restaurant.

ELAINE: You were going to invite me to dinner?

BENJAMIN: Yes.

ELAINE: Then what did you do?

BENJAMIN: I didn't invite you.

ELAINE: I know.

BENJAMIN: I just came up here. I got this room. I kind of wallowed around. I wrote you some letters.

ELAINE: Love letters?

BENJAMIN: I don't remember.

ELAINE: So what are you going to do now?

BENJAMIN: I don't know.

ELAINE: Where are you going?

BENJAMIN: I don't know.

ELAINE: Well, what are you going to do?

BENJAMIN: Are you deaf?

ELAINE: Excuse me?

BENJAMIN: I don't know what I'm going to do.

ELAINE: Well, will you get on a bus or what?

BENJAMIN: Are you concerned about me or something?

ELAINE: You came up here because of me. You messed up your life because of me, and now you're leaving because of me. You made me responsible. I don't want you drunk in some gutter because of me.

BENJAMIN: You want me to stick around?

ELAINE: I want you to have a definite plan before you leave, then I want you to leave.

BENJAMIN: I have no plans.

ELAINE: Then just make up your mind.

BENJAMIN: What?

ELAINE: Don't you have a mind?

BENJAMIN: Of course.

ELAINE: Then make it up.

BENJAMIN: I could go to Canada.

ELAINE: You want to go to Canada?

BENJAMIN: No.

ELAINE: You think I can study? You think I can think with you here?

BENJAMIN: Just tell me to leave and I'll leave.

ELAINE: I have so much work this semester.

BENJAMIN: Would you just tell me to leave, please?

ELAINE: Are you simple?

BENJAMIN: What?

ELAINE: I mean what do I have to say to you?

BENJAMIN: I don't know.

ELAINE: Can't you see the way I feel?

BENJAMIN: Shall I go then?

ELAINE: Why don't you.

BENJAMIN: Why don't I go.

ELAINE: Yes.

BENJAMIN: Alright. That's all you had to say.

(*ELAINE goes to the door.*)

ELAINE: You know what she gave me for my eleventh birth-
day? She gave me a bartender's guide. I made her cocktails all day.
BENJAMIN: She's a strange woman.
ELAINE: Is she attractive?
BENJAMIN: Yes. Not really.
ELAINE: Well is she or not?
BENJAMIN: I don't know.
ELAINE: You don't know which she is or you don't know which
I'd like to hear?
BENJAMIN: Either.
ELAINE: And am I?
BENJAMIN: I'm sorry?
ELAINE: Am I as attractive as her?
BENJAMIN: Oh, yes.
ELAINE: I have to go now.
BENJAMIN: Would you marry me?
ELAINE: Would I what?
BENJAMIN: Marry me. Would you?
ELAINE: Marry you?
BENJAMIN: Yes.
ELAINE: Marry you?
BENJAMIN: Would you?
ELAINE: Why would I?
BENJAMIN: I think we have a lot in common.
ELAINE: Well, that's true.
BENJAMIN: So will you?
ELAINE: Marry you?
BENJAMIN: Yes.
ELAINE: Hah. Ha ha ha. Oh Benjamin, you are something.
BENJAMIN: Am I?
ELAINE: Yes you are, but I don't know what. Why do you want
to marry me?
BENJAMIN: It's the way I feel. I feel we should.
ELAINE: What about the way I feel?

BENJAMIN: How do you feel?
ELAINE: Confused.
BENJAMIN: Are you fond of me? *(She sniffs.)* Are you?
ELAINE: Yes, fond.
BENJAMIN: Then let's get married.

Vincent in Brixton

BY NICHOLAS WRIGHT

SCENE 2

It is 1873 in London and twenty-year-old Vincent Van Gogh has come from Holland to work as a junior sales assistant for the international art firm, Gospil and Co. (it is years before Vincent will discover his own passion and talent as an artist). He is living in a rented room in the quiet neighborhood of Brixton because he liked the sincere and plain service in the nearby Congregational church, and because he was enchanted by the beautiful eighteen-year-old Eugenie whom he saw coming out of a house with a room-for-rent sign on it.

The owner of the house, Eugenie's mother Ursula Loyer, is a free-thinking, melancholy widow in her forties, who also runs a small preparatory school for young boys in her front room. When he inquired about renting a room, Vincent, being an inexperienced man in the world, and especially with woman, told Ursula of his instantaneous love for Eugenie. She responded that she would rent him the room only if he agreed to never bother Eugenie (who loves another boarder, an artist named Sam). Vincent consented.

It is now some months later on a sunny Sunday afternoon. Vincent has been told that Sam has gone to Kent to sketch and Eugenie has gone to visit her aunt in Broadstairs, also in Kent. After working in the garden, Vincent comes into the kitchen and sees Ursula sitting at the table, clearly despondent (she feels that life has passed her by). She offers him tea but he asks for a beer instead. They chat about various things, including a book Vincent is reading (*L'Amour* by Jules Michelet) and his plans to bring his sister to London. After a while Ursula again offers Vincent some tea.

··

URSULA: Mr. Vincent . . .
VINCENT: What?
URSULA: Are you quite sure you wouldn't like some tea?
VINCENT: I'll have a beer.
URSULA: I'll get it.

(She gives him a beer, makes tea for herself.)

I knew there was something odd going on when I found you digging up the garden.
VINCENT: In Holland I work in the garden all the time . . .
URSULA: I'm sure you do.
VINCENT: I sow not only flowers but turnips, potatoes, cabbage . . .
URSULA: Listen to me. I realised then that you didn't intend to leave. And now that you talk of staying on into the summer . . .
VINCENT: Well?

(Pause.)

URSULA: Mr. Vincent, do you still love my daughter?
VINCENT: Yes.
URSULA: Are you quite certain of that?
VINCENT: Of course.
URSULA: Then I think you should move. Move out. As we agreed.
VINCENT: But that was months ago.
URSULA: Exactly.

VINCENT: No. I can't accept this. If you want to throw me out, you should have done it the day I arrived.

URSULA: You're right. I should have.

VINCENT: Why didn't you?

URSULA: I don't know.

VINCENT: I've kept my promise.

URSULA: You have.

VINCENT: I've said nothing to her, nothing!

URSULA: No I know you haven't.

VINCENT: It isn't a nice position, being the rejected lover who hasn't even had the chance to be rejected.

URSULA: That's why I think we ought to end the situation.

VINCENT: But you've never once said that. Never till now. Why's that?

(Pause.)

You see? You haven't an answer.

URSULA: In fact I do.

VINCENT: What is it?

URSULA: It's that I cannot believe you're anything like as much in love as you imagine.

VINCENT: Why not?

URSULA: Because . . . well, if your feelings are as strong as you said they were, I don't see how you could suppress them. It isn't your nature.

VINCENT: So you know my nature?

URSULA: I think so.

VINCENT: You've never said *that* before.

URSULA: I haven't needed to.

(She pours tea for herself.)

VINCENT: So . . . if I wasn't . . . as I am . . .

(He laughs.)

It's strange I even consider it. If your daughter was just your daughter to me . . . then I could stay.

URSULA: But why would you want to?

VINCENT: That's what I ask myself.

URSULA: It's not my cooking.

VINCENT: In fact I'm getting to like your cooking. And there's you. We both speak French. We read the same books. *Jude the Obscure. Felix Holt, the Radical.* What would I know about the lives of working people, if it wasn't for you?

URSULA: And Sam.

VINCENT: And Sam. Oh well, I'll never be Sam. But isn't there something deeper than that between us?

URSULA: What?

VINCENT: Don't you know?

URSULA: I think you should tell me.

(Pause.)

VINCENT: When I came in just now, you had your head in your hands. I knew you were feeling bad. Then you denied it. Now tell me, which of us was telling the truth?

(Pause.)

URSULA: I got the tram back from the station, and it stopped at the ponds. There were crowds of people milling about in the sunlight. Boys and girls, all eyeing each other. One young man came out of the pub with so many glasses of beer in his hands and up his arms that he looked like an acrobat. Everyone clapped and cheered, and I can honestly say that I felt more wretched than I've felt in months. All I could see was youth and Spring and life renewing itself, and what for?

(She laughs.)

What for? It's futile, it's a mockery. That's why you found me as you did. Of course I wish you hadn't.

VINCENT: I have known for months. On the day I arrived, I was having a beer with Sam. He asked me, why were you dressed in black? I discovered the reason soon enough. It was in February. The snow was melting.

URSULA: Go on.

VINCENT: You had a black mood. That was his name for it. You wouldn't talk, or eat, or look at us. One day you shouted at Eugenie. She was angry. I was the only one who understood. You'd fallen into the darkness of your soul. Have I offended you?

URSULA: No.

VINCENT: One night, I came downstairs at one in the morning and saw a light under your door. Then again at two, then again at three. I slept for a while, then something woke me. I came downstairs and as I got to the landing, I saw a white shape moving below me. It was you in your nightdress. I tiptoed back to my room, I looked out and I saw you sitting on the step of the garden shed. Like this.

(He indicates, his head in his hands.)

You looked up. I didn't move. We were like statues. Did you see me?

URSULA: No.

VINCENT: All that week, I woke at the quietest sound. The click of your door, the creak of a stair. I watched you. I watched *over* you. One day there was a bandage on your wrist. I hid the carving-knife. I hid the disinfectant. I went to the medicine chest, and hid the morphine and the laudanum. Did you not know it was me?

URSULA: No. I'd no idea. What on earth were you playing at?

VINCENT: I was protecting you.

URSULA: Oh for God's sake.

(She gets up. Reaches for her exercise-books. He puts them further away. She reaches for them and he moves them again.)

VINCENT: Where are you going?

URSULA: I can't stay here. Hand me those.

VINCENT: Not till you tell me . . .

URSULA: *(loudly)* I was no risk to myself at all, none whatso-
ever. Now give me those books!

VINCENT: Here.

(He gives her the books. She stands with them in her arms.)

You knew it was me. Admit it.

(She nods.)

You see! We have a mental affinity! But I still don't know what
made you so unhappy.

URSULA: Neither do I.

VINCENT: There must have been something.

URSULA: Yes, I'm sure there was.

VINCENT: What was it?

URSULA: I don't remember.

VINCENT: How could you not . . . ?

URSULA: *(interrupts)* It was probably something unimportant.
That's what it's like. It starts with something small and then it becomes about everything. And it's the 'everything' that makes me feel
as I do. I can't explain it any better. I know it's awful for everyone else.

(She sits, drinks her tea.)

The stupid thing is that if I were asked in a court of law to swear
it was genuine, that I wasn't just putting it on, I'd have to refuse. Because it could be mere indulgence. Perhaps it is. Perhaps I'm just a
self-pitying old baggage. I don't know. I don't. I haven't the faintest.

VINCENT: I know these feelings.

URSULA: Let me assure you, Mr. Vincent, that whatever you
feel is utterly different.

VINCENT: Who can say? I know I've sat in this kitchen, unable
to open my heart. That hurt me. And it hurts to feel my life is
wasted. I try to write poems, but all I can do is copy out other peo-

ple's. I thought, if Sam can draw, then why not me? But the results were shameful. There's only one thing that gives me hope. That's you. You're like a mirror of my unhappiness. When I've watched you, like a big white moth in the moonlight . . . when I look at your face . . . your hands . . .

(He looks at her hands. They're still for a moment.)

Your ring. Your wedding ring. Where is it?

(She looks at her left hand. Glances at the kitchen sink.)

URSULA: I must have taken it off for safety.

(He goes to the sink, looks.)

VINCENT: No, it's not here.
URSULA: It must be somewhere upstairs.
VINCENT: I'll get it.

(He goes to the door.)

URSULA: Eugenie has it.

(Pause.)

I said Eugenie has it.
VINCENT: I heard you. Why does she have it?
URSULA: I lent it to her.
VINCENT: No, I don't understand
URSULA: Mr. Vincent, is it possible that you are as naive as you seem?
VINCENT: Of course!
URSULA: Then let me explain. In order to register at a hotel as man and wife, it's necessary for the woman to wear a wedding ring.

My daughter, it seems, had bought a sixpenny ring to take to Broadstairs. But she forgot to take it to the station. I noticed her distress, and guessed the reason and I lent her mine.

VINCENT: You said she was staying with your sister.

URSULA: That's what *she* said. The truth is that she's sharing a hotel room with somebody else, someone very well known to you.

VINCENT: Who?

URSULA: Sam.

VINCENT: No. Sam is in Rochester.

URSULA: He *went* to Rochester. It's only thirty miles to Broadstairs on his bicycle. If he . . .

(Stops, starts to laugh.)

VINCENT: Why are you laughing?

URSULA: I don't know. I'm very upset.

VINCENT: Eugenie and Sam are staying as man and wife?

URSULA: Yes.

VINCENT: No, this is incredible. I cannot believe I'm hearing this. Do you mean they're married?

URSULA: They're in love.

VINCENT: Since when?

URSULA: Last winter.

VINCENT: But I was *here* last winter.

URSULA: It began before you arrived.

VINCENT: But *when* I arrived. *Still* nobody told me.

URSULA: We thought we wouldn't reveal the situation till we knew you better. Then once we did, we thought we'd better not.

VINCENT: Why?

URSULA: Because it's obvious that you cannot keep a secret.

VINCENT: Why is it secret?

URSULA: I run a school for young children. If it were known that my daughter was sleeping under the same roof as a young man with whom she had an understanding, I would have no more pupils. It's as simple as that.

VINCENT: Sam could have moved out.
URSULA: He could, but he didn't.
VINCENT: They could get married.
URSULA: Don't be absurd.

(*She gets up, moves about impatiently.*)

Think what it would mean for Sam. He'd be trapped. He'd be a common-or-garden painter and decorator till the end of his days. He'd be Mr. Bloggs who comes to paint the bathroom ceiling. Sam's better than that.
VINCENT: What about her? What kind of joy does it bring to a girl, to . . . No, I can't say it.
URSULA: She understands.
VINCENT: And did you . . . ? Did you know that they were going to . . . be together?
URSULA: One can know these things and not. I wasn't certain about it till this afternoon.
VINCENT: That's why you're sad.
URSULA: Oh, no, there's no connection. If two young people love each other, and they've waited as they have done, it would be wrong, quite wrong of me to take a contrary view. I believe that very strongly, Mr. Vincent.

(*She goes to pour tea.*)

I know it's a shock for you. I'm sorry.
VINCENT: No, it's fine.

(*Pause.*)

The funny thing is that I'm not upset. I feel quite pleased in a way. This house, that I thought was an empty place, was filled with love. And if the world contains some people who don't approve of what it's led to . . . we needn't worry about them. We can do as we like, and say as we like. So thank you.

(Pause.)

URSULA: It's getting dark.
VINCENT: I left the spade outside.

(Pause.)

I'll clear the shed out for you, if you . . .

(He stops.)

Maybe not.

(Pause.)

URSULA: It was a new departure for me. Sitting outside, I mean. I'd crouch on the step, hunched up, and . . . oh, so desperate. As though a storm was raging inside my brain. It was bitterly cold, but the air had a kind of bite to it. I liked that.

(She rubs an arm.)

I'd look at things around me, perfectly humdrum things, a patch of snow, or a knot in a piece of wood. I'd stare and stare, and every bit of it would have a meaning. Heaven knows what. It's odd, looking back on it. The nights were clear, not a hint of fog. I've never seen so many stars in London. I'd look up and . . . what I saw was the way I felt. The sky was so black that there seemed to be no end to it, but it was dotted with these brilliant, blazing lights. It was the blackness and the brightness, both so different in a way, but . . . No, I can't describe it. Then I'd think of myself, so run-of-the-mill, so dreary . . . No, don't interrupt. It's fifteen years since I talked about any of this. I'd look at the sky and think, if you're worthless, if you despise yourself, but you're able to see the best, most beautiful things that the world can offer, then you'll never get there yourself, how could you? But you can point the way. In my school, there's always one boy worthy of being brought on. Although he may not know it. Sam had no idea, when he first came to live here, what he was capable of. I think, for them, it's like those dreams . . . You're sitting at home, and you suddenly see an unfamiliar door. You tease it open, and there's a room you've never seen before, full of furniture and dust-sheets. Quite wonderful, really.

VINCENT: Is that why you let me stay?

URSULA: No, that was different. When you told me about my daughter, I thought you were mad. I thought that nobody falls in love like that. I was just on the point of throwing you out, when I turned and looked . . . I thought I'd never seen anyone quite so . . . raw and suffering, yes, but quite so ruthless. I couldn't resist it. That was the moment, I suppose. And now you really will have to leave.

VINCENT: Let me tell you something. For months and months I've thought about your daughter. Now I can't remember what she looks like. All I can see is you. Her hair in yours, her eyes in yours . . .

(She moves away.)

Where are you going?

URSULA: Mr. Vincent, have you any idea how old I am?

VINCENT: Listen.

(He opens the Michelet. Searches, finds the passage, reads:)

"I see her still, modest and serious, with her black silk dress scarcely enlivened by a simple ribbon."

(He glances at her.)

"This woman has been in my mind for thirty years, so innocent, so honest, so intelligent, yet lacking the cunning to see through the stratagems of this world." . . . *"Il n'y a point de vielle femme, tant qu'elle aime et est aimé."* "No woman is old, as long as she loves and is loved." I love you. I love your age. I love your unhappiness. And now, God help me, have I courage enough to cross this room?

URSULA: Why don't we sit for a moment?

(They sit at opposite ends of the table.)

VINCENT: So now we love each other.

URSULA: Yes.

VINCENT: And you are smiling.

URSULA: I was thinking of Ginny and Sam. I feel like children do when they're left alone in the house.

VINCENT: I feel that too. Have you had lovers since your husband died?

URSULA: No.

VINCENT: Do you mind my asking?

URSULA: No.

VINCENT: I've never been with a woman.

URSULA: I didn't think you had.

VINCENT: Someone in Holborn took me back to her room, but the atmosphere was not very *sympatique*, so I paid her the money she asked and went away.

(Pause.)

Let me tell you a story while you're still in love with me. My mother had a son who died on the day he was born.

(He approaches her slowly.)

They buried him at the door of my father's church. I was born one year later to the day. I used to read his gravestone every Sunday. His name was the same as mine. "Vincent van Gogh, died March 30th, 1852." I'd stand and read until they pulled me in to hear my father preach the sermon. Then I'd think about the amazing fact that I'd been born, and buried, and born all over again. That God had given me all my second chances rolled into one. And I'd never again have any others. Do you see what I'm saying? For me, it's once or never. Let me kiss you.

(He reaches her. They kiss.)

Do you hear my heart? It's beating so loud that I think it must make you deaf. You are a saint. An angel. No, I don't care about that. You are more beautiful than she is. I never loved her.

URSULA: You did.

VINCENT: Oh, *once* I did. I thought . . . how can I say it? Half of me thought I was in love. Now half of me knows. Don't puzzle your head about it.

(He has unbuttoned her dress. Stands back.)

URSULA: What is it?

VINCENT: Let me look at you.

The Shape of Things

BY NEIL LaBUTE

When Evelyn became Adam's girlfriend everything about him began to change. Under Evelyn's tutelage, his hair and clothes became more stylish, and he improved his physique through exercise and healthier eating. Adam, a not very confident young man, feels lucky to have a lovely, sexy, and sophisticated girlfriend like Evelyn and will do anything to please her. They both attend the same small college. Adam is majoring in English. He is twenty-two but still a junior because he had to work to save money for school. Evelyn is a passionate artist, studying for an MFA.

What Adam doesn't realize is that *he* is Evelyn's latest work of art; she will present his transformation, including videos of their lovemaking, as her graduate thesis—and he will learn that most of what she has said to him has been a lie. In the following scene, they are in a doctor's lounge. (Note: "P D A" refers to public displays of affection.)

....

(The doctor's lounge.)

(A glistening white room with relaxing color schemes on the walls and furniture. End tables filled with magazines.)

(ADAM and EVELYN sit on opposing couches, flipping through separate

copies of InStyle. *After a moment,* ADAM *glances up and checks his watch.)*

ADAM: . . . what time did they say?

EVELYN: Like, ten-thirty . . .

ADAM: And it's ten-fifty now . . .

EVELYN: No big deal, you always wait at the doctor's office.

ADAM: I know, I just have to be at work by twelve.

EVELYN: Today?

ADAM: Yeah, I told you that . . .

EVELYN: No, you didn't.

ADAM: I did . . . I always work Wednesday.

EVELYN: Really?

ADAM: Yeah, every Wednesday.

EVELYN: Damn. I hope they . . .

ADAM: It's okay. I guess I could be a little late if I have to . . .

EVELYN: Sure?

ADAM: Uh-huh. It's alright. . . . I mean, they hate it but I can make something up.

EVELYN: We can go.

ADAM: No, I wanna do this. I do . . . *(beat)* Who wouldn't want to get their nose chopped off?

EVELYN: Come on! It's not . . .

ADAM: I'm kidding. No, I think you're right about it . . .

EVELYN: It's just shaving it . . .

ADAM: Yeah, that's much better. "Shaving" your nose off . . . that settles the nerves.

EVELYN: You're only talking to them, anyway, that's all.

ADAM: I know, it's just weird to think . . .

EVELYN: People do it all the time. Especially out *here* . . .

ADAM: Right, no, you're right, I just never imagined myself one of those people . . .

EVELYN: I'm one of those people. Would you ever've guessed that?

ADAM: What? You are not . . .

EVELYN: Bullshit. Take a look . . .

ADAM: Where . . . ? *(He moves over to her, studies her nose.)* I don't see anything.

EVELYN: Exactly.

ADAM: You had your nose done? Honestly?

EVELYN: At sixteen. My parents' birthday present . . .

ADAM: Thoughtful.

EVELYN: No, I asked for it. I has this terrible hook. "The Jewish Slope," we called it in Lake Forest . . . the only ski run for miles around!

ADAM: *(smiling)* I can't believe it . . . I can't tell . . .

EVELYN: That's the idea, isn't it?

ADAM: Yeah, but . . . you could be lying to me.

EVELYN: And what would be the point of that?

ADAM: To get me in here. To watch chunks of my flesh get torn away . . . you could be a sadist, for all I know . . .

EVELYN: Hey, quit sweet-talking to me . . .

ADAM: Well, they did an amazing job. *(beat)* Wait a minute, your name's "Thompson," that's not Jewish . . .

EVELYN: On my mother's side, you dope. That's what makes me Jewish . . . her maiden name is "Tessman."

ADAM: Oh.

EVELYN: We don't have to stay here, Adam . . .

ADAM: No, it's alright, it just makes me a little jumpy . . .

EVELYN: It's cosmetic, not corrective . . . it's no big deal. I promise . . .

ADAM: If it's cosmetic, why can't I just put some powder on it or something, or shade it in on the side like they do for Richard Gere in photos . . .

EVELYN: You mean, before?

ADAM: . . . he had it done?!

EVELYN: Take a look at *American Gigolo* and then at any picture of him today. I'm serious. Lots of guys do it . . . Joel Grey.

ADAM: Okay, that's it, let's go . . .

EVELYN: *(laughing)* Kidding! What about Sting?

ADAM: Yeah, I knew he did. Looked totally different in *Quadro-phenia*. I used to rent that video all the time, my "Mod" phase . . .

EVELYN: That must've been cute . . . *(beat)* Does he look better now? Sting, I mean?

ADAM: I suppose so . . . maybe it's just all that yoga, though.

EVELYN: I think you'll look great. You have a good face, a nice shape to your nose, actually, but it's just got that bit of . . .

ADAM: What?

EVELYN: . . . bulb . . . at the end. Not a bulb, exactly, but . . .

ADAM: No, I got it, sort of the "Rudolph" effect. At least I can guide your sleigh tonight . . .

EVELYN: You can guide my sleigh any night.

(They look at one another, kiss.)

ADAM: P D A.

EVELYN: Indeed . . .

ADAM: Shall I check the men's room?

EVELYN: I dare you . . .

ADAM: Shut up!

EVELYN: I'm serious . . .

ADAM: You're crazy . . .

EVELYN: Quite possibly. I still dare you . . .

ADAM: What if they call us?

EVELYN: Then they'll just have to wait, won't they?

ADAM: I suppose they would . . .

EVELYN: Can you afford to be late, that's the question. Will you take the risk . . . ?

ADAM: Is this, like, my last meal or something? A conjugal visit before I'm drawn and quartered . . .

EVELYN: Stop being so morbid . . . it's just flesh.

ADAM: Yeah, I see what you mean . . . "It's just flesh," that's not morbid at all.

EVELYN: It isn't. It's one of the most perfect substances on earth. Natural, beautiful. Think about it . . .

ADAM: I'd rather not.

EVELYN: Oh come on . . . you've bitten more skin off from around your fingernails than a doctor would ever trim off your nose. It's true . . .

ADAM: Yeah, but that's just . . .

EVELYN: . . . what? It's the same thing. Now, that grows back and this wouldn't, but that's about the only difference. *(Beat)* How did you get that scar on your back?

ADAM: Which, the . . . ?

EVELYN: Yes. The raised one . . .

ADAM: A kid, ummm, threw a stick at me . . . first grade.

EVELYN: Stitches?

ADAM: Yeah. Thirty-three . . .

EVELYN: And is that terrible? Are you disfigured because of it . . . ?

ADAM: Well, I don't like to wear tanktops . . .

EVELYN: . . . and you should be respected for that . . .

ADAM: *(giggling)* I'm serious . . . it bugs me . . .

EVELYN: Okay, but why? Because it looks ugly or because you think other people will think it looks bad? Which?

ADAM: I dunno . . .

EVELYN: What's the matter with scars? Not a thing . . . *(Pulls up sleeve)* Look at these, see there?

ADAM: What're those?

EVELYN: They're scars . . . lots of little scars. You didn't notice them before?

ADAM: Yeah, I guess I did, but I didn't think anything . . .

EVELYN: Sure, you did. Of course you would, they're on my wrist. You know what they are . . .

ADAM: . . . did you try to . . . ?

EVELYN: No, not really. I mean, I cut on myself a little, tried to get attention when I was a teenager, but I didn't want to slit my veins open. Or I would have . . .

ADAM: Oh.

EVELYN: I'm a very straightforward person.

ADAM: Yeah, I'm getting that . . .

EVELYN: It's the only way to be. Why lie?

ADAM: You're right.

EVELYN: Exactly. *(beat)* So, is my arm unattractive to you, then, because of those, or not? Tell me . . .

ADAM: No . . .

EVELYN: Are you lying?

ADAM: No, not at all, I love your arm.

EVELYN: "Love" is a big word . . .

ADAM: I know that. That's why I used it. I don't throw it around, believe me . . .

EVELYN: Either do I.

ADAM: I love your arm. It's beautiful . . .

(He takes hold of her wrist gently, kisses it.)

EVELYN: They're like rings on a tree. They signify experience . . . make us unique.

ADAM: I can see that.

EVELYN: And that's all this is, the idea of you having some surgery. It's an experience . . .

ADAM: I know, it just makes me . . .

EVELYN: . . . what, nervous? Of course you should be nervous, why not? It's something you've never done . . . but that's the adventure.

ADAM: "It's a far, far better thing I do than I have ever done . . ."

EVELYN: Something like that. Is that from a book?

ADAM: Yeah, Dickens . . .

EVELYN: Huh. Well, I don't know about better, but at least different.

(Another quick kiss.)

EVELYN: So, are you gonna go check?

ADAM: What? . . . You mean, the rest room?

EVELYN: Uh-huh.

ADAM: Ummm . . . okay. What if they call my name, though? Seriously . . .

EVELYN: What if they do?

ADAM: *(smiling)* I smell trouble . . . which I may not be able to do after this.

EVELYN: Just go . . .

ADAM: *(standing)* Okay, why not? Then I can show you something . . .

EVELYN: What?

ADAM: Just a little thing I had done. For you.

EVELYN: Wait, what . . . show me now.

(He looks around, can't wait. He pulls open his pants and lets her glance inside.)

ADAM: Look . . . a big religious no-no. *(Pulls at his waistband)* Nice, huh?

EVELYN: "Eat." Lemme guess . . . you couldn't afford the "me."

ADAM: No, you goof! Your *initials*. Like it?

EVELYN: *(touching it)* I do, I like it. And I love the gesture . . .

ADAM: "Love" is a big word.

EVELYN: I know that. That's why I used it . . . *(Beat)* Go check the "handicapped" stall. I'm suddenly very hungry . . .

(He slips off, out of the waiting room. EVELYN goes back to reading her magazine, when a voice calls out.)

VOICE: Mr Sorenson. Adam Sorenson, please . . .

(EVELYN looks up, glances toward where ADAM has disappeared but says nothing. She smiles.)

How I Learned to Drive

BY PAULA VOGEL

Li'l Bit—so called because she was a very small infant—is seventeen, pretty, smart, and having a romance of sorts with her Uncle Peck, who has been teaching her to drive. Li'l Bit lives in "suburban Maryland," is in her last year of high school, and plans to go to college to study Shakespeare and lots of other interesting things. Peck, her uncle by marriage, is an attractive, interesting, and sensitive man in his forties. So far their sexual encounters have been more playful than passionate, but she has let him fondle and kiss her breasts, and he has let her know that he would like to go further—but only when she feels ready.

To celebrate Li'l Bit's passing the test for her driver's license on the first try, Peck has taken her to a fancy restaurant in a historically famous inn. Li'l Bit has had a lot to drink, but Peck, who has vowed not to drink around her, hasn't. They are now in the parking lot headed back toward the car. Li'l Bit is quite tipsy.

....

(PECK *is slowly propping up* LI'L BIT *as they work their way to his car in the parking lot of the inn.*)

PECK: How are you doing, missy?

LI'L BIT: It's so far to the car, Uncle Peck. Like the lanterns in the trees the British fired on . . .

(LI'L BIT stumbles. PECK swoops her up in his arms.)

PECK: Okay. I think we're going to take a more direct route. *(LI'L BIT closes her eyes.)* Dizzy? *(She nods her head.)* Don't look at the ground. Almost there—do you feel sick to your stomach? *(LI'L BIT nods. They reach the "car." PECK gently, deposits her on the front seat.)* Just settle here a little while until things stop spinning. *(LI'L BIT opens her eyes.)*

LI'L BIT: What are we doing?

PECK: We're just going to sit here until your tummy settles down.

LI'L BIT: It's such nice upholst'ry—

PECK: Think you can go for a ride, now?

LI'L BIT: Where are you taking me?

PECK: Home.

LI'L BIT: You're not taking me—upstairs? There's no room at the inn? *(LI'L BIT giggles.)*

PECK: Do you want to go upstairs? *(LI'L BIT doesn't answer.)* Or home?

LI'L BIT:—This isn't right, Uncle Peck.

PECK: What isn't right?

LI'L BIT: What we're doing. It's wrong. It's very wrong.

PECK: What are we doing? *(LI'L BIT does not answer.)* We're just going out to dinner.

LI'L BIT: You know. It's not nice to Aunt Mary.

PECK: You let me be the judge of what's nice and not nice to my wife.

(Beat.)

LI'L BIT: Now you're mad.

PECK: I'm not mad. It's just that I thought you . . . understood me, Li'l Bit. I think you're the only one who does.

LI'L BIT: Someone will get hurt.

PECK: Have I forced you to do anything?

(There is a long pause as LI'L BIT tries to get sober enough to think this through.)

LI'L BIT: . . . I guess not.

PECK: We are just enjoying each other's company. I've told you, nothing is going to happen between us until you want it to. Do you know that?

LI'L BIT: Yes.

PECK: Nothing is going to happen until you want it to. *(A second more, with PECK staring ahead at the river while seated at the wheel of his car. Then, softly:)* Do you want something to happen?

(PECK reaches over and strokes her face, very gently. LI'L BIT softens, reaches for him, and buries her head in his neck. Then she kisses him. Then she moves away, dizzy again.)

LI'L BIT: . . . I don't know.

(PECK smiles; this has been good news for him—it hasn't been a "no.")

PECK: Then I'll wait. I'm a very patient man. I've been waiting for a long time. I don't mind waiting.

LI'L BIT: Someone is going to get hurt.

PECK: No one is going to get hurt. *(LI'L BIT closes her eyes.)* Are you feeling sick?

LI'L BIT: Sleepy.

(Carefully, PECK props LI'L BIT up on the seat.)

PECK: Stay here a second.

LI'L BIT: Where're you going?

PECK: I'm getting something from the backseat.

LI'L BIT: *(scared; too loud)* What? What are you going to do?

(PECK reappears in the front seat with a lap rug.)

PECK: Shhhh. (*PECK covers LI'L BIT. She calms down.*) There. Think you can sleep?

(*LI'L BIT nods. She slides over to rest on his shoulder. With a look of happiness, PECK turns the ignition key.*)

Dinner with Friends

BY DONALD MARGULIES

ACT I, SCENE 2

Tom, a lawyer, and Beth, an artist, have been married for twelve years and have two children. On the surface they appear to have a good marriage. But last week Tom confessed to Beth that he'd been unhappy for a long time, is in love with another woman—and is moving out.

Tonight Beth and Tom (and their children) were scheduled to have dinner with Karen and Gabe, their dearest friends, the friends who introduced them (Karen and Gabe are international food writers). Beth went with the children, made an excuse for Tom (who was going to Washington to be with his girlfriend), and tried to put on a cheery face. During the dinner, while the kids were off watching TV, Beth broke down and cried, and revealed to her shocked friends that her marriage was ending.

The following scene takes place later that same night in Beth and Tom's "messy bedroom." Beth, "seeming vulnerable and bereft," is wearing a T-shirt and panties and is preparing for bed. She hears her dog bark and shouts to quiet him. (Note: *Perdu* means "lost" in French.)

....

BETH: Sarge! (*Pause. More barking.*) Sarge! Quiet! (*Pause. The barking persists.*) Sergeant, dammit, be quiet!

(The bedroom door opens, startling BETH. *She gasps.* TOM *enters. He's in from the cold, dressed in winter gear and tracking in snow from his boots. He stands there. Light from the hallway spills in.)*

Tom! Jesus . . .

TOM: *(overlapping; whispers)* Sorry. I didn't mean to . . .

BETH: *(overlapping; normal volume)* Couldn't you at least knock?

TOM: I'm sorry.

BETH: You can't just come and go as you please anymore, TOM . . .

TOM: Shhh . . .

BETH: *(continuous)* . . . it's not fair; if you're gonna go, go.

TOM: I just wanted to . . .

BETH: *(continuous)* Otherwise, I'm gonna have to change the locks.

TOM: Come on, you don't want to do *that* . . .

BETH: I *am*, that's what I'm gonna have to do.

TOM: *(over "have to do")* Look, I didn't come here to fight. Okay? I saw the light on; I just wanted to say hi.

BETH: *"Hi"?!* Why aren't you in D.C.?

TOM: My flight was canceled; they closed the airport.

BETH: Why, the snow's not that bad.

TOM: No, but it is getting worse. See?, it's really starting to come down.

BETH: *(glances out)* Oh, shit, it is. Why didn't you get a room at the airport?

TOM: There *were* no rooms at the airport—you mean a motel?

BETH: Yeah.

TOM: There were no *rooms*, nothing, everything was booked.

BETH: Everything?

TOM: There was not a room to be had. I swear. You should've seen what was going on there. Everybody shouting and pushing . . . I just didn't have it in me to stay and sleep on the floor.

BETH: Why didn't you call your friend, the stewardess?

TOM: *(wearily)* Travel agent.

BETH: Whatever.

TOM: I did.

BETH: And? Couldn't *she* help you? With all her many connections?

TOM: Not really; no. I was forty-five minutes from home. All I could think about . . . was coming home.

(They make eye contact. Pause. Then, off her look:)

Don't worry, I'm sleeping in the den.

BETH: Who's worried?

TOM: Well, look, I just wanted to say hi.

BETH: You're melting.

TOM: Huh?

BETH: Your boots. You're making a puddle.

TOM: Oh. Sorry . . . *(He sits to remove his boots)* I looked in on the kids; they both look pretty wrecked.

BETH: Oh, yeah, they partied hearty. Sam fell asleep in the car. I made a successful transfer, though; he didn't budge.

TOM: He's snoring his head off in there.

BETH: He's getting a cold.

TOM: *(sympathetically)* Oh no . . .

BETH: His nose was runny all night. I gave him some Tylenol before we left Karen and Gabe's.

TOM: Liquid or chewable?

BETH: Liquid.

TOM: Wow. And he let you? He usually puts up such a fight. Remember how he'd make himself gag?

(BETH, discomfitted by the familiarity of their conversation, changes the subject.)

BETH: Yeah, well, look, I'd really like to be alone right now if you don't mind . . .

TOM: *(over "if you don't mind")* Yeah, sure . . .

BETH: Your bedding's in the dryer.

TOM: Oh. Thanks.

BETH: I threw everything in the wash. I wasn't expecting you back.

TOM: I know. Thank you. I'll . . .

BETH: You might want to grab an extra blanket while you're at it; sounds like it might get pretty cold in there tonight.

TOM: Good idea, thanks.

(*Tom gets a blanket from a chest. He sees the placemats.*)

What's this?

BETH: Oh. For us. From Italy. A little house gift. Very homey, no? Karen and Gabe, God love 'em, they know what a disaster I am in the kitchen so they're always giving me things like trivets and cookbooks.

TOM: (*smiles, then*) How was dinner?

BETH: Fabulous. *You* know. When is dinner there *not* fabulous?

TOM: What was it this time?

BETH: Oh, *you* know. These incredible recipes they picked up in Italy. Pumpkin risotto, grilled lamb . . .

TOM: Mmm. That *does* sound good. You didn't bring any home by any chance?

BETH: No; I did not.

TOM: The kids eat that, too?

BETH: Of course not, what do you think?, they would never eat anything that good. No, Gabe cooked up some macaroni and cheese for them. From scratch. That was almost as good as the risotto.

(*A beat.*)

TOM: So how are they?

BETH: They're fine. *You* know. As always. They went on and on about Italy. Thank God their slides weren't back yet.

TOM: (*smiles; then*) So what did you tell them?

BETH: About what?

TOM: Why I wasn't there.

BETH: I said you had to go to D.C.

TOM: And they accepted that?

BETH: Why shouldn't they accept that? You're always going *some*where . . .

TOM: Yeah, but they didn't suspect anything?

BETH: No.

TOM: What did they say?

BETH: What do you mean, what did they say? What did they say about what?

TOM: About my not being there.

BETH: They said they were sorry.

TOM: Sorry about what?

BETH: About your not being there! Jesus! Are you gonna cross-*examine* me now? Look, I'm tired, I'm going to sleep . . .

TOM: I just want to get an idea of what you all talked about, that's all.

BETH: I told you. Italy and stuff. They talked about this famous old Italian cook they're doing a piece on.

TOM: And?

BETH: I don't know, Tom, we talked about a lot of things; what do we ever talk about?

TOM: I don't know, what *do* we talk about?

BETH: Movies, kids, money, the news, I don't know, what we saw, what we read. Karen's mom has cataracts; she has to have surgery.

TOM: Is that it?

BETH: I don't know, I don't remember every single goddamn thing.

TOM: You were there like five or six hours.

BETH: Oh, please . . .

TOM: Right? Like from five to ten, ten-thirty?

BETH: So?

TOM: That's a lot of hours to fill with talk. You mean to tell me the whole evening went by without a word about us?

BETH: You are so paranoid, you know that?

TOM: Oh, really, am I?

BETH: *(gets under the covers, turns away)* Look, I'm really not in the mood for this . . .

TOM: You told them.

BETH: What?!

TOM: You did! You told them!

BETH: Oh, God . . .

TOM: I can tell by looking at you! I *knew* I shouldn't've trusted you!

BETH: Shhh! You want to wake up the whole house?!

TOM: *(continuous)* We were gonna get a sitter and tell them to-gether, face-to-face, remember?! That's all I asked: wait for me to get back, we'll tell them together.

BETH: *(over "we'll tell them together")*: If it was really so impor-tant to you, you should've just come tonight, instead of running off to be with your girlfriend!

TOM: Shit, where were the kids?

BETH: What?

TOM: Where were the kids when you told them?

BETH: I don't know . . .

TOM: You don't *know*?! Were they *sitting* there?!

BETH: No, of course not. They were upstairs, I guess, watching a tape.

TOM: What were they watching?

BETH: What?!

TOM: What tape were they watching?

BETH: Christ, I don't know, Tom . . .

TOM: You don't know what tape your own children were watch-ing?!

BETH: Oh, for God's sake . . . I don't know, some Disney thing. *The Aristocats.*

TOM: *(pacing, agitated)* So, the kids are upstairs watching *The Aristocats* and you're where?

BETH: This is ridiculous.

TOM: No no, I want to get the whole picture. The kids are up-stairs and you're in the living room? Huh?

BETH: *(reluctantly)* At the table.

TOM: Middle of dinner?

BETH: Right before dessert.

TOM: What was it?

BETH: What.

TOM: The dessert.

BETH: Some kind of lemon-almond cake, made with polenta.

TOM: Was it great?

BETH: Yes.

TOM: So you're sitting there . . .

BETH: I don't believe this.

TOM: Tell me.

BETH: We were sitting there . . . and I lost it. I just . . . lost it.

TOM: Oh, Christ . . . You *cried?* You actually *cried?*

BETH: Yes. What do you expect? Of course I cried.

TOM: Shit!

BETH: *You* try carrying that around with you. I'm only human. I mean, I'm sitting there with our closest friends . . .

TOM: I can't believe you did this . . .

BETH: *(continuous)* . . . eating their food, drinking their wine, making believe that everything is just dandy, and I couldn't do it!

TOM: I can't believe it . . .

BETH: So what? So what if they know? So they know! They were bound to find out!

TOM: That's not the point! *You've* got the advantage now!

BETH: What?! I do not!

TOM: Of course you do! You got to them first!

BETH: Tom . . .

TOM: *(continuous)* They heard your side of the story first! Of *course* they're gonna side with you, it's only natural!

BETH: Oh, come on, nobody's taking sides.

TOM: Don't be naive! You know how it is! I'm not gonna let you get away with this . . .

BETH: What?!

TOM: *(continuous)* Gabe and Karen mean too much to me, I'm not gonna let you turn them against me!

BETH: Tom, you're overreacting.

TOM: Don't tell me I'm overreacting! You've prejudiced my case!

BETH: I have not, Tommy. I was very even-handed.

TOM: How can you say that?! You're sitting there turning on the tears . . .

BETH: I wasn't turning on anything! Fuck you; I stated the facts. They were very sympathetic.

TOM: Of course they were sympathetic. You won them over.

BETH: I did not; stop saying that.

TOM: You *intended* to tell them.

BETH: That is not true! I tried, I really did. I couldn't help it! Everything just spilled out!

TOM: Tell me. What did you spill? I want to hear what you spilled.

BETH: Look, this is sick. I'm exhausted. Aren't you exhausted, Tom?

TOM: *(over "Aren't you exhausted, Tom?")* I want to know what was said. Do you mind? I'm entitled to know.

BETH: You know all this, we've been through this a dozen times.

TOM: *(over "a dozen times")* If you're gonna be speaking for the both of us, the least you could do . . .

BETH: I told them what happened. Okay?

TOM: Everything?

(A beat.)

BETH: Yes.

TOM: And what did they say?

BETH: They were shocked. They were sad.

TOM: They were?

BETH: What do you think? They're our best friends. Of course, they were shocked, they were terribly upset.

TOM: They were sad for *you*, though, right? Because *I'm* such a bastard.

BETH: They were sad for everybody. They were sad for the kids.

TOM: Did you tell them what you did to me, how you killed my self-confidence?

BETH: Oh, Christ, Tom . . .

TOM: *(continuous)* Did you? Did you tell them how you refused to hear me? How I tried to get you to listen to me—for years—but you wouldn't? Did you tell them that?

BETH: *(over "Did you tell them that?")* No more of this. Please?

TOM: I cried out for help, so many times . . .

BETH: How did you cry out, Tom, by fucking stewardesses?

TOM: Goddammit, she's not a stewardess!

BETH: Were your cries detectable by *human* ears, Tom, or could just the *dogs* in the neighborhood hear them?

TOM: That's right, go ahead, cut me down, castrate me all over again.

BETH: *(over "all over again")* Oh, please. You know, I hear you say this stuff, Tom . . . I can't believe that someone I could have been married to, for *twelve years!*, that I could have had *children* with!, would be capable of spouting such banal bullshit!

TOM: Even now! Even now you're doing it! Even now you refuse to hear me!

BETH: I "hear" you, I "hear" you! Christ! Tell me your girlfriend feeds you this crap, Tommy, I can't believe you came up with it on your own!

TOM: Don't patronize me; I don't need *Nancy* to tell me what I'm feeling . . .

BETH: *(over "I don't need Nancy to")* Don't talk to me about being patronized! You patronized *me*, all along! From the very beginning!

TOM: I patronized *you?*

BETH: Yes! Admit it, you never took me seriously as an artist! Never!

TOM: *(Over "Never!")* Oh, for God's sake . . .

BETH: You didn't! You never really supported me!

TOM: I supported you! I supported you our entire marriage, how can you say I didn't support you?! You got a great deal! You needed more time to yourself?, help with the kids?, I got you a nanny . . .

BETH: *Me* a nanny?

TOM: *(continuous)* You needed your own space?, I built you one over the garage! God only knows what the hell you *do* up there all day.

BETH: All I ever wanted from you was *respect*, you know that? For me, for my art . . .

TOM: Ah, your art, your art.

BETH: What's the use? Get out of here. Go. Get out.

TOM: *(over "Go")* You held this marriage *hostage* to your goddamn art!

BETH: Out!

TOM: Do you know what it's like having to support something you don't believe in? Do you, Beth? Do you? It's exhausting.

BETH: *(turning away)* I don't want to talk anymore . . .

TOM: The lying, lying to you, lying to myself . . .

BETH: Go away! Get out!

TOM: *(over "Get out!")* What was I supposed to tell you, that I thought your "art" sucked?

BETH: Bastard . . .

TOM: *(continuous)* Huh? Is that what I was supposed to say? That it was just an excuse not to get a fucking job just like everybody else . . .

BETH: You are such a fucking bastard.

TOM: *(continuous)* . . . and really *do* something with your life?!

BETH: How dare you! How *dare* you!

TOM: *(continuous)* I couldn't do that; how could I? Everything depended on perpetuating this myth of talent!

(BETH strikes TOM. He grabs her wrists.)

You wanna fight? Huh? You wanna hit me?

(He gets onto the bed and straddles her.)

BETH: *(overlapping)* Let go of me! Let *go* of me!
TOM: *(overlapping)* Hit me! Hit me! Go ahead and hit me!
BETH: Prick!
TOM: Bitch!

(She spits in his face. They wrestle, roll around on the bed, inflaming their conflicted passions.)

    Ballbreaker!
    BETH: Liar!
    TOM: Dilettante!
    BETH: You fuck!
    TOM: *Look* at me! Look what you've *done* to me!
    BETH: Look what you've done to *me*!
    TOM: I could kill you! Right now, I could fucking kill you!
    BETH: Try it. I dare you.

(They look at one another. Suddenly he kisses her hard on the mouth. Pause. Equally aroused, she quickly undoes his pants.
    The lights fade.)

The Tale of the Allergist's Wife

BY CHARLES BUSCH

ACT I, SCENE I

Marjorie and Ira, in their fifties, are a well-off married couple living in Manhattan. Ira is a successful allergist, now retired, who is described as good looking and highly energetic. Marjorie is attractive and stylish, and in the "throes of an epic depression. It's not quiet depression but raging frustration. She's a volcano that explodes, simmers down, and then explodes again." Marjorie feels she has not achieved anything special in her life (she is even disappointed in her daughters, one of whom has married an orthodox rabbi and moved to Jerusalem, while the other she refers to as the "troubled one").

It is late morning and Marjorie is still wearing her bathrobe—and has a bandage on one wrist. Ira, who has recently come in, is wearing a jogging suit and headband. Just before the scene, Marjorie had a chandelier replaced by a building worker. The worker has just left.

....

IRA: When I left this morning, you were sleeping on the sofa. Did you spend the whole night out here?
MARJORIE: Apparently so.
IRA: Was it my snoring? I don't know what to do.
MARJORIE: It's not the snoring.

IRA: Then what is it, darling? Please, tell me.

MARJORIE: *(a long sigh)* Perdu.

IRA: What?

MARJORIE: Perdu. Utter damnation. The loss of my soul.

IRA: I'm opening these drapes. *(He pushes apart the curtains.)* Marjorie, you've got to rouse yourself from this perdu. You've spent how many weeks lying out here in the dark? I'm really worried. Perhaps you should see someone.

MARJORIE: A therapist? My therapist died. I cannot replace that remarkable woman as easily as I would a dead schnauzer.

IRA: Marjorie, I did not mean to disparage your relationship with Reba Fabrikant. But you cannot allow her passing to be a catalyst for a complete breakdown. Am I the problem? I know I'm far from perfect. It took me over thirty years to get the point that you hated my jokes. Have you heard a single joke from me in months, a play on words, a pun?

MARJORIE: It was wrong of me to censor you. I should be ashamed of myself.

IRA: No, you were right. People who constantly make puns aren't really listening. I'm glad you criticized me. I am grateful.

MARJORIE: Please don't say that. Have you heard from the Disney Store?

IRA: Yes. Good news. They're not going to press charges. They're being very understanding.

MARJORIE: What do they understand?

IRA: Well, that you had just left a memorial service for your beloved therapist and you had a—

MARJORIE: The memorial service was nearly a month before.

IRA: Doesn't matter. You were out of control.

MARJORIE: It was an accident. People drop things.

IRA: Within three minutes, you dropped six porcelain figurines. They tell me the Goofy alone was two hundred and fifty dollars.

MARJORIE: And you had to pay for everything?

IRA: Forget the expense. What is money but a conduit to help people? It's you I worry about.

MARJORIE: It was an accident.

IRA: I know but they thought you were making some kind of political statement about the Disney Corporation. You know what? I think you should get dressed and go outside. (*eyes the calendar taped to the refrigerator*) Let's see what you had going for today. Tuesday the Seventh. One thirty, Lecture on the literary legacy of Hermann Hesse at Goethe House. "Hiroshima/ Vagina", Multimedia landscapes, Landsberg Gallery, Soho. Five o'clock, Regina Resnik opera symposium, Florence Gould Auditorium. You've got quite a day mapped out for yourself.

MARJORIE: I should be barred from all of those places. I'm of limited intellect. Never have I had even one original thought.

IRA: That is not true. If I were half as intellectually curious as you.

MARJORIE: Curious yes. Profound no.

IRA: What do you call "profound"?

MARJORIE: The ability to think in the abstract. Oh Ira, can't we just face it? We're Russian peasants from the schtetl. We have no right to be attending art installations at the Whitney. We should be tilling the soil, pulling a plow.

(*IRA's beeper goes off. He takes out his phone and dials the number.*)

IRA: Jeffrey Krampf, one of my grad students. Brilliant, tortured mind. I think he's on crack. What can I do? Let him flounder? Now, the line's busy. You're so tough on us. You know, that last production of "Waiting for Godot" affected me deeply. I had the sense that I finally understood what that play was about.

MARJORIE: You understood the story. You think it's about two guys who get stranded by the Tappan Zee Bridge. They're not waiting for Triple A. It's about—I can't even explain what it's about. That is my conundrum. I don't understand the play any better than you. I'm a fraud. A cultural poseur. To quote Kafka, "I am a cage in search of a bird."

IRA: You're hungry.

MARJORIE: Yes, I'm hungry. (*an agonized cry*) Hungry for meaning!

IRA: You need food, real food. You made that wonderful meat loaf and didn't eat a bite. You're gonna lose potassium. I'm cutting you off a square of this Entenmanns. Just to nibble. You'll end up in the hospital with an I.V. at this rate.

(*IRA hands her the piece of cake.*)

MARJORIE: Thank you, Ira. (*eating a bite and yielding a bit*) It is good.

This Is Our Youth

BY KENNETH LONERGAN

ACT II

Warren, an eccentric, thoughtful, awkward, pot-smoking, nineteen-year-old, is staying with his hip, slick, drug-dealing friend Dennis in Dennis's small Upper West Side apartment (in New York City in 1982). Yesterday Warren was thrown out of his father's apartment, but as he left he stole a suitcase with $15,000 in cash that his father was intending to use for a shady business deal. He also took his odd collection of personal belongings, including a cherished Wrigley Field Opening Day baseball cap from 1914 that his grandfather gave him.

Last night Dennis's girlfriend Valerie dropped off her friend Jessica at the apartment. Jessica is bright, touchy, socially aware, and very cynical—especially now that Reagan has become president. After a difficult beginning, Warren and Jessica discovered that they liked each other and went off to spend the night at the Penthouse Suite at the Plaza Hotel, paid for by Warren's stolen money.

It is the next morning and Warren, who had not had any prior success with women, returns to the apartment and tells Dennis about his sexual encounter with Jessica (he "came pretty fast" he admits) and his confusion about her postcoital moodiness ("But I don't even know you" she said). Warren expects to meet Jessica for brunch, but she shows up in the apartment, clearly in a bad mood.

After some caustic repartee, Dennis leaves to sell some of Warren's belongings to recoup the stolen money that has been spent (Dennis is afraid Warren's father will blame him for the theft and have him killed). Warren and Jessica are now alone in the apartment.

JESSICA: Where's he going?

WARREN: He just has a business transaction to perform.

JESSICA: What is he, like the big drug dealer or something?

WARREN: He's the big everything.

JESSICA: Well . . . Sorry to bust in on you like this—

WARREN: That's OK.

JESSICA:—but I actually just wanted to tell you I can't have brunch.

WARREN: Why not?

JESSICA: Well, when I got home this morning I got into this really huge fight with my Mom and I think I'd better just be at home today. She kind of freaked out that I never called last night, so now she wants to have some big Landmark Discussion about how we're gonna handle my *living* there this year . . .

WARREN: Well . . . Thanks for cancelling in person.

JESSICA: Well, I'm sorry, but my Mom's really upset and getting along with her is a really big priority for me right now. I tried to call before, but the line was busy.

WARREN: Do you want to make a plan for any time this week?

JESSICA: I think I'd better just chill out a little bit this week, actually.

WARREN: All right.

(Silence.)

JESSICA: Well . . . You seem like you're really angry . . .

WARREN: I'm not.

JESSICA: Well, that's not the impression you're *conveying*, but . . .

WARREN: No—I guess I just don't understand why you walked

ten blocks out of your way so you could be around the corner so you could buzz up and tell me you can't have brunch with me.

JESSICA: Uh, *no:* I told you I tried to call . . .

WARREN: Yeah—he was on the phone for like two minutes.

JESSICA: All right, I'm *sorry.*

WARREN: There's nothing to be sorry about.

JESSICA: All right. *(She goes slowly to the door and puts her hand on the knob.)* So . . . can I ask you something!

WARREN: Go ahead.

JESSICA: Did you tell Dennis what happened last night?

(Pause.)

WARREN: Um . . . I guess.

JESSICA: Really. What did you say?

WARREN: Nothing. I said we had a nice time.

JESSICA: That's all?

WARREN: Pretty much.

JESSICA: I find that really hard to believe.

WARREN: Why?

JESSICA: I don't know. Don't you guys get into like, comparing notes and stuff?

WARREN: I'm not really into that.

JESSICA: Well . . . OK . . . It's just—This is getting a little weird now, because when I talked to Valerie, she asked *me* if anything happened with us last night, and for some reason, I guess I didn't really tell her that anything did. So now she's gonna talk to *Dennis* and I'm gonna look like a total *liar* to someone I'm just starting to be close friends with and who I really care about . . . !

WARREN: Um . . . So . . . I don't really get . . . You're mad at me because you lied to Valerie?

JESSICA: No, I just should have figured that you would like rush off to tell your friends that you *fucked* me—

WARREN: Whoa!

JESSICA:—whereas I might be more inclined to be a little more *discreet* about it till I found out where I *stood* with you.

WARREN: I didn't fuckin' rush off *anywhere!*

JESSICA: Yeah, whatever, you know what? It doesn't matter—

WARREN: I came *back* here 'cause I'm *staying* here—

JESSICA: OK, but you know what? It really doesn't matter—

WARREN: And the minute I walked through the door he like totally *grilled* me—

JESSICA: Oh so you just tell him anything he wants to know no matter what the consequences are for somebody else?!

WARREN: No! Will you let me finish my—

JESSICA: *(on "let")* But honestly, Warren? I really don't care who you told, or what you told them, because people are gonna think whatever they think and you know what? There's nothing I can do about it.

WARREN: What people? What are you talking about?

JESSICA: I don't know, but whatever it is I must be wrong because of the way you're *yelling*.

WARREN: You're not anything!

JESSICA: Well, it really—I should just really listen to my instincts, you know? Because your instincts are never wrong. And it was totally against my instinct to come over here last night, and it was definitely against my instinct to *sleep* with you, but I did and it's too late. And now my Mom is totally furious at me, I probably ruined my friendship with Valerie, and now like Dennis *Ziegler* thinks I'm like, easy *pickins*, or something—!

WARREN: Nobody thinks *any*thing—

JESSICA: And it's not like I even care what he thinks, OK? Because I don't actually *know* him. Or you. Or *Valerie*, for that matter! So it doesn't really matter! I've made new friends before, I can make more new friends now if I have to. So let's just forget the whole thing ever happened, you can chalk one up in your *book*, or whatever—

WARREN: I don't *have* a book.

JESSICA:—and I'll just *know* better next time! Hopefully. OK?

(Pause.)

WARREN: I don't really get what you're so upset about.

JESSICA: Well: I guess I'm just *insane*.

WARREN: I thought we had a really good time together, and I was actually in a fairly Up state of mind for once.

JESSICA: I'm sure you were.

WARREN: Well, I didn't mean that in any kind of lascivious way, so I don't know why you want to take it like that. I really like you.

JESSICA: Yeah, whatever.

WARREN: No not whatever! I'm sorry I said anything to Dennis. I definitely caved in to the peer pressure. But I also definitely said as little as possible and was totally respectful of you in the way I talked about you. Even though I was pretty excited about what happened last night, and also about like, maybe like, the prospect of like, I don't know, like, going *out* with you—Which I would be very into, if you were. But if you want to think the whole thing meant nothing to me, then go ahead, because that's not the case.

JESSICA: Well . . . You know, I really—

WARREN: It's totally weird, like taking all your clothes off and having sex with someone you barely know, and then being like, "What's up *now?*" You know? Like it's such an intense experience, but then nobody knows what to fuckin' say, even though nothing really bad actually happened. You know?

JESSICA: . . . Well . . . I don't know . . .

WARREN: But I really like you . . . I don't really agree with most of your *opinions* . . .

JESSICA: Oh, thank you.

WARREN: . . . but I don't meet a lot of people who can actually make me *think*, you know? And who can hold their own in an interesting discussion. And who I'm totally hot for at the same time. You know? It's a fairly effective combination.

(Pause.)

JESSICA: I don't know, Warren. Things are just really weird in my life right now. And everything you're saying is really sweet, but I have literally no idea whether you mean it or not. It's like my instinct is just *broken* . . . And I guess sometimes actions speak louder than words . . .

WARREN: But what action could I possibly take except to say that I'm sorry for whatever it is you think I've done?

JESSICA: *(a joke)* Presents are always nice. Just kidding.

WARREN: You want a present?

JESSICA: I'm just kidding.

WARREN: Why? I'm sitting on twelve thousand *dollars.* I'll buy you a *sports* car. OK?

JESSICA: That's OK. I don't even have a license yet.

WARREN: Well, what do you want?

(Pause.)

JESSICA: . . . Are you serious?

WARREN: *Name* it.

JESSICA: OK . . . *(Pause. She looks around the room. Her eyes light on the baseball cap.)* Um . . . Could I have the hat?

(Pause.)

WARREN: Definitely.

(Pause.)

JESSICA: Really?

WARREN: It's yours. *(He picks up the baseball cap and holds it out to her.)* Here.

JESSICA: *(looks at him uncertainly)* . . . Don't if you don't want to.

WARREN: I really want to.

JESSICA: Why?

WARREN: Because I really like you. *(Pause. She reaches out slowly and takes the hat.)*

JESSICA: Well—I don't know what to say . . . *(WARREN does not respond.)* I mean—I can't believe it . . . ! I can't believe that you would give me something that means this much to you—I don't even know what to say.

WARREN: Good. *(She puts it on her head and self-consciously "models" it for him.)*

JESSICA: What do you think?

WARREN: . . . Looks great on you . . .

JESSICA: You think?

WARREN: Definitely. *(She looks at him. He is clearly in distress and can't hide it.)*

JESSICA: Well, you look totally miserable.

WARREN: I'm not.

JESSICA: *(taking off the hat)* Well I'm sorry, but I feel really weird taking your grandfather's hat.

WARREN: Then why'd you fucking ask me for it? *(JESSICA flushes a deep mortified red.)*

JESSICA: I was *totally kidding* when I asked you for something—   WARREN: No you weren't!

JESSICA: Yes I *was!* And then you *insisted* I pick something! Only why did you *give* it me if you don't want me to *have* it!?!

WARREN: Because I really want you to have it!

JESSICA: But why do you keep SAYING that when you obviously DON'T!?

WARREN: NO! God *damn!* What do I have to do, like *BEG* you to take it from me?!

(A long moment.)

JESSICA: OK. Sorry. *(She puts the hat back on her head. Silence.)* Well . . . I mean . . . Should I just go home?

WARREN: *(looking at the floor)* I don't know . . . Do whatever.

JESSICA: Well, then I guess I will. *(She goes to the door.)* Should I assume you no longer want to go out this week?

WARREN: I don't think we can. I'm all out of baseball hats.

JESSICA: *(She takes off the hat.)* Can I please say something?

WARREN: You try to give me that hat back one more time, I swear to God I'll fuckin' *burn* it!

(Pause. JESSICA puts the baseball cap down on the table.)

JESSICA: Well . . . That would be up to you. *(She turn and exits.)*

Heartbreak House

BY BERNARD SHAW

ACT I

Thé setting is a room that resembles "the after part of an old-fashioned high-pooped ship with a stern gallery." Through the windows we see that it is a lovely evening in the country near Sussex, England. The house is owned by eighty-eight-year-old Captain Shotover, a doughty and eccentric former sea captain. He has two daughters. One, Lady Ariadne Utterword, has just returned to visit her father after a twenty-three-year absence. She is attractive, well dressed, and always has a lot to say. She left home to escape the Bohemian disorder and freedom in her father's household—to become a proper and respectable lady. She married a dull but successful government official and found order and happiness.

Now that she has returned, she is disappointed to find that disorder still reigns and the servants are still not deferential. Moreover, her father refuses to acknowledge that this woman who is approaching middle age is, in fact, his daughter, since the last time he saw her she was a young woman.

The Captain's other daughter, Hesione, has married Hector, "a very handsome man of fifty," well dressed, self-possessed, and frequently in pursuit of women other than his wife. Hesione knows about Hector's extramarital pursuits, and actually encourages them. Indeed, when Hesione introduced her sister, Lady Utterword, to

Hector, she suggested that he kiss her "like a good brother-in-law."
Lady Utterword was instantly attracted to him.

Now the others have all gone off to one place or another, leaving
Lady Utterword and Hector alone. She questions him about something he had started to say to her before, but had not completed.

LADY UTTERWORD: *(not interested in ELLIE)* When you saw
me what did you mean by saying that you thought, and then stop-
ping short? What did you think?

HECTOR: *(folding his arms and looking down at her magneti-
cally)* May I tell you?

LADY UTTERWORD: Of course.

HECTOR: It will not sound very civil. I was on the point of saying "I thought you were a plain woman."

LADY UTTERWORD: Oh for shame, Hector! What right had
you to notice whether I am plain or not?

HECTOR: Listen to me, Ariadne. Until today I have seen only
photographs of you; and no photograph can give the strange fasci-
nation of the daughters of that supernatural old man. There is some
damnable quality in them that destroys men's moral sense, and carries them beyond honor and dishonor. You know that, dont you?

LADY UTTERWORD: Perhaps I do, Hector. But let me warn
you once for all that I am a rigidly conventional woman. You may
think because I'm a Shotover that I'm a Bohemian, because we are
all so horribly Bohemian. But I'm not. I hate and loathe Bohemianism. No child brought up in a strict Puritan household ever suffered
from Puritanism as I suffered from our Bohemianism.

HECTOR: Our children are like that. They spend their holidays
in the houses of their respectable schoolfellows.

LADY UTTERWORD: I shall invite them for Christmas.

HECTOR: Their absence leaves us both without our natural
chaperons.

LADY UTTERWORD: Children are certainly very inconvenient
sometimes. But intelligent people can always manage, unless they
are Bohemians.

HECTOR: You are no Bohemian; but you are no Puritan either: your attraction is alive and powerful. What sort of woman do you count yourself?

LADY UTTERWORD: I am a woman of the world, Hector; and I can assure you that if you will only take the trouble always to do the perfectly correct thing, and to say the perfectly correct thing, you can do just what you like. An ill-conducted, careless woman gets simply no chance. An ill-conducted, careless man is never allowed within arm's length of any woman worth knowing.

HECTOR: I see. You are neither a Bohemian woman nor a Puritan woman. You are a dangerous woman.

LADY UTTERWORD: On the contrary, I am a safe woman.

HECTOR: You are a most accursedly attractive woman. Mind: I am not making love to you. I do not like being attracted. But you had better know how I feel if you are going to stay here.

LADY UTTERWORD: You are an exceedingly clever lady-killer, Hector. And terribly handsome. I am quite a good player, myself, at that game. Is it quite understood that we are only playing?

HECTOR: Quite. I am deliberately playing the fool, out of sheer worthlessness.

LADY UTTERWORD: (*rising brightly*) Well, you are my brother-in-law. Hesione asked you to kiss me. (*He seizes her in his arms, and kisses her strenuously.*) Oh! that was a little more than play, brother-in-law. (*She pushes him suddenly away.*) You shall not do that again.

HECTOR: In effect, you got your claws deeper into me than I intended.

Flyovers

BY JEFFREY SWEET

SCENE 2

Oliver has done much better in life than Ted, who tormented him when he was a "geek" in their small-town high school. Oliver, who lives in New York City, has become a famous TV film critic, while Ted, who still lives in the town, is bitter about how his life turned out, especially because he is now unemployed (the local plant that he worked in closed recently). Oliver has come back to town for his high school's twenty-five-year reunion and has accepted Ted's invitation for drinks at his home. The scene takes place in the evening on Ted's deck.

Ted has just left to take his wife Lianne to her mother's house. Lianne, a simple, troubled woman, is very worried about money now that Ted is unemployed, and Oliver, sensing her desperation, gave her one hundred dollars for a (probably worthless) stamp from her recently deceased father's collection. Oliver, who has hinted that his marriage has not been going well, is left alone with Iris, an attractive, tough-talking woman who he felt was way out of his league in high school.

Iris, like Ted, has remained in the town and she too lost her job when the plant closed. At the end of the scene, Iris seduces Oliver, and in the next scene we learn that her seduction was part of a blackmail scheme that Ted conceived: He threatens to send photos of Oliver and Iris in bed together to Oliver's wife. The scheme falls apart when Oliver reveals that his wife left him a few weeks ago.

....

IRIS: She was on good behavior. You should take that as a compliment. Something about you calmed her down. I have to hand it to Ted, his patience. I mean, you saw—

OLIVER: How long—?

IRIS: Well, she's always been a little unsteady. But it's been worse lately—first, the plant closing, then her father dying. The things that have always been there suddenly not.

OLIVER: Losing a parent's hard.

IRIS: Your folks?

OLIVER: Both gone. Yours?

IRIS: My dad's still hanging in there. He and an old buddy named Hank and Hank's wife share a place down in the Florida keys. I went down to visit, and I got the feeling that they'd moved a lot of stuff around before I got there, for my sake.

OLIVER: Cleaned up?

IRIS: More hiding the evidence.

OLIVER: Evidence of what? They running drugs or something?

IRIS: I think when it comes to Hank's wife, it's share and share alike.

OLIVER: Hank's wife puts up with this?

IRIS: Actually, I think it was more or less her idea. Apparently Hank has slowed down some.

OLIVER: Oh.

IRIS: And she hasn't.

OLIVER: And your father?

IRIS: Well, he's always tried to make himself useful.

OLIVER: They didn't want you to know this?

IRIS: I guess they thought I might have opinions.

OLIVER: You don't?

IRIS: At this point in their lives, jeez, if they can put together something that works for them, who am I to—

OLIVER: Sure.

IRIS: Kind of a hoot though, when I think back to how hard I tried to hide the stuff I was doing from *him*—my dad. And that he threw me out of the house for being a tramp.

OLIVER: Did he?

IRIS: Yeah.

OLIVER: That's kind of harsh.

IRIS: Well, I got knocked up. The summer after I got out of high school. He wasn't too happy about that.

OLIVER: Ken the drummer?

IRIS: Somebody else. I was smart enough not to marry him, though. What can I tell you—I was a wild kid. And now my kid's a wild kid. My daughter. Twenty-four now, not such a kid. You're looking at a grandmother.

OLIVER: I don't believe it.

IRIS: You're not the only one. But the same guy, you know—my dad—same guy who gave me grief about what I did back then, now here he is in a seniors threesome. And it seems kind of OK. They're all getting along, nobody's getting hurt—

OLIVER: Maybe different rules apply at different ages. There's stuff that we think is OK for people over eighteen to do that we think twelve-year-olds shouldn't. So maybe there's a later stage where stuff that would be upsetting, disturbing in people in their thirties, forties, fifties—maybe there's a point where it starts being almost—cute?

IRIS: That's just the word I never want to associate with sex. "How's you sex life?" "Cute." You got kids?

OLIVER: Nope.

IRIS: You came here alone. Your wife—

OLIVER: This wouldn't be her scene.

IRIS: She stayed in New York.

OLIVER: My reasons for coming here weren't anything she'd be interested in. Tell you the truth, our interests don't overlap all that much at the moment.

IRIS: Oh, I'm sorry.

OLIVER: It'll either work itself out or it won't.

(He gets up and pours himself another drink.)

You want another?

IRIS: Actually, yes, I would. How much is it really worth?

OLIVER: What? The stamp?

IRIS: How much?

OLIVER: Oh, maybe four thousand dollars.

IRIS: Gee, I would have thought more.

OLIVER: Well, maybe I underestimate. Maybe six, seven—

IRIS: Maybe six or seven *cents*.

OLIVER: You think Lianne might have put one over on me?

IRIS: That's right, it was her doing.

OLIVER: *(handing her the drink, smiles)* You were wrong about my not remembering you.

IRIS: Oh?

OLIVER: I think you might be surprised how much I used to think about you—

IRIS: About me how, as if I can't guess.

OLIVER: Well, aside from that.

IRIS: You never said anything.

OLIVER: What was I going to do, ask you for a date?

IRIS: People do. People did.

OLIVER: But there was something about you—

IRIS: What was about me?

OLIVER: This is going to sound sort of—

IRIS: Never mind what it sounds—

OLIVER: I thought—the crowd you hung out with?—I thought you were better than them.

IRIS: Better?

OLIVER: Not to put down the gang you hung out with—

IRIS: Even if they were lowlifes like Ted?

OLIVER: Well—but that there was more there. That you—

IRIS: I wasn't just a wild kid.

OLIVER: There was something—

IRIS: I had potential. I was a diamond in the rough. If you had the nerve, you would have shown me there were better things in life, finer things—

OLIVER: Put it that way, I sound like an asshole.

IRIS: *(waving his comment aside)* You'd introduce me to symphonies and the Mona Lisa. Expand my horizons. That it?

OLIVER: And poetry. Don't forget poetry.

IRIS: Shakespeare.

OLIVER: Emily Dickinson.

IRIS: So you'd introduce me to Shakespeare and Beethoven and that crowd. And what was I supposed to introduce *you* to?

OLIVER: Oh, I didn't think directly about that. Not straight on. I didn't paint any pictures. I just thought that I'd show you this world of higher thought and beauty and it would awaken in you this desire to—

IRIS: Jump your bones?

OLIVER: Not exactly the words I would have used then. Or now.

IRIS: What words *would* you use now?

OLIVER: *(not answering the question)* And what if I *had* asked you for a date—? Back then.

IRIS: I probably would have been flattered. That you looked down and noticed me.

OLIVER: Oh, come on, "down." I was a geek. How can a geek look down on anyone?

IRIS: You think everybody didn't know good stuff was going to happen for you? Why do you think Ted beat you up? He was paying you back ahead of time.

OLIVER: But you would have gone out with me? If I'd asked?

IRIS: No, actually, I probably would have made some kind of crack, and then I would have told the gang, and they would have given you shit, too.

OLIVER: You would have told them?

IRIS: Yes, I would. You had too high an opinion of me. I mean, I wasn't that nice a person.

OLIVER: Oh, don't do that. I mean, *kids*, for Christ's sake, teenagers—not an age for perspective, kindness, any of that. You can't expect, much less blame—You must have seen it in your own kid, your daughter. What's her name?

IRIS: Natalie.

OLIVER: Nice.

IRIS: You realize, she's older now than you and I were the last time we saw each other?

OLIVER: Wait a second, let me—say that again—

IRIS: You're older, no, *she's* older now than you and I were—

OLIVER:—the last time we saw each other. Right.

IRIS: It's true.

OLIVER: *(very directly)* You and Ted—the two of you—you never—

IRIS: What? Did he ever get into my pants? No. Somehow I missed that treat. Why? Would it damage your opinion of me—

OLIVER: I didn't think you had.

IRIS: Is that a load off your mind?

OLIVER: I hoped you hadn't.

IRIS: You hoped—?

OLIVER: It's something that—it's none of my business—something I couldn't help but wonder.

IRIS: When?

OLIVER: Back then, in school. And tonight.

IRIS: Wondering tonight about back then, or wondering tonight about—what—now?

OLIVER: The thought, the question occurred. Some of the looks you were giving each other—

IRIS: You're reading in.

OLIVER: It's none of my business anyway.

IRIS: Believe it or not, he's pretty nuts about Lianne. Whatever else there is about him, that part—I've never heard anything but that he walks the real straight and narrow when it comes to his marriage.

OLIVER: I'm glad to hear that. She's somebody who needs to be cared for. Looked after.

IRIS: From what you can see.

OLIVER: Which, yeah—Here I am, shooting my mouth off. Fifteen minutes and I'm—Sorry. But, you know, my heart went out to her.

IRIS: Oliver?

OLIVER: OK.

IRIS: She's not yours to rescue.

OLIVER: No, of course not.

IRIS: The hundred bucks was a nice gesture, but let it go at that.

OLIVER: No, of course. It would be presumptuous. Of course.

IRIS: And, about me and Ted—news flash: it is possible to be friends with a guy without making it with him.

OLIVER: I'm sure.

IRIS: Or don't you have any women friends?

OLIVER: Many.

IRIS: And do you sleep with all of them?

OLIVER: Hardly any.

(A beat.)

Gee, I wonder if I've had enough to drink. What do you think?

IRIS: Loosen your leash. You're not driving.

OLIVER: Yes, true. Do you think he's going to be long? Dropping off Lianne?

IRIS: Her mama's just down the road. But, you know, there's a chance he might get stuck in one of those family things.

OLIVER: Yeah, I've heard about them.

IRIS: Family things?

OLIVER: No, I was just wondering. See, Ted gave me a lift out here—

IRIS: Oh, right.

OLIVER: Not that I haven't enjoyed myself.

IRIS: Sure, how often do you get conversation this profound in New York?

OLIVER: When I think of how afraid I used to be of him—Do you know—well, maybe I shouldn't say this—

IRIS: Say anything you feel like—

OLIVER: He said earlier, before you were here—he made this comment about how I probably haven't thought about him in years. I wasn't going to tell him, but I think about him every day.

IRIS: Really?

OLIVER: When I was a freshman, I was standing in the boys' john, you know, at the—

IRIS: Urinal?

OLIVER: There was a whole row of these ones that go all the way down to the floor.

IRIS: OK, I get the picture.

OLIVER: So I'm standing there, and I'm—

IRIS: —yes, and?

OLIVER: —and suddenly I feel this hand in the middle of my back and a push. I step forward to catch my balance, and my foot's in the thing now, and down my right leg there's this trail.

IRIS: Ted?

OLIVER: He laughs. I go into one of the stalls and close the door and wait for it to dry. I was late to class, and I was sure everybody knew, could tell. All the times he pounded me, those I've mostly forgotten. But I go into a public john, particularly if there's a lot of noise and rowdiness—at a ballpark?—I feel my back tense up—

IRIS: Waiting to be pushed again?

OLIVER: Like that's something you needed to know, right? Well, maybe this visit will turn out to be therapeutic.

IRIS: Because you've made peace with Ted, you'll stop tensing up in the men's room?

OLIVER: You know, it would be worth the whole trip.

(IRIS *laughs*.)

IRIS: Would you like a lift back? Where are you staying, the Taylor Arms?

OLIVER: Good guess.

IRIS: I'll take you back.

OLIVER: If it's no trouble.

IRIS: It's what I have a car for.

OLIVER: Well, great. What about Ted? He comes back, we're not here—

IRIS: We'll leave a note.

OLIVER: Right.

IRIS: Or call him when we get where we're going.

OLIVER: "When we—"?

IRIS: Or however it turns out.

OLIVER: Sure.

IRIS: Ted is not a problem in any case. You ready?
OLIVER: Let me finish my drink.

(He is sitting in his chair as he drinks. She drifts over. He puts down his glass. She swoops down and kisses him on the lips, then stands up straight again. He is a little startled, but not displeased. He looks up at her, a little bemused. Lights fade.)

In the Moonlight Eddie

BY JACK LoGIUDICE

Gil Landau is a famous playwright whose new play opened on Broadway tonight. The reviews have come out and it looks like Gil has his first hit after a series of flops. He has brought his agent Max and his leading lady Abby (who is also Max's fiancée) back to his Central Park West apartment for a late-night celebration. Abby is beautiful, though no longer young, and she drinks a lot.

Gil wakes his son Eddie, who is staying with him, and invites him to join the festivities. Eddie, a serious and awkward young man who comes out in a sport coat and tie and mismatched shoes, had a nervous breakdown not long ago and tried to kill himself by jumping off a building. Eddie was living with his mother at the time, never having received much attention from his father, who has always been consumed by the ups and downs of his career.

After a few minutes with the group, Eddie gets upset at Abby's teasing him about his mismatched shoes and what he calls her condescending way of speaking to him. He goes out to the terrace, worrying the group that he might jump off. Abby soon follows him. (As the story proceeds, we learn that Gil didn't actually write his new play. It came to him as a gift from an unknown admirer and he simply put his name on it. The admirer turns out to be Eddie, who wanted to find a way to help his father and bridge the gap between them.)

(EDDIE is standing at the railing, looking out over the city. ABBY appears behind the glass door of the living room. She taps on the glass causing EDDIE to notice her. She then makes a funny face by placing her face up against the glass. ABBY walks onto the terrace.)

ABBY: It took me three months to get that face right, now I don't want a smile, I want a laugh!

EDDIE: You're right, I should have laughed. It was funny . . . really funny. I should have laughed.

ABBY: Do you mind that I'm out here?

EDDIE: No. Do you mind that I'm out here? I'll leave if—

ABBY: Eddie, I'm sorry if I embarrassed you in there.

EDDIE: Oh, you didn't do anything. I embarrassed myself. Making a good first impression was never one of my strong points.

ABBY: Me neither. Believe me, I understand. Would you like me to get you some more champagne?

EDDIE: No. No, thanks.

ABBY: So, I hear that half the city has wrenched their necks looking up to see if you've jumped.

EDDIE: They have?

ABBY: That was a joke, Eddie.

EDDIE: Oh, I get it! Don't you hate that when you tell someone something that's really a sidesplitter and they don't laugh? I hate that. I'll laugh next time, I promise, 'cause you're funny all right, believe me!

ABBY: You don't have to laugh unless you think something is funny. *(looking down at the street)* Look, is that your father standing on the street down there?

EDDIE: *(bursting into a laugh)* Yep, that's Dad all right!

ABBY: Is that funny?

EDDIE: I don't know, but I didn't want to take any chances in case it was.

ABBY: Does he often just stand on the street like that?

EDDIE: Only when I'm on the terrace. Don't stare at him. If he wants to stand alone on the street, that's his business.

ABBY: Does he think he'll catch you? It's five flights!

EDDIE: Why should he want to catch me? I'm not going to jump!

ABBY: Well, he thinks you might!

EDDIE: No, he doesn't.

ABBY: Why do you think he's standing alone on the street in his tuxedo? Are you crazy?

EDDIE: I guess so, look at my shoes! See, I have a sense of humor. Dad looks great tonight in his tuxedo, doesn't he?

ABBY: Yes, he does. I bet you'd look smashing in a tuxedo.

EDDIE: Not me. I just look like a lost usher. (ABBY *studies ED-DIE, making him uneasy.*) Something wrong?

ABBY: (*laughs*) No. I'm just trying to figure you out, that's all.

EDDIE: I don't think it's such a hot idea for you to laugh at me. At least that's what I've been told.

ABBY: Oh, Eddie, lighten up.

EDDIE: Are you aware that I had a nervous breakdown?

ABBY: Ah, show and tell. Are you aware that I'm an alcoholic? I like this. What else can we reveal about ourselves? I hate the color blue, how about you?

EDDIE: Can you be serious?

ABBY: Can you be drunk? (*a beat*) Eddie, let's go back inside so your father won't worry.

EDDIE: He's not worried, I'm telling you. How many times do I have to tell you that? I mean, he might have been worried in the beginning, but I wasn't right then. I'm better now. See, Dad's on the street because he wants me to know that everything's all right, that's all. I made a fool of myself in there with you and Max. He's just saying that it's okay. That's the way we communicate. Sometimes, when he makes a fool of himself, he walks out here and I go down and stand on the street. We've watched that moon a lot together. Funny thing, it's been a long time since we've carried on a decent conversation. But I'll tell you one thing . . . My old man and me . . . we always did enjoy a good full moon together. Now that's something, isn't it?

ABBY: Yeah, that's something, Eddie. What do you mean that it's been a long time since you two had a conversation? How long?

EDDIE: Well, a real long time . . . but that's all going to change now. It's all going to change. He's got a hit, and that's what he wanted.

ABBY: Personally, I think he just missed wearing that tuxedo. Maybe he should have been a waiter?

EDDIE: You know, you shouldn't drink so much. My God, you really used to be a knockout!

ABBY: I wonder if your father'd catch me if I jumped?

EDDIE: I said the wrong thing. See, I had two thoughts running through my head at the same time. I didn't necessarily mean that you look older because you drink. Now that could be the case, I don't know . . . I was just remembering how you looked ten years ago. You don't look bad now, but I mean, you were extraordinary. See what I mean?

ABBY: Did you really want to jump off that building, or did some girl try to push you off?

EDDIE: I messed up again, huh?

ABBY: Yep!

EDDIE: I'm sorry. Do you want me to get you another drink?

ABBY: No, I'll survive. Eddie, do I make you nervous?

EDDIE: Everybody makes me nervous.

ABBY: I see. Tell me, Eddie, what type of girl interests a fellow like you?

EDDIE: The type that says "yes." My grades aren't too hot in that department.

ABBY: I don't think you should worry about it.

EDDIE: Why, do you have a girl in mind? (*They laugh together.*) Hey, we talk all right together, don't we?

ABBY: Yes, Eddie, we talk all right.

EDDIE: This is great. I mean this is really great. Especially with you. I can't believe it!

ABBY: So, come on, Eddie. Tell me the kind of woman that would be special to you . . . besides the ones that say yes?

EDDIE: I don't know.

ABBY: For instance . . . for me it was Gable. What a feeling it was just to dream about him. Those eyes!

EDDIE: I had one of those once . . . an actress.

ABBY: Do you remember her eyes?

EDDIE: When I was 13, girls didn't have eyes. Her breasts are what I remember. I'm sorry, I—

ABBY: There's nothing wrong with that!

EDDIE: But I never saw them. I just knew that they were perfect. And the way they moved when she walked. And the way she walked . . . Man! I remember when she was in a play at the Martin Beck. Funny, I must have seen that play ten times, but now I don't remember the name, only the place. I'd wait outside and when she'd come out, I'd reach my hand out real quick, hoping she'd touch it. Sometimes she would, too! I didn't want her to sign anything, I just wanted her to touch me. I'd make sure to put a little powder on my hands so she wouldn't feel that I was sweating. Never worked. The powder'd always mix with my sweat and turn to paste, every time! I even did it when she was in a play of my father's. Each time, I'd disguise myself so she wouldn't recognize the jerk that left her hands all white.

ABBY: (after a pause) Eddie . . .

EDDIE: I can't believe I told you that. The doctor told me to be honest with my feelings. That's honest, huh? Sorry about your hands.

ABBY: How grateful I am to know that the sticky white stuff was only powder and sweat.

EDDIE: I think I'd better go back inside now.

ABBY: Eddie . . . don't go back yet.

EDDIE: I think I'd better. I want to get my father off the street.

ABBY: I'm flattered that you dreamed about me. I always wanted men to dream about me. Every man. See, I can be honest too. (Pausing.) I was pretty, wasn't I?

EDDIE: Oh man. But you're still . . . you know . . .

ABBY: Yes, I know. Eddie, with all the opportunities that you had to talk to me . . . How come you didn't?

EDDIE: Who wants to talk to the woman of their dreams? That'd mess it all up! You know what I mean? Not that you wouldn't be great and all.

ABBY: Sure. Hate to find out she's a worn-out old drunk.

EDDIE: It's not that. I just—

ABBY: Forget it, Eddie. I understand. *(a long awkward beat)*

EDDIE: It was . . . uh . . . good talking to you, Miss Norman. Real good. *(He begins to exit.)*

ABBY: Eddie?

EDDIE: What? *(With her back to the audience, ABBY drops the top of her dress for EDDIE to see.)*

ABBY: Your dream girl doesn't look that bad, does she?

EDDIE: Oh my.

ABBY: Please tell me.

EDDIE: Could you kindly remember that I'm getting over a nervous breakdown. *(Embarrassed, ABBY pulls the top of her dress up.)*

ABBY: Oh, Eddie . . . I'm sorry. *(EDDIE walks to the door, then stops and looks back.)*

EDDIE: Miss Norman . . . My dream girl . . . she still looks great.

Impossible Marriage

BY BETH HENLEY

Floral and her husband Jonsey have come to her mother's posh country estate near Savannah for the wedding of her younger sister to a much older man. Floral's efforts to dissuade her sister from the marriage have been unsuccessful and the couple have just gone off, leaving Floral, Jonsey, and other guests behind.

Floral's own marriage to Jonsey has not been happy. She is pregnant and soon to give birth, but Jonsey is definitely not the father, since they have not had sex in a very long time. Floral and Jonsey are very mismatched. She is smart and direct, and he tries too hard to ingratiate himself to others and is frequently baffled about what is really going on between people. Floral and Jonsey are now alone in the garden.

....

JONSEY: An odd man. He thought jasmine were honeysuckle.

FLORAL: I want to ask you a question.

JONSEY: Naturally, I wish them well and hope they have a most pleasant life. People deserve such things.

FLORAL: Your lovers? Which ones have been your lovers?

JONSEY: Floral. How strange.

FLORAL: Everyone knows about your infidelities. I've known for some time. I suspect even my mother suspects.

JONSEY: But I don't have lovers. Darling, you, of all people, must know. You know I cannot . . . It's quite clear I cannot.

FLORAL: With me.

JONSEY: With everyone.

FLORAL: I thought only me. You flirt with so many.

JONSEY: So they won't know. So you won't be ashamed.

FLORAL: My. You see, all along I thought it was only me.

JONSEY: I beg your pardon. I thought it was all apparent. I assumed you knew that my attention to others was merely a guise to make us appear normal.

FLORAL: No. I missed that.

JONSEY: Now you understand.

FLORAL: Yes.

JONSEY: Good.

FLORAL: I think I have to leave you.

JONSEY: No. Impossible. You're my wife. That's my child.

FLORAL: It's not.

JONSEY: We'll say it is. I'll love it like it is.

FLORAL: Love can't make it so.

JONSEY: What can?

FLORAL: It has to be.

JONSEY: I see. I see. There's nothing I can do.

FLORAL: About what?

JONSEY: Anything. Everything. I give up. I surrender. Wrap me in a white flag and ship me towards death. Better than whining and wanting like an undignified dog. Don't you agree?

FLORAL: Well, I do believe it has been your character.

JONSEY: Best not be without character.

FLORAL: People can change.

JONSEY: Who told you that? They were lying.

FLORAL: I've seen it happen.

JONSEY: Well, best believe your own eyes.

FLORAL: *(a beat)* What are you thinking?

JONSEY: I'm trying to recall if you said anything clever yesterday. Something I could compliment you on today.

FLORAL: Ah.

JONSEY: So rarely do I look people in the eye and wonder what they are thinking. What if it were something that could spoil the day? Because what you are thinking is exactly the opposite of what I am thinking. It's diametrically opposed. That's not to say I believe you to be wrong and me to be right or vice versa. Truthfully, my belief system is lenient to a grave degree. There is no point at which my spine is not wholly gelatinized. And yet I'm so handsome.

Life During Wartime

BY KEITH REDDIN

ACT I

Tommy is a young man with a new job selling home security systems. His first sale was to Gale, a divorced mother with a sixteen-year-old son. Despite the fact that Gale is older than he, they fall madly in love. Tommy's boss recently revealed to him that there is a darker side to their enterprise—that since they know the security codes of the systems they've installed, they are able to rob the houses with little effort or risk. They have some "professionals" who take care of this aspect of the business, he confided, and no one gets hurt because they know when the homeowners go in and out. Since Tommy has made some good sales, his boss wants him to "take home a piece of the action." Tommy has agreed to think about it.

In this scene he is at Gale's house for dinner and has tried without success to open up a dialogue with Gale's son Howard. Dinner isn't ready yet, so Howard goes off, leaving Tommy and Gale alone in the living room.

....

TOMMY: He hate's me, doesn't he?
GALE: Why do you say that?
TOMMY: Because he does. That was incredibly painful. We had nothing to say to each other.

GALE: It's alright. He likes you.

TOMMY: Now, you're being . . .

GALE: He does. He said so.

TOMMY: He did?

GALE: Yes. It just takes time. He'll . . . with some time, you'll both loosen up.

TOMMY: Because I want him to feel comfortable with me being around. I want him to feel like I'm not . . . like I'm here to steal his mother, or . . . God, he's bigger than me. I look . . . this is embarrassing.

GALE: How do you think I feel.

TOMMY: Nobody cares.

GALE: Oh really.

TOMMY: Nobody does.

GALE: People see you and me together and they say, oh is that your son? And what am I supposed to say, no that's my lover who looks like he's twelve.

TOMMY: You tell people that I'm your lover?

GALE: No, but you know what I'm saying.

TOMMY: I don't look twelve.

GALE: You do. Tommy . . .

TOMMY: Say Tom.

GALE: Maybe we should give it a rest.

TOMMY: What are you talking about?

GALE: Maybe we should slow down. Things are happening very fast and I think we should not . . .

TOMMY: What?

GALE: I like you very much, but I think . . .

TOMMY: I thought we were getting serious.

GALE: That's what I'm talking about. I'm scared. I find myself thinking about you a lot, too much to be good for me and I'll only get hurt.

TOMMY: You won't really.

GALE: You don't know what you want.

TOMMY: I do. I want to spend my life with you.

GALE: I want to believe this. But I'm older than you and I know a little something about people . . .

TOMMY: About men.

GALE: Alright, men, and you're young. You should find somebody . . . look this is a lot of fun. You feel naughty and it's fun. But it's going to end. Sooner or later it will end. And if I set myself up to get . . . I'll only be . . .

TOMMY: I won't leave. I'll be here for you.

GALE: I wish I could believe that.

TOMMY: Look, at some point you got to trust somebody. Otherwise you spend your life . . . Okay, I gathered your ex was this major shit, but not everybody is like that. They're not.

GALE: Oh really?

TOMMY: I'm not. There are a few decent people left. There are people you can put your trust in, that care for you and . . . if you let them, but you got to let them, sure that's scary, but so is life, it's scary and there's plenty of bad people running around, but I am not one of them. You got to believe that.

GALE: Why?

TOMMY: Because I know what I want.

GALE: Which is what?

TOMMY: Which is you. Do you think you're a good person?

GALE: Honestly? I don't think about it.

TOMMY: Well you are. And I'm a good person. Let's blow everybody's mind and live happily ever after. (*GALE smiles.*) Who makes you laugh?

GALE: You.

TOMMY: And who makes you hear colors during sex?

GALE: Okay, you.

TOMMY: I'm smart, I've got three suits and I have this mouth, this mouth that you asked me to keep here, so what's the problem?

GALE: I don't know . . .

TOMMY: You lose.

GALE: Well I . . .

TOMMY: (*He makes a buzzer noise.*) . . . Time's up. I win. Now kiss me. Come on, plant one right here.

GALE: Those lips there?

TOMMY: No, the lips in your garage. Right here. (*They kiss.*)

Blithe Spirit

BY NOEL COWARD

ACT I, SCENE 2

Charles Consodine, a successful writer living in Kent, England, invited Madame Arcati, a professional psychic, to his home to conduct a séance. His goals were to gather material for his new novel and to provide an evening's entertainment for himself, his wife Ruth, and some friends. But Charles got more than he bargained for. Somehow Madame Arcati managed to summon from the "other side" Charles' dead wife Elvira—but only Charles is able to see or hear her. Charles had been married to the puckish and willful Elvira for five years, until her untimely death seven years ago. For the past five years he has been married to the more staid Ruth.

Ruth, who doesn't see or hear Elvira, gets upset with Charles when he converses with Elvira in her presence, especially because she thinks that some of the snappy things he says to Elvira are directed at her. Ruth accuses him of having had too much to drink and storms off, leaving him alone with Elvira.

....

CHARLES: *(following RUTH to the door)* Ruth—
ELVIRA: That was one of the most enjoyable half-hours I have ever spent.

CHARLES: *(putting down his glass on the drinks table)* Oh, Elvira—how could you!

ELVIRA: Poor Ruth!

CHARLES: *(staring at her)* This is obviously an hallucination, isn't it?

ELVIRA: I'm afraid I don't know the technical term for it.

CHARLES: *(coming down center)* What am I to do?

ELVIRA: What Ruth suggested—relax.

CHARLES: *(moving below the chair to the sofa)* Where have you come from?

ELVIRA: Do you know, it's very peculiar, but I've sort of forgotten.

CHARLES: Are you to be here indefinitely?

ELVIRA: I don't know that either.

CHARLES: Oh, my God!

ELVIRA: Why? Would you hate it so much if I was?

CHARLES: Well, you must admit it would be embarrassing?

ELVIRA: I don't see why, really. It's all a question of adjusting yourself. Anyhow, I think it's horrid of you to be so unwelcoming and disagreeable.

CHARLES: Now look here, Elvira—

ELVIRA: *(near tears)* I do. I think you're mean.

CHARLES: Try to see my point, dear. I've been married to Ruth for five years, and you've been dead for seven . . .

ELVIRA: Not dead, Charles. 'Passed over.' It's considered vulgar to say 'dead' where I come from.

CHARLES: Passed over, then.

ELVIRA: At any rate, now that I'm here, the least you can do is to make a pretence of being amiable about it.

CHARLES: Of course, my dear, I'm delighted in one way.

ELVIRA: I don't believe you love me any more.

CHARLES: I shall always love the memory of you.

ELVIRA: *(crossing slowly above the sofa by the armchair to downstage left)* You mustn't think me unreasonable, but I really am a little hurt. You called me back; and at great inconvenience I came—and you've been thoroughly churlish ever since I arrived.

CHARLES: *(gently)* Believe me, Elvira, I most emphatically did not send for you. There's been some mistake.

ELVIRA: *(irritably)* Well, somebody did—and that child said it was you. I remember I was playing backgammon with a very sweet old Oriental gentleman, I think his name was Genghiz Khan, and I'd just thrown double sixes, and then the child paged me and the next thing I knew I was in this room. Perhaps it was your subconscious . . .

CHARLES: You must find out whether you are going to stay or not, and we can make arrangements accordingly.

ELVIRA: I don't see how I can.

CHARLES: Well, try to think. Isn't there anyone that you know, that you can get in touch with over there—on the other side, or whatever it's called—who could advise you?

ELVIRA: I can't think—it seems so far away—as though I'd dreamed it . . .

CHARLES: You must know somebody else besides Genghiz Khan.

ELVIRA: *(moving to the armchair)* Oh, Charles . . .

CHARLES: What is it?

ELVIRA: I want to cry, but I don't think I'm able to.

CHARLES: What do you want to cry for?

ELVIRA: It's seeing you again—and you being so irascible, like you always used to be.

CHARLES: I don't mean to be irascible, Elvira.

ELVIRA: Darling—I don't mind really—I never did.

CHARLES: Is it cold—being a ghost?

ELVIRA: No—I don't think so.

CHARLES: What happens if I touch you?

ELVIRA: I doubt if you can. Do you want to?

CHARLES: *(sitting at the left end of the sofa)* Oh, Elvira . . . *(He buries his face in his hands)*

ELVIRA: *(moving to the left arm of the sofa)* What is it, darling?

CHARLES: I really do feel strange, seeing you again.

ELVIRA: *(moving to right below the sofa and round above it again to the left arm)* That's better.

CHARLES: *(looking up)* What's better?

ELVIRA: Your voice was kinder.

CHARLES: Was I ever unkind to you when you were alive?

ELVIRA: Often.

CHARLES: Oh, how can you! I'm sure that's an exaggeration.

ELVIRA: Not at all. You were an absolute pig that time we went to Cornwall and stayed in that awful hotel. You hit me with a billiard cue.

(Light Cue No. 5. Act 1, Scene 2)

CHARLES: Only very, very gently.

ELVIRA: I loved you very much.

CHARLES: I loved you too . . . *(He puts out his hand to her and then draws it away.)* No, I can't touch you. Isn't that horrible?

ELVIRA: Perhaps it's as well if I'm going to stay for any length of time. *(She sits on the left arm of the sofa.)*

CHARLES: I suppose I shall wake up eventually . . . but I feel strangely peaceful now.

(Light Cue No. 6. Act I, Scene 2)

ELVIRA: That's right. Put your head back

CHARLES: *(doing so)* Like that?

ELVIRA: *(stroking his hair)* Can you feel anything?

CHARLES: Only a very little breeze through my hair . . .

ELVIRA: Well, that's better than nothing.

CHARLES: *(drowsily)* I suppose if I'm really out of my mind they'll put me in an asylum.

ELVIRA: Don't worry about that—just relax.

CHARLES: *(very drowsily indeed)* Poor Ruth.

ELVIRA: *(gently and sweetly)* To hell with Ruth.

The Nina Variations

BY STEVEN DIETZ

SCENE 29

Nina and Treplev are the central characters in Anton Chekhov's *The Seagull*. Treplev was deeply in love with Nina and dreamt of writing great plays for her to star in. But she ran off with Trigorin, an older man and successful writer, who was Treplev's mother's lover. Trigorin eventually abandoned Nina and since then she has supported herself as a minor actress in the Russian provinces. Near the end of the play she returns home and pays a surprise visit to Treplev in his study where he has been writing. She tells him about her disappointing life and he tries, unsuccessfully, to convince her to stay with him. After she leaves, he kills himself.

In *The Nina Variations* Steven Dietz uses various elements from *The Seagull* to imagine many other possibilities for this final encounter between Nina and Treplev (who is also called Kolya and Konstantin). Here is one of them.

....

TREPLEV rushes on, embraces Nina, passionately. NINA remains seated at the desk.

TREPLEV: Nina! Nina—it's you . . . it's you . . . all day long I've

thought this would happen! Just like my mother, I had a premonition—a premonition that you would come to me!

NINA: I never left, Kostya.

TREPLEV: How I've *waited*, Nina! How I've waited for you to
return! I came looking for you every day! I called out your name! I
kissed the ground you walked on!

NINA: I've been here all along. Sitting right here, at your desk.

TREPLEV: I've been in such agony. Cold as a man in a dungeon.
Alone with my words—my colorless, melancholy words. I cursed
you! I hated you! I tore up your letters and your photographs— but
now—Nina, my darling—you've come to me!

NINA: Don't cry, you musn't cry.

TREPLEV: Are we alone?

NINA: We're alone.

TREPLEV: Lock the door, so no one will come in.

NINA: No one will—

TREPLEV: Mother is here, I know it! Lock the door. (*He closes
his eyes. She does not move.*)

NINA: There. It's locked. Is that better?

TREPLEV: (*eyes still closed*) Put a chair against it.

NINA: Kostya—

TREPLEV: Please! (*She does not move.*)

NINA: How's that? (*TREPLEV slowly opens his eyes.*)

TREPLEV: Much better. (*He turns and looks at her.*)

NINA: May I kiss you?

TREPLEV: Oh, my love . . . (*He approaches her, hopefully*)

NINA: I want to light three candles and kiss you. (*He stops.*)

TREPLEV: Why three candles? (*She removes three small candles from her bag [or the desk] during the following.*)

NINA: It is my wish.

TREPLEV: Yes, but—

NINA: Do you not wish to kiss me?

TREPLEV: Certainly. I wish it, Nina, I wish it day and night—
but I was asking about the—

NINA: When I kissed Trigorin—in that stolen interval when my life seemed whole and possible—there were no candles lit. We kissed in wet, dark air. And from that kiss, our life to this moment ensued. So, now, Kostya . . . I want to kiss near a flame. *(She begins to light the candles.)*

TREPLEV: My mother is very superstitious. She has an unfounded fear of many things.

NINA: I am almost ready, Kostya—

TREPLEV: The number thirteen is one. It terrifies her—silly old woman!

NINA: There. Now, I will dim the lights. *(She closes her eyes and reaches an arm into the air, as—the lights fade out—leaving the candles prominent.)*

TREPLEV: And she has one other fear—her *greatest* fear, actually: *(NINA approaches him.)* That of three lit candles.

NINA: Yes. One for me. One for you. And one for mystery. *(She prepares to kiss him. He is fearful, motionless.)*

TREPLEV: Mother warned me—all my life . . .

NINA: Yes?

TREPLEV: "Three lit candles," she always says . . .

NINA: Yes?

TREPLEV: "Bring emptiness and despair." *(She kisses him, gently, seductively, on the mouth. She whispers . . .)*

NINA: And so, Kostya, who do you wish to believe? Your heart? *(She kisses him again.)* Or your mother? *(He stares at her. Then, he kisses her with great passion. She responds in kind. After a few moments, NINA pulls back and looks at his face.)* It's so warm here. So warm and so good. *(She blows out one of the candles.)* Do I look different to you now?

TREPLEV: Yes.

NINA: I was afraid you would hate me. Every night I have the same dream: You look right at my face and you don't recognize me. *(She blows out a second candle.)* And now, Kostya? Do I look different to you now?

TREPLEV: Yes.

NINA: Tell me that's only a dream. Tell me it's not true. Tell me you see me—that you see me *right now*—and that you know who I am.

TREPLEV: I *see you*, Nina. I swear it. *(She blows out the third candle. The stage sits in darkness.)*

NINA: And now? Do you see me now?

TREPLEV: Yes. *(Silence. Words from the darkness.)*

NINA: Never forget me, Kostya. No matter how black the night, no matter how deep the years—remember that I have written my name on you. I am the last face you will see before your death.

The Last Night of Ballyhoo

BY ALFRED UHRY

SCENE 5

It is late in the evening in Adolph Freitag's home in Atlanta, Georgia in December 1939. Adolph is a German Jew and a very successful businessman (he owns a bedding company), but Jews are a small minority in Atlanta and the Freitags have worked hard to assimilate into genteel (and gentile) Atlanta society. They even have a Christmas tree. The Freitags (*Freitag* is the German word for *Friday*), like all of Atlanta, are excited because *Gone With the Wind* is premiering in the local movie house. They are also troubled by the news that Hitler has begun to attack Jews in Europe. It is also of great concern to some that the daughters of the family, Sunny and Lala, get invited to Ballyhoo, the upcoming major social event of the season.

Adolph's pretty and very bright twenty-year-old niece, Sunny Freitag, is home from Wellesley College for Christmas break (she has an A-average and finds Ballyhoo "asinine"). She recently met Joe Farkas, who began working for her uncle a few weeks ago. Joe is in his twenties, hails from Brooklyn, New York, and has never heard of *Gone With the Wind*. He too is Jewish but of Eastern European background, which is generally considered lower status by German Jews.

Joe stopped by the Freitag home late this evening after returning from a business trip. Some family members have gone to the kitchen to make him some food, leaving Joe and Sunny alone in the living room. In a previous scene he asked her to go to Ballyhoo with him.

....

SUNNY: Can I ask you something?

JOE: Shoot.

SUNNY: How did you get to Atlanta? And don't tell me you came on the train.

JOE: Actually I drove down. Okay, okay. I was selling mattresses at Macy's Herald Square and they offered me assistant bedding buyer at their store in D.C. and then the store across the street asked me to assistant manage and then that chain got taken over by Dixie Bedding and one day your Uncle Adolph came in to check us over and he hired me to work for him. That answer your question?

SUNNY: Yes.

JOE: Can I ask you something?

SUNNY: All right.

JOE: Are you people really Jewish?

SUNNY: 'Fraid so. A hundred percent all the way back—on both sides.

JOE: 'Fraid so?

SUNNY: Oh, you know what I mean.

JOE: Yeah. You mean you're afraid you're Jewish.

SUNNY: No. Of course not. That's just an expression.

JOE: Okay. What do you mean?

SUNNY: I don't think I mean anything. It was just something to say. Can we please talk about something else?

JOE: Sure. (*a beat*) Nice Christmas tree.

SUNNY: Thank you.

JOE: Old family tradition, is it?

SUNNY: I've had Christmas trees my whole life, if that's what you mean.

JOE: That's what I mean.

SUNNY: Is there something wrong with that?

JOE: Hey, I'm just trying to get the lay of the land down here. You know, smoke out the local customs.

SUNNY: Everybody I know has a Christmas tree. It doesn't mean we're not Jewish.

JOE: Right. It just means you don't wanna be.

SUNNY: Whether I want to be or not, I am, and there's not much I can do about it.

JOE: Sure there is. For starters you can anglicize your name.

SUNNY: Sunny Friday. Sounds like a weather report.

JOE: Or a striptease artist.

SUNNY: I could call myself Sunny O'Houlihan and everybody around here would still know what I am.

JOE: So what?

SUNNY: It hurts sometimes.

JOE: I know.

SUNNY: No. I don't think you do.

JOE: What do you mean?

SUNNY: I imagine you grew up in a Jewish neighborhood. You were like everybody else. I grew up on Habersham Road.

JOE: Only two Jewish mailboxes and the other one is down at the tacky end of the street where it doesn't count.

SUNNY: You've been talking to Lala.

JOE: Yep.

SUNNY: Well, see? That's all we wanted—to be like everybody else.

JOE: And you are.

SUNNY: Oh no. No we're not.

JOE: Whaddaya mean?

SUNNY: The summer between sixth and seventh grade my best friend was Vennie Alice Sizemore. And one day she took me swimming at the Venetian Club pool. Her parents were members. So we were with a whole bunch of kids from our class and the boys were splashing us and we were all shrieking—you know—and pretending we hated it, when this man in a shirt and tie came over and squatted down by the side of the pool and he said, "Which one is Sunny Freitag?" and I said I was, and he said I had to get out of the water. And Vennie Alice asked him why and he said Jews weren't allowed to swim in the Venetian pool. And all the kids got very quiet and none of them would look at me.

JOE: What did you do?

SUNNY: I got out of the pool and phoned Daddy at his office. When he came to get me all the color was drained out of his lips. I remember that.

JOE: And Vennie Alice?

SUNNY: Oh, her mother called up Mama and apologized. We stayed friends—sort of. Neither of us ever mentioned it again, but it was always there. So believe me, I know I can't hide being Jewish.

JOE: Yeah, so how come you try to camouflage it so much?

SUNNY: Oh, stop it! You think being Jewish means you have to run around in one of those little skullcaps and a long white beard?

JOE: Not in your case.

SUNNY: I'm serious!

JOE: Well, I guess I think being Jewish means being Jewish.

SUNNY: I wish you could've sat in on my comparative religions class last semester.

JOE: Why?

SUNNY: Professor Brainard made so much sense. She believes that all faiths are basically the same with different window dressings.

JOE: Really?

SUNNY: Yes. And I agree with her. I don't think what religion a person happens to be matters all that much in the modern-day world.

JOE: Oh, I think it matters to some pretty important people.

SUNNY: Like who?

JOE: Like Hitler.

SUNNY: No fair. Hitler's an aberration. Let's limit the discussion to human beings.

JOE: Tell you what. Let's drop it altogether.

SUNNY: Why?

JOE: Because I don't want to spend my first date with a pretty girl talking about Hitler.

SUNNY: This isn't a date.

JOE: Not yet.

SUNNY: What do you mean?

JOE: If I'm not mistaken, there's a White Castle right up there in Buckhead.

SUNNY: There is.

JOE: You hungry?

SUNNY: A little.

JOE: Great. Now it's a date!

SUNNY: Joe, I can't just go to Buckhead at this hour of the night.

JOE: Why not?

SUNNY: Mama wouldn't know where I am.

JOE: Leave her a note.

SUNNY: She's asleep.

JOE: Then what's the difference?

SUNNY: I don't do things like that.

JOE: Like what? Eat hamburgers?

SUNNY: I wouldn't feel right. I'm sorry.

JOE: Okay.

SUNNY: I know you're probably used to girls who—

JOE: Who what?

SUNNY: Take more chances.

(He thinks a minute.)

JOE: You think going out with me tomorrow night would be taking too big a gamble?

SUNNY: No, I imagine I can handle that.

JOE: White Castle in Buckhead?

SUNNY: Sure. And maybe a movie first.

JOE: One qualification.

SUNNY: What?

JOE: Not *Gone With the Wind*.

SUNNY: Agreed.

JOE: Good first date.

SUNNY: Yes.

JOE: And the second one is going to be even better.

SUNNY: Second one?

JOE: Ballyhoo. We made a deal, remember?

Fresh Horses

BY LARRY KETRON

ACT II

The play takes place in the rural south, and twenty-two-year-old Larkin has dropped out of college to figure out his future (he is determined to avoid the "prison" of working at a job he hates). He moved into an abandoned railroad maintenance station, invents board games that he hopes to sell to Parker Brothers, and spends most of his time making love to and arguing with his sexy girlfriend Jewel (he met her at the home of a woman named Jean, a place where young people hang out, drink, and have sex).

Larkin recently learned that Jewel is sixteen, not nineteen as she told him, and is married to a thug named Green who has been away in the Navy. Upon Green's return, Larkin borrows money from his mother so Jewel can get her marriage annulled. Last night things came to a head for Larkin. His friend showed up with some bright college girls and he soon realized what has been missing in his relationship with Jewel (who has dropped out of high school and can converse about very little).

As the scene begins, the girls have gone and Larkin is alone in his shack. He has been up all night waiting for Jewel to return with his car, which she borrowed to meet Green at a bar to get him to sign the annulment papers.

(The light begins to turn green. Tremendous sound now of a jet air-plane and: Daybreak, Thursday morning. LARKIN alone in the shack, cuddled in the Indian blanket in the chair. Enter JEWEL. She comes into the shack, closes the door. She tosses the car keys down. She picks up a can of cola left over from last night:)

JEWEL: Can I have one of these? *(LARKIN is shaking his head. She slams can down.)* Okay, I won't have one.

LARKIN: *(looking at his watch)* I'm not shaking my head you can't have a Coke. I'm shaking my head I don't believe you. Or me *with* you. Or anything else. Or that I been sitting here like a fool all fucking night long.

JEWEL: Then you don't even want to give me a chance to ex-plain?

LARKIN: I gave you a chance, too many chances. This whole five months I've known you has been *me* going slowly down into a hole. Because you don't have brain one or any social grace and no-body wanted to be around us except others of the same type like Jean McBaine and her daughter Laurel. And you have a bad temper, I think you even scare people. And you haven't even finished high school so you have this pervasive dumbness which follows you around like a dog. And hitting the bottom of the hole was finding out you were married. But I even tried to work *that* out somehow. Then you break up a night I'm having, you take my car for a few minutes, and I sit here all night long! Bullshit! I've had it. I had fun here last night for the first time in a long time.

JEWEL: *(sarcastically)* No, you never had *fun* with me.

LARKIN: I had fun with you. But not like last night. Last night was *fun*. It was loose. There was . . . happiness in it. That group that was here, we were all on the same planet.

JEWEL: What am I, on Mars?

LARKIN: Yes. As a matter of fact, you're on fucking Mars. Those kids and me, we have things in common to talk about. We have school in common. They were refreshing. Fucking wasn't the *only* thing I wanted to do with them.

JEWEL: That's *all* you want to do with me.

LARKIN: It's all we *do!* There's nothing else *to* do! We can't *talk.* I can't, for example, discuss with you, the, the, the . . . or when's the last time we were together somebody had an *idea?* Never.

JEWEL: I can't talk good to you. You get me all nervous inside with butterflies. But those girls that were here? I told them a whole story I heard over at Jean's about a little girl fell into the river and this guy tried to save her but couldn't.

LARKIN: Over at Jean's. We try to talk and the only thing you can say is something you heard somebody *else* say over at Jean's.

JEWEL: I don't hear you no brilliant conversation!

LARKIN: Don't argue with me! You shouldn't have left me alone all night, Jewel. After I had such a good time with those people here, I started getting more and more angry at you until I popped. Then I settled down. And I sat here all night. And I realized what a good time I had had earlier before you showed up to spoil everything.

JEWEL: Yeah, everywhere I go.

LARKIN: Whose fault is that?

JEWEL: I hate those girls who were here.

LARKIN: Of course you do, that's you!

JEWEL: Life is handed to them. Life is not handed to me. I got no advantages. Everything's always been against me.

LARKIN: Who wants to listen to that? I want to listen to some-body who wants to *help* herself, not somebody who all she can do is twist your guts out.

JEWEL: No you don't! You don't know what it was like growing up like I did with that—

LARKIN: Don't start!

JEWEL:—with this *body!* Looking seventeen when I was four-teen, looking nineteen at sixteen. I never fit in with anybody.

LARKIN: Don't do this to my sympathy, not anymore!

JEWEL: You don't even care what happened to me last night. You're as cruel and awful as everybody else I ever met.

LARKIN: I'm not going to listen to something from you that may or may not be true.

JEWEL: You think I wouldn't have got back here quick if I could?

LARKIN: I don't know. That's the thing, I do not know. Okay, why couldn't you?

JEWEL: I drove out and met Green at the back of the Blue Devil Drive-In Restaurant.

LARKIN: See, that you would even *go* to a hangout like the Blue Devil! It's just a hangout for thugs.

JEWEL: That's where he told me to meet him! I had to if I wanted him to go along with the annulment.

LARKIN: Why didn't you tell me you were going to meet him *there*, I wouldn't have let you go or I would have gone with you.

JEWEL: You didn't ask me. *(pause)* I parked in the back where he was with some other guys.

LARKIN: Thugs. Hoodlums.

JEWEL: And he come over to my car.

LARKIN: To *my* car! And he *came* over. He didn't *come* over, he *came* over, it's past tense, it's already happened, Jewel.

JEWEL: Don't correct my English!

LARKIN: Did he ask you where you got the car?!

JEWEL: He knew it was somebody else's car. And he made me get in the back seat with him. He said just to talk. I give him the paper this lawyer give me for him to sign it. And he did sign it. But by then a bunch of these other guys had started gathering around and some of them got in with us.

LARKIN: Got in the car?

JEWEL: Some of em in the front seat and in the back. One of them was Green's old man, he was there. He's even more awful than my stepfather ever was. Everybody's drinkin cans of beer and I was so a-scared I could have died. I didn't know what they were going to do.

LARKIN: Well what did they do, Jewel!

JEWEL: They all started grabbing me and touching me. Or tryin to cause I was strugglin. Then Green made them stop and I thought he was gonna protect me but I should of known better. He was only keeping them off a me till they paid him.

LARKIN: Paid him what?

JEWEL: Till they gave him money. Cause he had told them he would show me off for money from them.

LARKIN: What?!

JEWEL: So they started paying him. And one would hold me and he would pull up my shirt and bra and show me off to one or two of them, then others would pay and he'd show me off to *them*. Then one or two would get out of the car and others would get in and the same thing. And the windows were all fogged up and I was getting dizzy and shaken and bruised and I couldn't even struggle any more or think straight. Then I know people paid *more* money and Green pulled my pants down and my underwear down and every one of them was laughing and slappin each other around and crawling over each other to get a better view of me and drinkin beer and passin liquor around and then some would get in and some would get out and Green with his whole fist full of money. I was in shock, I swear I was.

LARKIN: *(his hands on her shoulders)* Jewel . . . Jewel, did they rape you? Are you telling me you were raped in the back of my car?

JEWEL: I don't know!

LARKIN: Of course you know!

JEWEL: I was in shock, I said! I said it was awful and I am only clear about it as much as I've told you!

LARKIN: How long did this go on, Jewel?

JEWEL: I don't know, I don't know! It seemed like a long time. At one point they held my nose and made me drink liquor.

LARKIN: You were assaulted! If you were raped, too, that's—we'll have to get the cops!

JEWEL: No! Just, no! I want to be done with it and forget about it. I went through it and it's over. I passed out, I must have passed out. I woke up this morning in the back seat with my clothes every-which-a-way. I straightened myself up and come right here.

LARKIN: Did you recognize any of the others besides Green and his old man?

JEWEL: One. That friend of Tipton's was one of them.

LARKIN: Who?!

JEWEL: Sproles. That guy Sproles.

LARKIN: Sproles!?

JEWEL: He was one of them. He paid his money to see me. I swear it. (*Pause.* LARKIN *is blown away.*)

LARKIN: I can't go out and, I don't know, avenge this for you.

JEWEL: Who asked you to?

LARKIN: Because everybody's going to have a different story, aren't they, Jewel? Everybody's going to have a different tale to tell. (*Then.*) Will you let me take you to a *doctor*?

JEWEL: NO! JUST SHUT UP ABOUT IT! (*pause*) Now that I've said my piece, I'll leave. Now that I've lost any chance I had of having you, I'll just leave. I know you don't want me now, I'm used, I'm worn-out as far as you're concerned. I'm bad goods. Ya can't trust me. I'll get your money back to you somehow. I don't *know* how. But if it takes ten years, I'll do it. (*pause*) You deserve one of those college girls. Somebody new. Somebody really up there. One of those you can be proud of to take around with you places. You think I'm a dope. But deep down I've always been smart enough to know it wouldn't last.

LARKIN: Everything you told me about last night, was it true?

JEWEL: You're not going to believe me if you don't want to.

LARKIN: See . . . even the way you *reply* to me, I feel like I'm being manipulated. Even the way you reply. I can't let somebody manipulate me.

JEWEL: What does that mean?

LARKIN: Draw stupid emotions out of me by telling me stories of bad luck all the time and manipulating me.

JEWEL: Bad luck, yeah . . .

LARKIN: Whatever it is, then, whatever it is! But they're horror stories one right after the other and you've used them to suck me in and suck me in deeper. It's got to stop. I even feel it right now, Jesus Christ, I feel it right this second! I don't have any damn respect for myself. I don't feel like I'm making decisions based on anything but sex and sympathy, it's stupid. I'm sleepwalking with a hard-on.

JEWEL: (*sarcasm and anger*) Then why don't you just wake up?

LARKIN: That's the plan.

JEWEL: (*softer*) I'm going to walk over the hill. And if I never see you again ever, I don't worry about it. I'm used to it. I'm going over to Jean's house and get as drunk as I can.

LARKIN: Good, you go on.

JEWEL: I will. *(as she starts out)*

LARKIN: Jewel!?

JEWEL: What?

LARKIN: *(a beat, then:)* Please don't go over to Jean's.

JEWEL: Ha . . . *(She walks out the door and disappears.)*

Sorrows of Stephen

BY PETER PARNELL

SCENE 6

Stephen Hurt is a romantic young man living in New York who finds inspiration and solace for the ups and downs of his love life in famous literary heroes. His girlfriend has moved out, which was painful but, of course, there are other women out there. He is very attracted to his best friend's fiancée Christine, he has met a lovely and mysterious woman at the opera, and he has picked up a waitress (Sophia) who has spent the night with him in his apartment. As the scene begins, the apartment is dark.

....

(Sound of alarm clock ringing. It is turned off. In the darkness:)

STEPHEN: Calm! Calm! . . . Oh, du calme, Christine . . . We will find a way . . . Christine . . .

(Lights up. STEPHEN asleep in bed. WAITRESS (SOPHIA PICKLE) beside him.)

SOPHIA: It's Sophia, Stephen Hurt. Sophia Pickle. And I have to go now, too.

(She gets up and starts to dress. STEPHEN rolls over and opens his eyes.)

STEPHEN: What time is it?

SOPHIA: Eight o'clock.

STEPHEN: Where are you going?

SOPHIA: Home.

STEPHEN: It's early yet.

SOPHIA: My boyfriend is waiting for me . . .

STEPHEN: Your boyfriend! You didn't tell me . . .

SOPHIA: Would it have made a difference?

STEPHEN: Where does he think you've been all night?

SOPHIA: With you. Or someone like you.

STEPHEN: With me?

SOPHIA: Asleep with another man. *(pause)* We have a very free relationship.

STEPHEN: That's nice.

SOPHIA: Yes.

STEPHEN: Why will he be waiting for you?

SOPHIA: He likes me to pour him his coffee.

STEPHEN: What are you, a waitress or something? *(pause)* Don't answer that. *(pause)* I'd like you to pour me my coffee.

SOPHIA: I can't. Find a waitress of your own. *(pause)* What about your girlfriend?

STEPHEN: What about her?

SOPHIA: Didn't she pour you your coffee?

STEPHEN: I suppose, in a manner of speaking. *(pause)* Actually, both of us drank tea. *(pause)*

SOPHIA: You didn't tell me you missed her.

STEPHEN: I don't.

SOPHIA: You do. You were saying her name in your sleep all night. "Be calm, Christine . . . it will be alright . . . We will find a way . . ."

STEPHEN: Did I call her Christine?

SOPHIA: Yes.

STEPHEN: Is that what I called her?

SOPHIA: You think about her a lot, don't you?

STEPHEN: I suppose. *(pause)*

SOPHIA: This is a very nice place you've got here.

STEPHEN: Thank you.

SOPHIA: You must do very well.

STEPHEN: What does your boyfriend do?

SOPHIA: He handles money.

STEPHEN: A financier?

SOPHIA: A teller.

STEPHEN: Oh.

SOPHIA: He works hard.

STEPHEN: Yes.

SOPHIA: Though maybe not as hard as you. *(pause)*

STEPHEN: Listen, I want to apologize . . .

SOPHIA: For what?

STEPHEN: For last night.

SOPHIA: What about it?

STEPHEN: The fact that I couldn't, well . . .

SOPHIA: *(shrugs)* It happens.

STEPHEN: Not to me.

SOPHIA: To everyone.

STEPHEN: Yes, but still . . .

SOPHIA: Was it the first time?

STEPHEN: That it happened?

SOPHIA: Yes.

STEPHEN: No.

SOPHIA: Oh.

STEPHEN: But I mean, it's not something I'm known for.

SOPHIA: Don't worry. I won't tell. *(pause)*

STEPHEN: I think it was my rushing into things that did it.

SOPHIA: Yes.

STEPHEN: The fact that I'd only just met you.

SOPHIA: Mmn.

STEPHEN: I mean, normally I'm used to rushing into things, but this . . . this was quite a rush! *(pause)* I've had a lot on my mind lately.

SOPHIA: It's alright, you know. I understand. *(pause)* A lot of men find me very attractive in the restaurant, and then, when they get me home . . . well . . .

STEPHEN: It's not that I didn't find you attractive, because I did. I do.

SOPHIA: This one man brought me up to his apartment and told me the only thing he really liked about me was my lips. He said a woman's lips were the most beautiful thing in the world. It was very nice for starters, but, well, nothing to make a night out of.

STEPHEN: I think your lips are very beautiful, too. *(pause)*

SOPHIA: You're feeling a little lonely, aren't you.

STEPHEN: A little, yes.

SOPHIA: Lost, almost. *(pause)* Don't worry. Someone will find you.

STEPHEN: You think?

SOPHIA: You're too good not to be found.

STEPHEN: Good?

SOPHIA: Honest. Open. Innocent, almost. It's very unusual.

STEPHEN: Is it?

SOPHIA: Yes.

STEPHEN: Is it good?

SOPHIA: To be good?

STEPHEN: Mmn.

SOPHIA: Why not? I'd like to meet some more good men. The thing about good men is, often they're the most passionate.

STEPHEN: Are they?

SOPHIA: Mmn. When they're not acting good, that is.

(STEPHEN looks bewildered. SOPHIA moves to bed. Kisses him.)

Come on.

STEPHEN: What?

SOPHIA: Come here.

STEPHEN: But . . .

SOPHIA: We'll be alright this time.

STEPHEN: What about your boyfriend?

SOPHIA: There isn't one.

STEPHEN: There isn't?

SOPHIA: I made him up.

STEPHEN: Why?

SOPHIA: In case you didn't want to apologize. *(Pause. She gets under the covers.)* You're shaking.

STEPHEN: Yes.

SOPHIA: What's the matter?

STEPHEN: I'm afraid.

SOPHIA: Don't be.

STEPHEN: I am.

SOPHIA: Of what?

STEPHEN: I don't know.

SOPHIA: Being alone?

STEPHEN: Yes.

SOPHIA: But you aren't.

STEPHEN: No.

SOPHIA: You're with me.

STEPHEN: Yes. *(pause)* But I know I will be.

SOPHIA: Alone?

STEPHEN: Yes.

SOPHIA: When?

STEPHEN: Soon.

SOPHIA: You mean later?

STEPHEN: Mmn.

SOPHIA: Later today? *(pause)*

STEPHEN: Yes.

Camille: The Lady of the Camellias

BY ALEXANDRE DUMAS (FILS)

ACT I, SCENE I

Camille was written by Alexandre Dumas (fils) in 1852, adapted from his novel. It tells the story of Marguerite Gautier, a beautiful, impetuous, self-centered woman, who is at the center of Parisian society—and who has been ill for a long time with consumption (she is called the Lady of the Camellias because camellias, which have no smell, are the only flowers that she will allow in her home).

The play depicts a decadent group of upper-class Parisians whose main concerns are their sexual liaisons and maintaining their social positions (through an odd circumstance, Marguerite is supported by a wealthy Duke, but she spends much more than he provides and is deeply in debt). Many men have loved Marguerite but none has won her heart, and she treats none of them very well. Tonight, some friends have come to visit her and brought with them a Monsieur Armand Duval, a young man who told them that he has been a secret admirer of Marguerite for two years (he reveals that, a year ago, when she was hospitalized for three months, he went to the hospital every day to inquire about her health but never made his presence known to her). After dinner, Marguerite and the others—dance, but she becomes short of breath and asks everyone to leave the room (her lavish boudoir) so she can rest. But Armand soon returns and the scene that ensues depicts the beginning of a love affair that is one of the most moving and tragic in dramatic literature.

....

MARGUERITE: *(alone, tries to get her breath)* Ah! *(looks in the mirror)* How pale I am!—*(She leans against the fireplace, her head in her hands.)*

ARMAND: *(entering)* And now, Madame, are you better?

MARGUERITE: Yes, M. Armand! Thank you, I am better.—I am used to it, anyway—

ARMAND: You are killing yourself! I wish I were your friend, or relative, so that I could keep you from harming yourself.

MARGUERITE: You would not succeed!—But what is it? What's the matter?

ARMAND: *(tears in his eyes)* What I see—

MARGUERITE: Oh! You're very kind. Look at the others, they don't worry much!

ARMAND: The others do not love you as I do.

MARGUERITE: Oh, that's true, too!—I had forgotten about that great love!

ARMAND: It only amuses you—!

MARGUERITE: God forbid! Every day I hear the same thing;—it no longer amuses me.

ARMAND: As you wish.—But that love is worth at least one promise from you.

MARGUERITE: What promise—?

ARMAND: That you will take care of yourself.

MARGUERITE: Take care of myself! Is that possible?

ARMAND: Why not?

MARGUERITE: But, my dear boy—if I took care of myself, I should die. What keeps me going is the feverish life that I lead. Take care of myself! It's only ladies of fashion with families and friends can afford the luxury of taking care of themselves; but we others must go on, for as soon as we stop playing up to the pleasure and vanity of men, we are abandoned. Long evenings follow long days. How well I know it! I was ill in bed for three months. At the end of three weeks, not a soul came to see me.

ARMAND: I know that I mean nothing to you, but if you would let me, Marguerite, I would take care of you. I would never leave you, I would make you well. Then when you had the strength, you could take up your life again—if you still wished to. But I am sure that by then a quieter, more regular existence would appeal to you!

MARGUERITE: The wine has made you sad.

ARMAND: Have you no heart, Marguerite?

MARGUERITE: A heart! That's the one thing that could wreck a life like mine! *(a silence)* It's really serious then?

ARMAND: Very—serious.

MARGUERITE: Prudence didn't lie to me when she told me you were sentimental. You would actually take care of me?

ARMAND: Yes.

MARGUERITE: Stay with me day in and day out?

ARMAND: As long as I did not bore you.

MARGUERITE: And you call that——?

ARMAND: Devotion.

MARGUERITE: And why this devotion?

ARMAND: I am irresistibly drawn to you, Marguerite.

MARGUERITE: Since——?

ARMAND: Two years ago—one day, when I saw you pass, beautiful, proud, smiling—since that day I have followed you silently, from afar.

MARGUERITE: Why haven't you told me this before?

ARMAND: I did not know you, Marguerite.

MARGUERITE: Why, when I was so ill and you came every day to inquire about me, why didn't you come up?

ARMAND: What right had I to intrude upon you?

MARGUERITE: Right! One does not stand upon ceremony with a woman like me.

ARMAND: One always stands upon ceremony with a woman.— Then, too—I feared the influence that you might have upon my life.

MARGUERITE: It really looks as if you were in love with me!

ARMAND: *(looking at her and seeing her laugh)* If I am ever to tell you so, this is not the moment.

MARGUERITE: Never tell it me.

ARMAND: Why?

MARGUERITE: Because only two things can come. Either I won't believe you, in which case you will hold it against me; or I will believe you. Then you would have the saddest of lives—the companionship of a sick, nervous woman—sad, gay with a gayety more sad than sorrow—a woman who spends a hundred thousand francs a year; that's good enough for an old Crœsus like the Duke, but it could only prove boring for a young man like yourself. But there—we are talking a lot of nonsense! Give me your hand and let's join the others. They will be wondering what's keeping us.

ARMAND: Join them, if you wish. I ask your permission to remain here.

MARGUERITE: Why?

ARMAND: Because your gayety hurts me.

MARGUERITE: Do you want me to give you some advice?

ARMAND: Give it me.

MARGUERITE: Take the first coach and run away, if what you have told me is true; or else love me as a good friend, but not otherwise. Come to see me, we shall laugh and talk; but do not exaggerate my worth, for I am not worth much. You have a good heart. You need to be loved. You are too young and too sensitive to live in our world; love some other kind of woman, or marry. You see, I am a decent sort—I want to be quite frank with you.

PRUDENCE: *(half-opening the door)* What the devil are you doing here?

MARGUERITE: We are talking sense; leave us a moment—we'll join you later.

PRUDENCE: Oh, all right, my children. Talk away. *(Exit.)*

MARGUERITE: So—it's settled—you don't love me any more.

ARMAND: I will take your advice—I will go away.

MARGUERITE: Is it as bad as that?

ARMAND: Yes.

MARGUERITE: Many people have said that—but they haven't gone.

ARMAND: Because you held them back?

MARGUERITE: Good God, no!

ARMAND: Then you've never loved any one?

MARGUERITE: Never, thank God!

ARMAND: Thank you!—Thank you!

MARGUERITE: For what?

ARMAND: For what you have just told me; nothing could have made me happier.

MARGUERITE: What a child!

ARMAND: Supposing I told you that I have spent entire nights under your windows, that I have kept for six months a button fallen from your glove?

MARGUERITE: I would not believe you.

ARMAND: You are right—I'm quite mad. Laugh at me, that's the best thing to do.—Good-bye.

MARGUERITE: Armand!

ARMAND: You are calling me back?

MARGUERITE: I'm not calling you back but I do not want you to go away angry with me.

ARMAND: Angry with you? Is that possible?

Scenes for Two Women

Collected Stories

BY DONALD MARGULIES

SCENE 3

The play begins in September 1990, when Lisa Morrison, in her mid-twenties, becomes Ruth Steiner's student. Ruth, in her late fifties, is a celebrated short story writer who teaches writing in NYU's graduate program. Lisa, who shows promise as a writer, soon becomes Ruth's assistant and, before long, her friend and confidant. Ruth tells her things she has not told anyone, nor written about— like her love affair with the poet Delmore Schwartz when she was twenty-two years old.

It is now October 1996 and Ruth's and Lisa's relationship has changed. Lisa has become more confident and assertive—even to the point of sharply criticizing one of Ruth's latest short stories. Lisa's first novel has just been published and tonight she read an excerpt from it to an enthusiastic audience at the 92nd Street Y. Ruth, who has been ill (and has taken in a visiting nurse to help her) did not show up for the reading, and Lisa, who has not come by for weeks, stops in to check up on her.

Lisa tells Ruth about her reading and the two make small talk for a while, but Lisa "senses the chill in the air." Ruth, who never married, has been saying that she would have liked to have had a child (Lisa has just returned from the kitchen "holding a saucer and a cup of tea").

RUTH: I'm telling you it's been *weeks*; Monica's been coming for weeks.

LISA: Has it really been that long?

RUTH: Yes!

LISA: I'm sorry; I've been busy. The book.

RUTH: Yes. Of course. The book. *(pause, re: LISA's tidying)* Leave it.

LISA: You have junk mail here from Christmas.

RUTH: You don't have to pick up after me, I can still pick up after myself.

LISA: I'm just straightening up.

RUTH: Whenever *you* straighten up, things disappear.

LISA: *(flips through a* New Yorker*)* Did you read the Janet Malcolm piece in here?

RUTH: Life's too short for *The New Yorker*.

LISA: It's good; you should read it. *(She puts it beside RUTH's chair.)*

RUTH: I don't have time to read. I have all the time in the world and no time at all. My life is a paradox. That's quite a lovely dress you have on.

LISA: Oh, thank you.

RUTH: Looks expensive.

LISA: It was.

RUTH: That's what you wore tonight?

LISA: Uh huh. I wanted to look *serious*—but sexy. Too much?

RUTH: For the 92nd Street Y? Perhaps. How'd it go?

LISA: Actually, it went fine. It was fun.

RUTH: Good.

LISA: There were a couple of candy-wrapper-crinklers I wanted to kill, but aside from that. . . .

RUTH: I used to love readings. I always found them exhilarating. I loved playing all the parts. And getting laughs. I loved the laughter. I'm just an old ham, you know that.

LISA: Yes; I do.

RUTH: And it isn't just any old laughter; it's the self-congratulatory laughter of people who want you to know that they get *every*thing.

LISA: *(smiles, then:)* This Barnard undergrad cornered me afterwards, saying she couldn't *wait* to meet me? It was really weird finding myself in a position of being pursued, when all my life I've been the pursuer—but she really wasn't interested in what I had to say; all she wanted was to talk about herself! *(LISA observes Ruth lost in thought, not really listening. Pause.)* Ruth? Would you like some tea?

RUTH: It would have been good for me, I think, having a child.

LISA: Yes?

RUTH: I might have become a different person. A better writer, maybe; a better human being, possibly. My life surely would have been *different*. Instead, I spent many many years, too many years, nurturing other people's gifted children. *(a beat)* The first day of every class I ever taught—thirty-two years, thirty-two first days— I'd scan the faces and try to predict who out there would one day dazzle me. Who would thrill and astonish me with their promise? Who will it be this year? I'd want them, like a vampire wants fresh blood. I'd want to fill them up with what I know, these beautiful hungry empty vessels, and watch them grow. I've had a succession of chosen daughters through the years, mostly daughters. A few sons. Unformed, talented, as susceptible to my wisdom as I was to their youth. But none I loved as much as you.

LISA: Ruth. *(pause)*

RUTH: I read your book.

LISA: Yes. I figured.

RUTH: Well, most of it, anyway. As much as I could possibly read right now. My eyes are stinging. There are tons of typos in the copy you gave me, tons.

LISA: *(over "... tons.")* I know, it's an advance copy.

RUTH: I hope they're planning on correcting them.

LISA: Of course they are.

RUTH: I marked the margins anyway. Force of habit. There are some truly egregious errors in there.

LISA: I know.

RUTH: One whole section is suddenly repeated. I thought I was losing whatever mind I have left. Either that or you'd gone Joycean on me. And experimental fiction, as we both know, is not your style. (*silence*) Lisa Lisa. If you had only asked me what I thought. If you had only asked me.

LISA: Ruth.

RUTH: I would have told you you were making a mistake.

LISA: I didn't know what to do, I didn't know how to handle it.

RUTH: Stay away from Schwartz; leave him out of it. He's mine, not yours. Besides, he's been done to death, picked-over by so many vultures in the name of literature, and Bellow finished him off for everyone. If you had *asked* me. If you had only *asked* me.

LISA: Ruth.

RUTH: If you had only asked my advice. Forget my permission. If you had asked my advice. I'd have told you to look elsewhere, leave him alone, leave him out of it. They'll compare you to Bellow and your work simply can't support it, darling. It can't. You're not good enough. You may never be good enough. Why call attention to it? If you had asked me what I thought, I would have told you. But you didn't ask. Instead you skulked like a thief. Avoided me for two and a half years,—

LISA: No, I didn't. . . .

RUTH: (*continuous*)—evaded my questions, failed to look me in the eye.

LISA: Ruth. . . .

RUTH: You did, you did, my darling, I knew something was up: When you *did* come to see me, you couldn't *look* at me. I thought it was my appearance, that I was looking so awful you couldn't look me in the eye.

LISA: No!

RUTH: I could have used your friendship but you were too busy going through my panty drawer, scavenging through my personal effects.

LISA: That's not what I did!

RUTH: Then why did you skulk? Why couldn't you look at me?

LISA: I don't know, I . . . I needed some distance.

RUTH: "Distance"!

LISA: I needed to separate from you.

RUTH: *(amused)* That you did, my darling, that you did.

LISA: *(over "... that you did")* You wouldn't know what it's like, to have to get out from under you, from under your influence, you couldn't possibly know what that's like!

RUTH: *(over "... what that's like!")* Everything I told you. Everything I shared.

LISA: Ruth.

RUTH: What a fool I was.

LISA: No.

RUTH: It was all *material* to you! That's all it was.

LISA: That's not true.

RUTH: Here I was, regaling you with stories from my life like the pitiful old woman you've made me out to be . . .

LISA: *(over "... you've made me out to be ...")* "Pitiful"?! No no. . . .

RUTH: *(continuous)* . . . and all the while you were taking notes!

LISA: That isn't true! I was listening! I was cherishing every minute!

RUTH: I'm sure.

LISA: If I had told you and you'd disapproved—*(RUTH turns away, busies herself.)* Listen to me: If you had disapproved, I don't know what I would've done.

RUTH: Uh huh.

LISA: I never could've written it. How could I have written it? I might have lost *you* and I would have lost my novel, too. I was scared.

RUTH: Poor thing.

LISA: I didn't know what to do! You were the one person who could advise me but I couldn't discuss it with you.

RUTH: Clearly you listened. You listened all right. You took it all in. And set it all out for the world to see.

LISA: What, what did I do that any good writer wouldn't have done?, that you wouldn't have done yourself? A story grabbed me and wouldn't let go.

RUTH: *(over . . . "wouldn't let go")* No, no, dear, that's where you're wrong: it didn't grab *you*; you *seized it*, it didn't seize *you*. Have you no conscience?! Have you no moral conscience?!

LISA: I have a conscience.

RUTH: *Do* you? *Do* you? You went ahead and did it anyway! That's what's so remarkable. You did it anyway.

LISA: What did you teach me: You taught me to be ruthless.

RUTH: *(struck by the unintentional pun)* So to speak.

LISA: If something captures your eye, you told me, grab it. Remember? Like a good photojournalist: Go in and shoot. *(RUTH is evading her, LISA follows her around the room.)* Remember, Ruth?—Don't walk away!—That's what you taught me! Don't worry about feelings, you taught me that, worrying about feelings is sentimental and God knows we mustn't be sentimental.

RUTH: You've crossed the line, though, sweetie. You've crossed the line.

LISA: Why, because it involves you?

RUTH: I would think that would enter into it, yes! I was a fellow *writer* telling you these stories, not a longshoreman or a, a *waitress*, for God's sake! A fellow writer! It's a matter of professional courtesy, I would think. What did I need to do?, proclaim them off-limits? Plant a flag? Make you *sign* something? You were my friend, goddammit!

LISA: I wish you wouldn't use the past tense.

RUTH: Once upon a time writers made things up, you know. Can you imagine?

LISA: *(over "Can you imagine?")* Oh, come on. You used people all the time! Don't give me that shit. Whatever you could get your hands on, you took.

RUTH: *(over ". . . you took")* If I used people for my stories, my dear, they were people who *had* no voice, no outlet for expression.

LISA: *(over ". . . for expression")* Oh! Well! Is that so! That's awfully condescending of you, Ruth, really. How do you know? How do you know that?

RUTH: It's the truth!

LISA: *(continuous)* You're always making these *pronounce-*

ments! When did the Little People you built your *career* on choose *you* as their advocate?!

RUTH: I gave them a voice where they had none.

LISA: Well, there you go: We all play God. Don't we? We all put words into people's mouths. You taught me that, Ruth.

RUTH: (*over "You taught me that, Ruth"*) No no no, what you've done is something else, it's something else. I *have* a voice. I *have* the tools.

LISA: Ruth. . . .

RUTH: Use your own goddamn life! If yours isn't rich enough, too bad; that's not my problem. Don't thumb a ride and hop aboard mine. Hitchhiker!

LISA: Ruth! What do you make me out to be? You make me sound like the most mercenary person imaginable. The last thing I wanted was to hurt you.

RUTH: *Was* it? Oh, I don't know, I think you might be deceiving yourself, dear.

LISA: How?

RUTH: (*continuous*) I think there's something terribly Freudian going on here, don't you? The Oedipal struggle to the finish. You destroy me and claim my lover for yourself, take him to bed with you. I think you *wanted* to destroy me.

LISA: That's ridiculous.

RUTH: You wanted to obliterate me.

LISA: No, no, I wanted to *honor* you!

RUTH: *Honor* me?!

LISA: It was my gift to you.

RUTH: Your *gift?!*

LISA: Yes! I was honoring you. For all you've given *me*.

RUTH: Well, I don't want your gift. How do you like that? I'm very sorry, that isn't very gracious, I know, but your gift doesn't honor me. I want the receipt so I can exchange it for something else but you're telling me there *is* no receipt. It's take it or leave it!

LISA: (*genuinely*) What exactly is so offensive to you? I don't understand it.

RUTH: You don't?!

LISA: No.

RUTH: You've stolen my *stories*, Lisa. My stories! What am I without my stories? I'm nothing. I'm a cipher. I'm as good as dead.

LISA: But they *aren't* your stories, Ruth. Not anymore. They stopped being your stories when you told them to *me*. They changed my life so how can they be solely your stories anymore? You don't *own* them.

RUTH: Oh, no?

LISA: No! You are a part of my life now, Ruth. Our lives intersect. My experience includes your experience. I am the sum of your experience and my experience and everybody else's experience I've ever come in contact with.

RUTH: *(over ". . . come in contact with")* Yeah yeah yeah.

LISA: I couldn't tell your stories, not the way *you* would, I couldn't *possibly* do that. But I *can* take your experiences, what I *know* of them, what I *make* of them, and extrapolate, *that* I can do, but my book doesn't pretend to be the *truth*. Miriam isn't *you*. *(RUTH scoffs.)* She *isn't*.

RUTH: I know that line, *bubeleh*; believe me, I've used it.

LISA: All right, she's as much me as she is you.

RUTH: That lonely, pitiful woman, pining for Delmore Schwartz?

LISA: No, no, the young, impressionable disciple who wants nothing more than the high regard of her mentor.

RUTH: Is *that* what you were going for?

LISA: Yes!

RUTH: Then you've failed miserably; I don't see that at all.

LISA: That's 'cause you don't *want* to see it! You've totally, willfully, misread her! Miriam isn't pitiful. She's vital, funny, self-ironical. She sees the affair for what it truly was, in ways you obviously cannot!

RUTH: What is that supposed to mean?!

LISA: *You're* the one who calls it the "shining moment" of your life, for Christ's sake, Ruth!, that's what you told me! You wear it like some kind of masochistic badge of honor.

RUTH: Who the hell asked *you?*

LISA: *(over ". . . asked you?")* You've let that one brief affair define your entire life!

RUTH: I have not! That is absurd!

LISA: *(continuous)* You're like a professional war widow or, or Miss Havisham in her wedding dress or something!

RUTH: That is not who I am! That's insulting!

LISA: I'm sorry.

RUTH: You gonna lay some post-feminist crap on me now? Huh, Lisa?

LISA: *(wearily)* No.

RUTH: *(continuous)* How only *you*, with the benefit of a modern, feminist perspective, can put *my* affairs in their proper place? Is that it?

LISA: *(over "Is that it?")* I wanted to reclaim for you a part of your life, okay? I wanted to give something precious back to you.

RUTH: Really! And who the hell asked you?! Who *asked* for your revisionism of *my* life?

Wit

BY MARGARET EDSON

Vivian Bearing, fifty years old, a renowned professor of English and expert on the sonnets of John Donne, has terminal ovarian cancer and has been participating in an experimental chemotherapy program. She has faced her painful illness and the indignities of her hospital stay with the same no-nonsense attitude that served her well throughout her life. As always, she has relied on her formidable intellect and caustic wit, with no sentiment allowed.

But she is finding it more and more difficult to bear her increasing pain and dependency, and her growing fear of death. Having lived a life of the mind without emotional ties to others, she now finds herself seeking comfort from her kind but unsophisticated nurse Susie. Susie is not an intellectual, but she raises the important question of whether the doctors treating Vivian and others in the hospital should be keeping suffering patients alive for the sake of their research.

(SUSIE enters, concerned.)

SUSIE: Ms. Bearing? Is that you beeping at four in the morning? (She checks the tubing and presses buttons on the pump. The alarm stops.) Did that wake you up? I'm sorry. It just gets occluded sometimes.

VIVIAN: I was awake.

SUSIE: You were? What's the trouble, sweetheart?

VIVIAN: *(to the audience, roused)* Do not think for a minute that anyone calls me "Sweetheart." But then . . . I allowed it. *(to SUSIE)* Oh, I don't know.

SUSIE: You can't sleep?

VIVIAN: No. I just keep thinking.

SUSIE: If you do that too much, you can get kind of confused.

VIVIAN: I know. I can't figure things out. I'm in a . . . *quandary*, having these . . . *doubts*.

SUSIE: What you're doing is very hard.

VIVIAN: Hard things are what I like best.

SUSIE: It's not the same. It's like it's out of control, isn't it?

VIVIAN: *(crying, in spite of herself)* I'm scared.

SUSIE: *(stroking her)* Oh, honey, of course you are.

VIVIAN: I want . . .

SUSIE: I know. It's hard.

VIVIAN: I don't feel sure of myself anymore.

SUSIE: And you used to feel sure.

VIVIAN: *(crying)* Oh, yes, I used to feel sure.

SUSIE: Vivian. It's all right. I know. It hurts. I know. It's all right. Do you want a tissue? It's all right. *(silence)* Vivian, would you like a Popsicle?

VIVIAN: *(like a child)* Yes, please.

SUSIE: I'll get it for you. I'll be right back.

VIVIAN: Thank you.

(SUSIE leaves.)

VIVIAN: *(pulling herself together)* The epithelial cells in my GI tract have been killed by the chemo. The cold Popsicle feels good, it's something I can digest, and it helps keep me hydrated. For your information.

(SUSIE returns with an orange two-stick Popsicle. Vivian unwraps it and breaks it in half.)

VIVIAN: Here.

SUSIE: Sure?

VIVIAN: Yes.

SUSIE: Thanks. (SUSIE *sits on the commode by the bed. Silence.*) When I was a kid, we used to get these from a truck. The man would come around and ring his bell and we'd all run over. Then we'd sit on the curb and eat our Popsicles.

Pretty profound, huh?

VIVIAN: It sounds nice.

(*Silence.*)

SUSIE: Vivian, there's something we need to talk about, you need to think about.

(*Silence.*)

VIVIAN: My cancer is not being cured, is it.

SUSIE: Huh-uh.

VIVIAN: They never expected it to be, did they.

SUSIE: Well, they thought the drugs would make the tumor get smaller, and it has gotten a lot smaller. But the problem is that it started in new places too. They've learned a lot for their research. It was the best thing they had to give you, the strongest drugs. There just isn't a good treatment for what you have yet, for advanced ovarian. I'm sorry. They should have explained this—

VIVIAN: I knew.

SUSIE: You did.

VIVIAN: I read between the lines.

SUSIE: What you have to think about is your "code status." What you want them to do if your heart stops.

VIVIAN: Well.

SUSIE: You can be "full code," which means that if your heart stops, they'll call a Code Blue and the code team will come and re-suscitate you and take you to Intensive Care until you stabilize again. Or you can be "Do Not Resuscitate," so if your heart stops we'll . . . well, we'll just let it. You'll be "DNR." You can think about it, but I wanted to present both choices before Kelekian and Jason talk to you.

VIVIAN: You don't agree about this?

SUSIE: Well, they like to save lives. So anything's okay, as long as life continues. It doesn't matter if you're hooked up to a million ma-. chines. Kelekian is a great researcher and everything. And the fellows, like Jason, they're really smart. It's really an honor for them to work with him. But they always . . . want to know more things.

VIVIAN: I always want to know more things. I'm a scholar. Or I was when I had shoes, when I had eyebrows.

SUSIE: Well, okay then. You'll be full code. That's fine

(Silence.)

VIVIAN: No, don't complicate the matter.
SUSIE: It's okay. It's up to you—
VIVIAN: Let it stop.
SUSIE: Really?
VIVIAN: Yes.
SUSIE: So if your heart stops beating—
VIVIAN: Just let it stop.
SUSIE: Sure?
VIVIAN: Yes.
SUSIE: Okay. I'll get Kelekian to give the order, and then—
VIVIAN: Susie?
SUSIE: Uh-huh?
VIVIAN: You're still going to take care of me, aren't you?
SUSIE: 'Course, sweetheart. Don't you worry.

(As SUSIE leaves, VIVIAN sits upright, full of energy and rage.)

Spike Heels

BY THERESA REBECK

ACT II, SCENE I

Georgie and Lydia are having a hard time with the two men in their lives, Andrew and Edward. Georgie, who comes from a poor background, lives in the apartment above Andrew's. Andrew, who teaches political philosophy, has become Georgie's mentor of sorts, has introduced her to serious books, and has gotten her a job in his friend Edward's law firm.

Lydia, who comes from Boston's posh Beacon Hill, has come to Georgie's apartment to see what she looks like since Andrew, who just broke off their engagement, constantly talks about her. Georgie, who wears sexy clothes and spike heels, loves Andrew, who, because of his vows to Lydia, refused to have sex with her when she tried to seduce him. Later, when she tried to seduce Edward as a way to hurt Andrew, he too declined (Edward had come on strong to her, but then decided he didn't want to be used).

Edward has just left Georgie's apartment to go downstairs to Andrew, leaving the distraught women alone.

....

(GEORGIE *turns and looks at* LYDIA, *who is very steely indeed.*)

GEORGIE: Look. It's been great meeting you, but you know, I am having one ripper of a day, you know, so—

LYDIA: Don't talk to me about bad days.

GEORGIE: Listen—

LYDIA: No. No. You listen. (*She puts down her purse decisively, crosses to the door and shuts it.*)

GEORGIE: HEY—

LYDIA: I don't know you. You and I have never met. And you are wreaking havoc on my life.

(*LYDIA crosses back to her purse, reaches in and pulls out GEORGIE's jacket, blouse, slip, skirt, pantyhose and shoes from the previous day. She folds these items and stacks them neatly as she speaks. GEORGIE watches, amazed.*)

LYDIA: At first, I admired Andrew's interest in your welfare. He cares about people; he truly cares and I think that's wonderful. But these past few months, I must admit, I have become less interested in his interest. Not only do I listen to him talk about you incessantly, any time I come over to have dinner or spend the night here, I am bombarded by you. When you come home at night, we hear your little heels clicking on the ceiling. When you leave in the morning, we hear your little heels. When you go to bed we hear you brush your teeth, and talk on the phone, and listen to the radio and on certain evenings I could swear that we can even hear you undress. I am not enjoying this. For the past two months, I have been under the distinct impression that any time I spend the night here, I am actually sleeping with two people—Andrew, and yourself. In fact, when you came home with Edward tonight my first thought was, my God, the bed is already crowded enough; now we have to fit Edward in too? Now. I don't know what went on between you and Andrew.

GEORGIE: Nothing. Nothing at all.

LYDIA: Excuse me, but that clearly is not the case. And I want you out of my life! Is that understood?

GEORGIE: Where am I supposed to go?

LYDIA: I don't care! I'll find you a better apartment! It will be my pleasure!

(They glare at each other for a moment.)

GEORGIE: Listen, I am really sorry but I am just not up to this right now, okay? I mean, if I get mad one more time tonight I might just die from it. So, can we chill out for a minute? You want a cup of tea or something?

LYDIA: Do you have anything stronger? Scotch? Is that scotch?

GEORGIE: Yes. It is.

LYDIA: I'll have scotch.

GEORGIE: Fine. *(She exits to the kitchen and reenters a second later with a glass. She pours LYDIA a shot of scotch.)* Here. You knock that back, you'll feel much better.

LYDIA: Thank you. *(She drinks and studies GEORGIE.)* That's an interesting outfit you have on.

GEORGIE: Excuse me?

LYDIA: I guess men really do like that sort of thing, don't they? You'd like to think some of them, at least one, or two, are above it, but that just doesn't seem to be the case. All of them, they're like Pavlov's dogs; you provide the right stimulus and the next thing you know, they're salivating all over you. Don't those shoes hurt?

GEORGIE: Yeah, as a matter of fact, they kind of do.

LYDIA: But I guess you don't wear them for comfort, do you? You wear them for other reasons. You wear them because they make your legs look amazing. *(She puts the second pair of heels on and walks around the room for a moment and picks up a large book under the table.)* And I see you're also studying law.

GEORGIE: *(crosses and takes the book from her)* No, I am not "studying law." I stole that from the library at work so I could figure out what the fuck was going on down there.

LYDIA: Really. How remarkable.

GEORGIE: Look—

LYDIA: Could I have another?

GEORGIE: Another?

LYDIA: Please.

(GEORGIE *takes* LYDIA'S *glass from her and pours scotch into it, looks at her, and then continues to pour an enormous amount of scotch into the glass. She gives it back to her.* LYDIA *looks at it, and knocks back a solid drink.* GEORGIE *stares.*)

LYDIA: God, I wish I still smoked.

GEORGIE: You used to smoke?

LYDIA: Two packs a day. It was disgusting.

GEORGIE: You know—you're very different from what I thought. It's weird, meeting you. It's just—weird.

LYDIA: Oh, really? Well, what did you think I'd be like?

GEORGIE: I don't know. I mean, you're very—forceful. I guess I thought you would be kind of formal and polite. Maybe like Dracula, or something.

LYDIA: Oh. Edward told you that; that's where you got that. He is so awful. Ever since I dumped him he's been telling everybody I'm some kind of vampire. He thinks it's witty.

GEORGIE: Wait a minute. You went out with him, too?

LYDIA: Didn't you know that?

GEORGIE: Man, what do those two do, trade off girlfriends once a year or something?

LYDIA: It's certainly starting to look that way.

GEORGIE: Wait a minute, that's not what I—

LYDIA: (*overlap*) Really, there's no need to explain. In fact, I would prefer not to know the details.

GEORGIE: I'm just trying to tell you—

LYDIA: And I'm trying to tell you: What I've had with both of them is substantially more real than whatever this is, and I don't want to know about it. All right? I just want it to stop. All right?

GEORGIE: Right.

LYDIA: As long as we understand each other.

GEORGIE: Oh, I understand you all right. This part, I think I got down solid.

LYDIA: Good.

GEORGIE: (*finally angry*) But what I don't have, you know—what I want to know is—if you're so fucking real, Lydia, then what the hell are you doing here? I mean, if you're so much better than me, then why even bother? You could just wait it out and I'll drift away like a piece of paper, like nothing, right? 'Cause that's what I am. Nothing. Right? So why the fuck are you up here, taking me apart?

LYDIA: I don't think I have to justify myself to you.

GEORGIE: Oh, yeah? Well, I think you do. All of you. What an amazing fucking snow job you all are doing on the world. And I bought it! We all buy it. My family—they're like, all of a sudden I'm Mary Tyler Moore or something. I mean, they live in hell, right, and they spend their whole lives just wishing they were somewhere else, wishing they were rich, or sober, or clean; living on a street with trees, being on some fucking TV show. And I did it. I moved to Boston. I work in a law office, I'm the big success story. And they have no idea what that means. It means I get to hang out with a bunch of lunatics. It means I get to read books that make no sense. (*She pushes the law book off the table.*) It means that instead of getting harassed by jerks at the local bar, now I get harassed by guys in suits. Guys with glasses. Guys who talk nice. Guys in suits. Well, you know what I have to say to all of you? Shame on you. Shame on you for thinking you're better than the rest of us. And shame on you for being mean to me. Shame on you, Lydia.

LYDIA: (*pause*) I'm sorry.

GEORGIE: I think you'd better go.

LYDIA: Yes. Of course. (*pause*) I am sorry. I just—Andrew postponed our wedding tonight, and I'm a little—my life is in a bit of a shambles, tonight, and I know that's no excuse, but I'm just not myself. Please. Forgive me. (*She goes to the door.*)

GEORGIE: Oh, God. Wait a minute.

LYDIA: No. You're right. I've been behaving very badly. You're right. I'm sorry. (*She turns and opens the door.*)

GEORGIE: No, I'm the one. Come on, I'm being a jerk. He postponed the wedding? Fuck me. I'm sorry, you said that before and it went right by me. I'm sorry. I got a bad temper, and—whatever. Just sit down, okay?

(GEORGIE brings her back into the room. LYDIA pulls away.)

LYDIA: Really, I think I'd best go. Please. Please don't be nice to me. I don't want to be friends with you.

GEORGIE: Yeah, I don't want to be friends with you either. I'm just saying. I didn't mean to, like, yell at you. I think you better finish your drink.

(She hands her scotch to her. LYDIA looks at it for a moment then sits and drinks.)

GEORGIE: He's probably just nervous. Weddings make boys nervous.

LYDIA: I think it's worse than that. He—we haven't had sex in quite a while.

GEORGIE: You mean *none* of us are getting laid? No wonder we're all so uptight.

LYDIA: You mean you and Edward didn't—

GEORGIE: No.

LYDIA: No?

GEORGIE: No. I swear to God, I worked on him for four hours and I couldn't get him *near* the bedroom.

LYDIA: Edward? You couldn't—Edward?

GEORGIE: You didn't have that problem, huh?

LYDIA: As a matter of fact—never mind.

GEORGIE: He wanted it.

LYDIA: Yes, dear, he always wants it. Well. If he wouldn't sleep with you, I think you must've really made an impression on him.

(They laugh a little.)

LYDIA: And I know you've made an impression on Andrew.

GEORGIE: *(awkward)* Oh. I don't know.

LYDIA: Please. Could we not—? *(pause)* I'd prefer not to pretend. I'd also prefer not to talk to you about it, but I just don't know who else to talk to.

GEORGIE: Hey—

LYDIA: I'm not crying! It's just, I can't talk to my family about this; they'll simply gloat. They never liked Andrew. He wasn't "good" enough. Is that unbelievable? He's the best man I've ever met, and he's not *good* enough for them. He doesn't make enough money. And they certainly don't like his politics. Edward was the one they liked. Well. You can imagine. You know what my father told me, when Andrew and I decided to get married? Never trust a man who thinks he can change the world. That's what he said! I don't care, really, I don't—but how can I tell them this? I always told him, he didn't understand, just didn't understand. Andrew saved me. He is my best self; he makes me my best self. How can I tell them they were right?

GEORGIE: They're not.

LYDIA: No, I know. They're not. I know. It's just—I'm confused.

GEORGIE: Yeah. Me too. *(pause)* You want to dance? *(She crosses to the boombox and puts in a tape. Romantic music comes up.)*

LYDIA: Excuse me?

GEORGIE: Come on. Dance with me.

LYDIA: What?

GEORGIE: It'll make you feel better. I'll lead and you can just dance—

LYDIA: Oh, no—

GEORGIE: Come on. Let me do this—*(She unties LYDIA's bow and takes her in her arms.)*

LYDIA: I don't—aw, no—I don't dance—

GEORGIE: No, it's not silly. It's just nice. Haven't you ever danced with a girl before? It's nice. Come on.

(GEORGIE takes her by the arms and they begin to slow dance.)

GEORGIE: I love to dance. It's so fucking romantic. You know? It always makes me want to have sex. Men are so dumb, they're so

busy trying to get you in bed they can't even figure that out. I
mean—I'm not making a pass at you.

LYDIA: I understand.

(GEORGIE *nods, and they begin to dance more freely.* GEORGIE *leading
and coaxing* LYDIA *into the moves. As they turn through the room
their movements become looser, more hilariously erotic. They laugh
for a moment, and end up slow dancing.*)

The Tale of the Allergist's Wife

BY CHARLES BUSCH

ACT I, SCENE 2

Marjorie is in her fifties, attractive, stylish, and married to Ira, a successful Manhattan allergist, now retired. But Marjorie is bitter and depressed because she feels she has not achieved anything special in her life. She goes to all the interesting, cosmopolitan places in New York, but is merely an observer, never a creator. Ira can't find a way to console her, and her mother's self-pity and suggestion that she "do some volunteer work" only increases her exasperation.

It is midday. Marjorie is alone in her apartment, reclining on a window seat when the doorbell rings.

....

MARJORIE: Who is it?

(*A woman's voice is heard outside the door.*)

WOMAN: I'm here to see the apartment.
MARJORIE: Beg your pardon?
WOMAN: I'm here to look at the apartment.

(MARJORIE *opens the door.* LEE GREEN *is an energetic, beautifully*

groomed lady of MARJORIE'S *age, with a very comfortable sense of
her own sensuality.)*

MARJORIE: I think there must be some mistake.

LEE: This is 12B?

MARJORIE: No. This is 12C. 12B is around the corner.

LEE: Please forgive me for disturbing you. *(peeks her head in)*
Nice place. May I?

MARJORIE: I don't know. I'm not dressed.

LEE: It looks like such a lovely jewel box of a room. Just for a
minute?

MARJORIE: All right. Come in. *(She shows LEE into the apartment.)* Please forgive the way I'm dressed. I'm never usually in my
robe this late in the—

LEE: Don't apologize. Are you having one of those days?

MARJORIE: I can't even—

LEE: No need to. I've spent whole weeks in bed. And you have a
view. Have you lived here long?

MARJORIE: Five years. We were around the corner before. I'm
sorry. I should introduce myself. I'm Marjorie Taub.

LEE: Marjorie. I'm very fond of that name.

MARJORIE: Really?

LEE: When I was a little girl, I had a best friend named Marjorie. Unfortunately, we moved away when I was ten years old. I
never saw her again. Lee Green.

MARJORIE: Lee, may I get you something to drink?

LEE. Anything sparkling would be wonderful.

MARJORIE: Seltzer?

LEE. Perfection.

(MARJORIE goes over to the kitchen area and pours a glass for LEE.)

LEE: I must say the city has changed since I last lived here.

MARJORIE: When was that?

LEE: Well, I gave up my apartment in eighty-six but I'm from
New York.

MARJORIE: I'm a native myself. Where did you grow up?

LEE: I'm from decidedly humble origins. The Bronx. Fleetwood.

MARJORIE: Isn't that funny? That's where I'm from. We lived in a tiny apartment on Bronx River Road.

LEE: Those Tudor buildings? (*MARJORIE nods.*) Marjorie, you're not—By any wild coincidence, your maiden name isn't Marjorie Tuchman?

MARJORIE: Yes.

LEE: Oh my God.

MARJORIE: Lillian?

LEE: Yes.

MARJORIE: Lillian Greenblatt. Oh my God. (*They tearfully embrace.*) I can't believe this.

LEE: It's amazing. After all these years. This is too much.

MARJORIE: I'm stunned.

LEE: The coincidence. I meant it when I said I've often thought of you.

MARJORIE: Well, you had a great impact on me. You really did. And your mother. She was so elegant. I can still hear her saying that a lady holds both her teacup and saucer.

LEE: My poor mother. The Duchess of Fleetwood. (*beat*) Now, I'm assuming you're married?

MARJORIE: For thirty-two years to Dr. V. Ira Taub. He's an allergist. He retired this year but he remains very active. He's started a free clinic for the homeless.

LEE: Admirable. Children?

MARJORIE: We have two daughters. Joan and Rochelle. Here they are.

(*MARJORIE takes a framed photo off a table and hands it to LEE.*)

LEE: Very attractive.

MARJORIE: Joan is a successful real estate lawyer. Rochelle is a lot slimmer now.

LEE: Rochelle. She's the troubled one.

MARJORIE: We've had our ups and downs.

LEE: Does she live in the city?

MARJORIE: Ashland, Oregon. She's a holistic healer. People swear by her. They say she can shrink tumors and cure stuttering.

LEE: Was she always interested in alternative medicine?

MARJORIE: Two years ago she was in a feminist avocado-farming commune. The year before that she had a cabaret act. I shouldn't be so judgmental. We bring our children into the world to fulfill a fantasy. The creation of the perfect human being. To quote Cocteau, "What are the thoughts of the marble from which a sculptor shapes a masterpiece?" It can't help but resent all the picking and chipping away.

LEE: You were always such a voracious reader. You were plowing through *The Grapes of Wrath* when the rest of us were playing Hopscotch. I always imagined that you became a writer.

MARJORIE: I tried. I wrote a novel. I worked on it for years. It became a joke. Marjorie and her book.

LEE: Tell me about it.

MARJORIE: I'd rather not.

LEE: I've waited forty years to find out.

MARJORIE: I don't want to sound pretentious.

LEE: I am truly interested. Please.

MARJORIE: It was a phantasmagoria. At the time I was heavily influenced by Thomas Pynchon. Some of it was composed as verse drama. There were chapters in various historical periods. Plato and Helen Keller were major characters. Allusions to *Anna Karenina* were woven throughout. I invented an entirely new form of punctuation. I was attempting to break away from conventional narrative structure.

LEE: I'd love to read it.

MARJORIE: I burned every copy.

LEE: Marjorie!

MARJORIE: I don't need tangible proof of my own mediocrity.

LEE: I'm sure you're being too harsh.

MARJORIE: Let's just say that my epic was given the thumbs down by thirty-two publishers. To be exposed as a sham was devastating.

LEE: Tell me, what's with the bandage?

MARJORIE: Not what you think. For some unknown reason I went into the Disney Store on Fifth Avenue. I was holding this large figurine and it slipped out of my fingers and smashed on the floor. I was compelled to pick up another. I think it was the Beast and then it too fell. I couldn't stop. Hercules, Aladdin's genie, the little mermaid's father. It looked like a bomb exploded. Ira had to pay a fortune.

LEE: I bet that felt good.

MARJORIE: Stop that. You're jumping to the wrong conclusion.

LEE: I can see with my own eyes that you're tight as a drum with frustration.

MARJORIE: My situation is far from grim.

LEE: Marjorie, it's perfectly understandable. Don't forget. I know your mother. I remember we put on a performance in the playground with all our little friends, *Pippi Longstocking*. All the parents said we were so clever and industrious. Your mother quipped "This piece of drek would close in New Haven." My God, with forty more years of that kind of negativity, no wonder you've become a retail terrorist.

MARJORIE: *(emotionally)* You are most presumptuous. How dare you? You don't know me. You don't know my mother. How dare you? She's endured incredible hardships. She was born into degrading poverty. She saw her father run over by a milk truck. Her mother was insane and went after her with a meat cleaver. We never had any money but she always managed to make us feel we were as good as anyone else. I'll be damned if I'll let anyone put her down!

LEE: Stop. I'm sorry. It was inappropriate for me to mouth off like that. I suppose I don't know you. How could I after all these years? It's just that in my mind our relationship has never really ended. I carry the memory of the wondrous, magical child that you were like a talisman. Can we start again? Friends?

MARJORIE: Friends. I'm sorry I blew up. Now, it's my turn to be the Grand Inquisitor. I hope you can take it. So Lil, you changed your name?

LEE: Lillian Greenblatt wasn't terribly euphonious. It's so—

shall we say it? So Jewish. I'm sorry. I just don't identify. Never have. Call me a terrible person. I hope I'm not offending you.

MARJORIE: No, I'm with you. I've always sought spirituality on a more individual basis. Joan, my eldest, is deeply religious. She's married to a Rabbi and lives in Israel. She calls herself Jonaya Taub-Ben-Shalom. I've just always felt alienated from every group, be it Jewish, American, The West Side Wine Tasters.

LEE: I've never even been a part of a couple.

MARJORIE: You never married?

LEE: Lee has led a totally selfish life, and had a helluva good time.

MARJORIE: May I ask what do you do for a living?

LEE: Oh gosh, what haven't I done? I've been in Public Relations. I've been an international food critic. Written a couple of coffee table books. *Balinese Masks*. That sort of thing. I worked for several years for Chanel in Paris. For awhile I ran a small discotheque in Hong Kong. I helped open a museum of contemporary art in Berlin. And I ran a clam bar outside Mendocino. Now I fundraise for political organizations.

MARJORIE: My, you've really been an adventuress. I would have loved to have traveled more, but with Ira's practice it's been difficult.

LEE: I live for travel. Mainland China, a revelation. Changed my entire perspective of the world, of the very essence of life itself.

MARJORIE: Did you go there alone?

LEE: No, I went with the Nixons. I was covering the event for a small gourmet food magazine.

MARJORIE: Oh my. Did you get to know the Nixons?

LEE: Yes, I did. I didn't agree with them politically but I grew very fond of Pat. In fact I was the first person that Pat Nixon phoned after the resignation. I felt as if I was in the midst of a tragedy of Shakespearean proportions.

MARJORIE: And you lived in Berlin. That must have been fascinating. I am a great devotee of twentieth-century German fiction. My favorite author is Hermann Hesse. My favorite book is *Siddartha*.

LEE: I've read every word he wrote. *Demian, Steppenwolf, Magister Ludi*. The examination of the dark side.

MARJORIE: So many people seem to—I don't know—live on the surface. Black is black, white is white. I delve, I reflect, I brood.

LEE: You're a figure of shadow and light.

MARJORIE: I have also found great solace in the writings of Heinrich Boll, Guntar Grasse, Thomas Mann.

LEE: I had a little affair with Guntar Grasse.

MARJORIE: No.

LEE: Very brief but in my safe deposit box, I have some very tender love letters.

MARJORIE: Did you ever meet Fassbinder?

LEE: Oh, many times. Have you ever seen the film *The Bitter Tears of Petra von Kant*?

MARJORIE: Indeed.

LEE: In the scene in the bar, I'm the weird chick who looks like she's got a pinata stuck on her head.

MARJORIE: My God. What a life you've led.

LEE: Well, it's easy in Germany. Never a dull moment. I'll never forget the night the wall fell.

MARJORIE: You were there?

LEE: Such joy. I was with a group of students from the University. We screamed and shouted and kissed each other, grabbing with our fists great chunks of stone and mortar. By dawn, we were drenched in sweat and cheap champagne.

MARJORIE: You certainly know where the action is.

LEE: Never intentionally.

MARJORIE: *(embarrassed to ask)* Did you um ever meet Diana?

LEE: Oh yes. Lee Green, would you cool it? Marjorie's gonna think you're an obsessive name dropper.

MARJORIE: No, no, no. How'd you meet her?

LEE: I met her several times. The most memorable was at a dinner party in London. Diana was seated to my left. She overheard my conversation with Henry Kissinger on the tragic situation of the landmines. She knew nothing about it and was quite fascinated. So I guess in my little way, I helped plant that seed.

MARJORIE: Thank God you did.

LEE: Now Marjorie, please take note that Lee's life has not been one long ride on the Orient Express. There were also years when she lived in a tiny cold water flat in the village.

MARJORIE: That sounds romantic too.

LEE: It wasn't all *La Boheme*. That's how I learned the fundamentals of cooking. I grew quite adept at whipping up a creative meal for two dollars. But we did have great fun in those days. Kerouac, Jimmy Baldwin, Andy.

MARJORIE: Andy Warhol?

LEE: He used to come over and we'd share a can of soup. He got such a kick out of the way I used to pile the empty Campbell soup cans on top of each other. I guess you could say, I planted a little seed.

Women in Motion

BY DONALD MARGULIES

Libby and Monica, two single women who work together, are taking their Christmas vacation together in the Caribbean. They are both in their thirties, and each in her own way is hoping for a glorious time—but they are beginning to grate on each other. Monica is enthusiastic and optimistic. Libby tends to be laid back and cynical. The scene takes place at poolside.

....

(The women, in bathing suits, on chaise lounge chairs. MONICA is reading a romance novel. LIBBY, lying on her stomach with her bikini straps undone, is reading a magazine.)

MONICA: Can you believe this place?

LIBBY: Mmm.

MONICA: It's gorgeous. It's like paradise. Looks just like the brochure. Doesn't it?

LIBBY: Yeah.

MONICA: Not a cloud in the sky, the water . . . Can you believe that water? This place is totally unreal. When I saw the water in the brochure I thought: can't be, there *is* no such color, they made up a color like that. But can you believe that color?

LIBBY: Mmm. I know.

(Pause.)

MONICA: I'm *so* glad we did this. Aren't you?

LIBBY: Oh, yeah.

MONICA: Uch, can you imagine being in the city?

LIBBY: Yeah.

MONICA: The crowds and the cold and everything? Uch, if I had to spend another Christmas with my family . . . *(pause)* I can't believe we just got here. I was just thinking to myself, isn't this funny? I feel like we've been here for days. Don't you? Don't you feel like you've been here for days?

LIBBY: Mmm.

MONICA: I feel like we've been here a week. I feel so relaxed. I can't believe how relaxed I feel. *(a beat)* You should put some stuff on, you know. You're burning.

LIBBY: I am?

MONICA: You want me to?

LIBBY: I *put* some stuff on. I put 25.

MONICA: I know but you're burning anyway. I can tell with these sunglasses. You're turning pink. Your shoulders. They say if you sweat or swim . . . You want me to do it?

LIBBY: You mind?

MONICA: Not at all.

LIBBY: Thanks, it's in my thing.

(MONICA gets a bottle of sun block out of LIBBY's bag and applies the lotion.)

MONICA: You have pretty skin.

LIBBY: Thank you.

MONICA: My back breaks out. *(a beat)* Wasn't lunch great?

LIBBY: It was all right.

MONICA: Just all right? Didn't you think it was delicious?

LIBBY: It was chicken salad with pineapple in it.

MONICA: Yeah, I know, I thought it was delicious. What an interesting combination. I'm gonna have to try that. Tropical chicken salad.

LIBBY: It was canned pineapple.

MONICA: That wasn't canned pineapple.

LIBBY: Yes it was. It was a ring. Like you get from Dole.

MONICA: Libby, that was not canned pineapple. This is the tropics. They *grow* pineapple here. What do they need to get it from cans for?

LIBBY: I'm telling you, mine had a piece of ring in it. Fresh pineapple doesn't come in rings, that much I know.

MONICA: So what if it was?

LIBBY: Was what?

MONICA: So what if it did come from a can? Does that mean it wasn't good?

LIBBY: All I'm saying, for what they charge you, they could at least give you fresh pineapple. That's all I'm saying.

(Pause.)

MONICA: *(quietly)* I thought it was very good. *(a beat)* I suppose you didn't like the dessert either?

LIBBY: No, the dessert was good.

MONICA: Oh. Well.

(LIBBY ties her bikini top and sits up.)

LIBBY: Monica. Why must you take everything so personal?

MONICA: I don't.

LIBBY: Yes, you do. I tell you it was canned pineapple and you get all huffy with me.

MONICA: I do not get huffy.

LIBBY: Okay. Whatever you say.

(Pause.)

MONICA: I'm sorry you didn't like the chicken salad.

LIBBY: I said it was all right! I didn't say I didn't like it! It's not like you *made* it!

MONICA: I know.

LIBBY: It's really no big deal!

MONICA: Okay!

(Long pause. Both resume reading.)

We're not having a fight, are we?

LIBBY: Who said we're having a fight?

MONICA: I'm only asking.

LIBBY: No we are not having a fight.

MONICA: Good. I didn't think so. *(pause)* I hate fights.

LIBBY: This isn't a fight.

MONICA: I know, I'm just saying. My parents used to fight all the time. It was horrible. The stupidest things they'd fight about. *(a beat)* Can we go dancing tonight please?

Fast Girls

BY DIANA AMSTERDAM

ACT I, SCENE I

It is ten A.M. in Manhattan. Lucy, in her mid-thirties, is in the doorway of her brownstone studio apartment. She is wearing a bathrobe and has just said goodbye to Joe, a twenty-three-year-old with whom she has spent the night. As she turns away from the door, we see that she is "relaxed and euphoric." Before the door shuts, her friend and neighbor Abigail (also mid-thirties) whirls in.

(*Exit* JOE. LUCY, *relaxed and euphoric, swings into the room. Almost immediately,* ABIGAIL *swings in after her.*)

ABIGAIL: And who was that?
LUCY: Joe! That was Joe! That, Abigail, was Joe!
ABIGAIL: I doubt it. I mean, millions of people call themselves Joe, but Lucy, nobody's really named Joe. What'd he say his last name is?
LUCY: Joe—I don't remember. Something very nice.
ABIGAIL: But . . . did you? I mean, it looks like you did, it seems like you did, you look like you did, you seem like you did, he looked like *he* did like you looked like you did, but if you can't re-

member his name I can't believe you did, but you did, didn't you, did you?

LUCY: O'Malley!

ABIGAIL: You did.

LUCY: Abby, please, I haven't even had my coffee yet. I gotta have lunch with a writer at two o'clock—what time is it?

ABIGAIL: Ten-oh-six.

LUCY: Thank God, I have hours—hours!—

(LUCY makes coffee. ABIGAIL begins to fold up the sleep bed.)

LUCY: Wait, wait, leave that open, I'm gonna need a nap.

ABIGAIL: Didn't you get any sleep?

LUCY: Not much.

ABIGAIL: How much not much? Six hours? Three hours? A coupla minutes? He was here nine hours and twenty-five minutes.

LUCY: You timed how long he was here?

ABIGAIL: My watch did all the work. Naturally I was concerned, Lucy, what do we really know about his person?

LUCY: His name is Joe. Joe C. O'Malley. He's twenty-three. He's assistant to Connie Stone at Dell. He lives in Brooklyn. And his thumbnails—you should see his thumbnails—they're wider than they are high!

ABIGAIL: That's important.

LUCY: And he's so sweet. With a face like that he could be stuck-up as all hell but he's not, he was so nervous around me, I don't know why he was so nervous—

ABIGAIL: Probably you remind him of his mother—

LUCY: At dinner—he kept making all these mistakes, first he put ketchup on his shrimp cocktail, then he takes his tea bag and opens it into the hot water—and drinks it!—Then he's trying to help me on with my coat and I look back and he's putting my arm into the pocket! That's when I decided to bring him home. *(laughs)* So you see. I know everything I need to know about him.

ABIGAIL: Oh, yeah? Do you know if he slept with anybody

who slept with anybody who slept with anybody who slept with anybody who's bisexual or an IV drug user in the past ten years? Do
you know his travel habits? Ever been to Haiti? Ever owned a
green monkey?

LUCY: Abigail—

ABIGAIL: Did you check out his arms for needle marks?

LUCY: I checked out his arms. And I checked out the rest of
him, too. Sorry, Abby. I just don't feel like worrying. I don't think I
could worry, even if I wanted to. Every cell in my body's been swept
clean of worrying like a street after a spring rain.

*(LUCY lies back, closes her eyes. ABIGAIL regards her, then rushes to a
closet, brings out the vacuum, and vacuums the walls, furiously.)*

LUCY: What are you doing?

ABIGAIL: Trying to bring your walls up to the level of your
cells.

LUCY: Don't! Abby! Stop it! I like those cobwebs! *(turns off
vacuum)*

ABIGAIL: Maybe I'd better go back to my apartment.

LUCY: No, that's all right, just don't vacuum.

ABIGAIL: No, I'd really better.

LUCY: Why?

ABIGAIL: *(explodes)* I've been worried sick over you, Lucy,
what do you think, you go out last night at nine-oh-five you tell me
you're just going to the corner for a beer you don't come in till two-
thirteen I practically called the police, I destroyed an entire finger-
nail and then you come in with this stranger, this absolute stranger,
and I couldn't even get a good look at him through the peephole,
the hall was so goddamn dark—

LUCY: You were watching—?

ABIGAIL: Only with one eye, and then you bring him in here
and the door slams and three o'clock, four o'clock, five o'clock, six
o'clock, seven o'clock, eight o'clock, nine o'clock, ten o'clock, ten-
oh-one, ten-oh-two, ten-oh-three—

LUCY: Abigail—

ABIGAIL: I mean he could be a Shiite terrorist, he could be a serial murderer, he could be a married orthodontist—anybody, anybody, oh sure, maybe your cells are squeaky clean, oh sure, maybe my cells haven't been washed or even dusted in year, maybe it looks to you like I'm miserable, maybe it looks to me like I'm miserable—maybe I am miserable—but at least I know it! At least I'm willing to admit that the only safe course for a woman today is to find a good, loving, successful man to marry in a city where the only men left are misfits or thumbsuckers, yes, it's difficult, yes, it's impossible, yes, it's a goddamn absurd maniacal joke perpetrated by a sadistic and vengeful God, but that's life! You can't escape it! With your flings! Lucy, the piper must be paid!

LUCY: Baby—I've brought men home before.

ABIGAIL: Not for a long time. Not complete strangers.

LUCY: I met him at the Dalton party.

ABIGAIL: Two weeks ago? . . . You didn't tell me.

LUCY: Honey, I can't tell you everything.

ABIGAIL: Yes, you can, about men, if you don't tell me about men I have no love life.

LUCY: Okay. This is what happened. I met Joe, but he didn't call me. So last night—remember how the air felt like velvet?—I tried to get you to come out with me, but as usual you found some excuse—

ABIGAIL: I had to wait for Ernest to call.

LUCY: Right. So I went by myself. I called Joe when—

ABIGAIL: You called him?

LUCY: Yes.

ABIGAIL: You called him?

LUCY: Yes.

ABIGAIL: From where?

LUCY: I'm trying to tell you. From Pete's. I was nursing a cold beer, I remembered Joe, seeing his mouth and thinking, "Destiny"—

ABIGAIL: And you called him? For the same night? Weren't your hands shaking? Wasn't your heart thumping? Didn't you throw up all over the phone booth?

LUCY: I knew he liked me.

ABIGAIL: How?

LUCY: I could tell—

ABIGAIL: How?

LUCY: There's a certain look—

ABIGAIL: What?

LUCY: I know you've seen it—

ABIGAIL: When?

LUCY: Anyway—he didn't have anything special to do so he came.

ABIGAIL: What a loser.

LUCY: And that's the whole story.

ABIGAIL: Hah!

LUCY: So please. Don't worry about me.

ABIGAIL: Of course I'm going to worry about you.

LUCY: No, please. I don't want anybody worrying about me right now.

ABIGAIL: You can't stop people worrying about you—

LUCY: Look! I just got out of a relationship where I was constantly being worried about and fussed over and truly, I mean it, Abigail, I'd appreciate a little time to do what I want without upsetting anyone! Okay?

ABIGAIL: Okay! Okay okay okay do what you want! Do what you want and pretty soon nobody'll care about you at all!

(Beat.)

LUCY: Ernest didn't call. Did he?

ABIGAIL: Ernest? What does Ernest have to do with this?

LUCY: If you were feeling good, you wouldn't be sitting around all night fretting over me.

ABIGAIL: You see what you do? You see this? You're totally un-aware—Whenever we start talking about your problems, we end up talking about my problems, like you don't have any problems, watch, just watch how we suddenly find ourselves talking about me. *(Long pause. Bellows.)* No! He didn't call! No! He never calls! And I wait. I wait and wait, listening to that silence. Phones are macho. They know when you need a good ring, and then they withhold. Pretty soon nobody calls you. Even your mother doesn't call you, even when you're sitting down to eat she doesn't call you. I swear, I'll strangle it with its own cord!

LUCY: I thought we were talking about my problems.

ABIGAIL: God, you're self-centered.

LUCY: Honey. How long have you been waiting for Ernest to call?

ABIGAIL: Oh, I don't know. Three months, two days and nineteen hours. *(checks watch)* And twelve minutes.

LUCY: Forget Ernest.

ABIGAIL: I would, if I wasn't hoping to marry him. Lucy, Ernest is the only man I've met in the past year who's even possible. Ernest is handsome. Ernest is successful. Ernest is ambitious, wealthy, intelligent, witty, punctual, not opposed to children and certified AIDS-free, Ernest meets nine of my ten essential requirements.

LUCY: And the tenth?

ABIGAIL: So he's not particularly nice, so what?

LUCY: That's the only thing that matters. Honey—if a man's not good to you, get rid of him. *(takes a big bite of chocolate donut)* Mm.

ABIGAIL: That's easy for you to say! *(viciously)* You don't get fat!

LUCY: *(sings)* "Too many fish in the sea, too many fish in the sea, tall ones, short ones, fat ones, skinny ones, too many fish in the sea—" *(throws open the window)* C'mere. C'mere. Look. C'mere, I just want to show you something.

(ABIGAIL goes to the window.)

LUCY: See that?

ABIGAIL: Eight potential muggers.

LUCY: No, look. Men.

ABIGAIL: That's what I mean.

LUCY: This town is crawling with gorgeous men! Men you can

have drinks with, men you can take walks with, men you can go out
with if only everything doesn't have to be about marriage . . .

ABIGAIL: But it does.

LUCY: No it doesn't! You can be happy by yourself, happier! We
are free! We don't need men! We may love them, we may want
them, but we don't need them, for the first time there are free
women walking this earth, and we are two of them!

ABIGAIL: You are two of them.

LUCY: . . . Look! Across the street! He's looking at us! At you!

ABIGAIL: *(Shuts window and closes blinds. Referring to blinds.)*
Let me clean this.

LUCY: What are you so afraid of? Pleasure is good for you.

ABIGAIL: Pleasure is bad for you. It's a natural law. If it feels
good, it's dangerous. Like that donut. Loaded with chocolate which
is not only high in cholesterol, it can also cause cancer.

LUCY: Take one bite. And you'll forget all about it.

ABIGAIL: *(looking at donut)* No, thank you . . . *(takes donut)*
Maybe I'll just hold it . . . What was it like?

LUCY: What?

ABIGAIL: *(looking at donut)* Making love with a 23-year-old
boy?

LUCY: Very nice. But I prefer older men.

ABIGAIL: You do?

LUCY: Definitely. Young boys have a boundless energy for sex,
honey, and they want it so bad it breaks your heart, but they think
there's only one thing that *is* sex. While a man—a man—he knows
that you can get to a place where everything is sex. Everything.
Every touch. Every look. Every sound. Every breath. Everything is
sex.

(ABIGAIL bites the donut.)

LUCY: Eat it slowly.

(The phone rings. ABIGAIL jumps up.)

ABIGAIL: *(toward her apartment)* You hear that? Pay attention, that's what you're supposed to do, see?

LUCY: *(picks up phone)* Hi! Did you get home already? From where? That's sweet. Sure I do. *(turns her back to ABIGAIL, and speaks softly into the phone)*

(ABIGAIL tiptoes to LUCY till she is right on top of her, trying to listen to the conversation. LUCY turns around.)

LUCY: . . . I can't—Abigail!?!?!? My neighbor. Sorry, baby, not tonight, wait—Just wait—A few days, *(sexily)* It'll be so much better. Okay, bye.

ABIGAIL: Was that him? The lousy lover?

LUCY: I didn't say he's a bad lover—

ABIGAIL: Already calling you? How come he didn't call for two weeks and now he's already calling you?

LUCY: Now he knows what he's calling for. *(The phone rings. Picks up.)* Hello? Oh, Joe. No, listen. I had a wonderful time last night, I really did, honey but please—I'll call you in a couple of days. Okay. Bye. *(hangs up)* Oh, dear. I hope he doesn't decide to fall in love with me.

ABIGAIL: That would be terrible, two in a row, how consecutive.

LUCY: I'm sorry—

ABIGAIL: No! Don't apologize! I enjoy living next door to the only thirty-six year old woman in New York whose biggest problem is men falling in love with her, very interesting, when will Lucy Lewis discover that her real worries are little things like loneliness, aging, and premature death?

LUCY: You know, Abigail, when you first came in here, I was floating on a cloud. And now I feel tense. And irritable. And snappy!

ABIGAIL: Well, these sexual highs never last—

LUCY: I think I need that nap now. I have to start reading manuscripts, real soon.

ABIGAIL: Oh. You're kicking me out. It always comes to this.

LUCY: Abigail, you practically live here!

ABIGAIL: *(goes to the door, opens door, turns)* Joe? All morning, I was waiting for him to leave so I could come in here, and then I blow it in the first *(checks watch)* ten minutes and thirty-three seconds. You're right. I must be really unhappy.

LUCY: . . . Stay.

ABIGAIL: No, I'm bringing you down.

LUCY: No, it's okay—

ABIGAIL: No, you're tired.

LUCY: I feel fine.

ABIGAIL: You look like hell.

LUCY: Stay, dammit! Only go easy! Today's the first day I've felt really happy since I broke up with Sidney, I just want to enjoy it! *(The phone rings.)* Okay?

ABIGAIL: Okay. Don't trouble yourself! *(picks up phone)* You know, on behalf of Lucy I think somebody ought to tell you, it's really not attractive, you calling like this, just because Lucy's nice to you—Lucy's nice to all the guys—It's your mother—Your mother! *(puts hand over receiver)* Lucy. I forgot. I called your mother—Last night—When you didn't come home—*(into phone)*. One minute!

LUCY: You called my mother? Didn't you call her back and tell her I was okay?

ABIGAIL: Yes—

LUCY: Fine—

ABIGAIL: But I told her you brought home a man.

LUCY: You—What?—Abigail—What is the matter with you? For Chrissake! *(regards phone for quite some time, takes it)* Mom? Yes. No. He's gone. No. You really don't have to do that. Mom. I'm fine. It won't do any good. What? *(listens intently)* Oh. Okay. *(hangs up)*

ABIGAIL: I guess . . . I'd better be going now. *(starts to exit)*

LUCY: No! Stay! Don't leave me!

ABIGAIL: What?

LUCY: My mother's coming to New York—She says she's going to make sure her daughter's married right away—

ABIGAIL: Would she adopt?

LUCY: She's got an article—from the Palm Beach Gazette—seems a girl I knew in grade school—Penny Trupotey—is—sick. She was divorced. Single. Kinda wild. I guess she must have slept with somebody who slept with somebody who slept . . .

ABIGAIL: Oh. This is terrible. We have to stay together now. I'll stay right here with you. Nothing can tear me away! *(The phone rings offstage, in* ABIGAIL'*s apartment.)* I'll be right back. *(exits)*

*(*LUCY *stands, suddenly very much alone.)*

Impossible Marriage

BY BETH HENLEY

PART I

A marriage is about to take place in the lush garden of Kandall Kinglsey's country estate outside of Savannah, Georgia. Her impetuous, romantic twenty-year-old daughter, Pandora, is about to marry Edvard Lunt, a successful novelist and worldly man who is well past fifty. Edvard, who is still attractive, swept Pandora off her feet by his passion for her and by the fact that he based the heroine in his latest novel on her.

Kandall and Pandora's thirty-year-old sister, Floral, are set against the marriage. Floral is smart, well read, in an unhappy marriage of her own, and "acutely pregnant" (but not by her husband). She has told her mother she will find a way to prevent the marriage from taking place. Her mother has just ushered the reverend and Floral's husband into the house for refreshments, leaving the sisters alone.

FLORAL: Pandora. Wait here a moment. I have something . . . Let them go. Let them get out of range.
PANDORA: What is it?
FLORAL: I love you.
PANDORA: Yes, I love you too.

FLORAL: I wanted you to know, in case you had any doubts. Having said that, I must ask you, why are you marrying this man?

PANDORA: He divorced his wife of twenty-three years and all of his children just for me.

FLORAL: Ask yourself ponderously, does that speak well of his character?

PANDORA: His character's not important. He's an artist.

FLORAL: So you have no doubts about your future? No gnawing concerns? I mean, the fact that he is over twice your age, myopic, rumored to be a drunkard, decidedly a philanderer, and has been known to wear a ponytail, makes no matter to you?

PANDORA: Not really, no.

FLORAL: Very well, as you wish.

PANDORA: Thank you, but you mustn't be concerned. He's everything I've ever wanted, all my heart desires, I couldn't be happier, if only he were more my age.

FLORAL: What can you do? He won't grow younger. I presume just older.

PANDORA: I wouldn't mind it, if only . . .

FLORAL: What?

PANDORA: His hands have spots.

FLORAL: Age spots, liver spots. Death spots.

PANDORA: Little brown ones. And there are grey hairs all over him. On his chest even. Another thing, he cries when he looks at me.

FLORAL: You're going to be his nursemaid.

PANDORA: I'm too young to be a nursemaid.

FLORAL: And yet it's your fate.

PANDORA: Oh, help me. You're my older sister. Please, save me. Make everything all right again. I'm too young for all this.

FLORAL: All right. I'll tell him. I'll break it off for you.

PANDORA: He's going to be so angry.

FLORAL: Then so he shall be . . . You must not sacrifice your life to some doddering relic, simply because he turned you into a silly legend.

PANDORA: I like being a legend.

FLORAL: But is it worth a bad marriage?

PANDORA: You have a bad marriage.

FLORAL: Why do you say that? Jonsey and I are very happy.

PANDORA: You seem to despise him. Yesterday you and I were going out to get malts, Jonsey asked to join us and you changed your mind immediately, saying you had no interest in a malt. When we returned with our malts, you cried, saying you had wanted one all along. Jonsey offered you his, but you shoved it away with such a force that it fell and splattered all over the cobblestones.

FLORAL: I suppose I simply did not want a malt after all. You don't understand being pregnant. There are cravings you cannot explain. These cravings are very deep and reason does not speak to them. Now shall I call off your wedding or not?

PANDORA: What do you think I should do?

FLORAL: Why ask me? It's your decision entirely. This will make or break your life and I won't be held responsible, only you can decide.

PANDORA: Ooh. Ooh. I don't know. Why ask me? Let's pull the petals off this flower. Whatever it says will be so. (*She picks a flower from the yard.*)

FLORAL: That is a childish way to make up your mind, a foolish solution.

PANDORA: I think it'd be fun to do it this way.

FLORAL: Fine. It's your life.

PANDORA: (*as she plucks petals from the flower*) Yes, I'll marry; no, I'll not. Yes, I'll marry; no, I'll not. Yes, I will. No, I won't. Yes. No. Yes, no. Yes, no. It stopped.

FLORAL: Fine.

PANDORA: But my heart.

FLORAL: Too late. Live by the flower, die by the flower. The wedding is off. (*Kandall enters from the manor.*)

Defying Gravity

BY JANE ANDERSON

SCENE 8

Defying Gravity imagines the life of the teacher who died in the 1986 *Challenger* spaceship disaster, and of other lives affected by this tragic event.

The teacher is in love with the human mind's ability to conceive grand possibilities, particularly the idea of flying to the heavens, and has tried to imbue her young students and her daughter with the same sense of awe and adventure.

Donna is an African-American bartender in a Cocoa Beach hangout near NASA's astronaut training facility. The teacher has begun her training for the space flight.

(Note: A slash [/] in the dialogue means that the next speech overlaps here.)

....

(*The bar.* DONNA *and the* TEACHER *are standing on either side of a bar stool.*)

TEACHER: Go ahead.
DONNA: Go ahead what.
TEACHER: Climb up.
DONNA: Uh-uh, no way.

TEACHER: What could happen?

DONNA: This thing could tip over, I could break my head.

TEACHER: You won't fall, I'll hold on to you.

DONNA: Uh-huh, can't do it.

TEACHER: Chicken.

DONNA: Hey, this is how I am. I'm an earth sign. I don't have any problem with my phobia. If I have to reach something high, I don't need a ladder, I get my boyfriend to do it.

TEACHER: What if he's not around?

DONNA: I get another boyfriend. Look, I get along just fine. My sister, she sent me a plane ticket to visit her in Pittsburgh. I said no thank you, I can drive. It only took me a day to get there. I was relaxed. I was alive. I don't need planes. Forget planes. Planes crash.

TEACHER: Oh come on, and cars don't? That is / so lame—

DONNA: I just read in the paper the other day about some jet/ taking a dive off the runway—

TEACHER: How often do you get your car serviced?

DONNA: On my salary? Honey, if it ain't broke.

TEACHER: Tell me about it. But to get back to my point—

DONNA: Here she goes.

TEACHER:—flying is much safer than driving because a jet is not allowed to leave the ground until / every moving part is checked.

DONNA: Oh come on, do you think the ground crew at an airport is really doing their job?

TEACHER: Absolutely.

DONNA: Those guys are looking at jets all day, they get bored with the routine,/ their minds are wandering all over the place, they're gonna get sloppy.

TEACHER: Oh, you're such a cynic. I'm not listening to you.

DONNA: (over her) Even the ground crew here, they're the creme de la creme, but they screw up all the time—oh shit, Honey, that's not what I was trying to say. I was just—that was just me going along with the argument. I don't even know where that came from. Listen, these boys have their hearts and souls wrapped up in those rockets. I swear to the Lord, they'd rather cut their own throats than let anything happen to you. You want a drink? (*The* TEACHER *shakes her head.)* You want to put me up on this stool? I scare the crap out of you, you get to scare the crap out of me, an even exchange? So what do I do?

TEACHER: Take my hand.

DONNA: *(The TEACHER helps DONNA up on the stool.)* I'm too big for this.

TEACHER: No you aren't.

DONNA: I'm gonna fall.

TEACHER: I have you. *(DONNA is now standing on the stool but is still bent over in panic.)* Straighten up.

DONNA: Don't let go.

TEACHER: I won't. Keep your eyes open, keep looking up. *(DONNA slowly straightens up.)* That's a girl. All right, I'm going to let go of your hand.

(The TEACHER does so. DONNA is standing by herself on the stool.)

DONNA: OK I did it, thank you, let me down now.

TEACHER: Not yet.

DONNA: I don't like where this is going.

TEACHER: Reach your hand up, try to touch the ceiling.

DONNA: Damn, why am I listening to you?

TEACHER: Because I'm the Teacher. Come on. Reach. *(DONNA reaches her hands up.)* How are you doing?

DONNA: I'm doing OK.

TEACHER: Just stay up there for a minute and take in the view.

DONNA: All right.

TEACHER: What do you see?

DONNA: Oh man, there's a bunch of dead bugs on top of the TV. What'd you send me up here for? Get me down, I don't need to look at that. *(DONNA gets down.)* I'm gonna send you up there next time, send you up with a broom . . . hey, are you all right. Oh man, is it that thing that I said? Come on sit down. What do you take, ginger ale?

TEACHER: I wet my pants in training today.

DONNA: Oh don't worry about that, happens to the regulars all the time. Which ride did they put you on?

TEACHER: The escape basket.

DONNA: The one with the twenty-story drop?

TEACHER: Straight down, eighty miles per hour.

DONNA: *Oh* yeah, I know about that one.

TEACHER: They told me to keep my eyes open.

DONNA: What for, the scenery?

TEACHER: I kept my eyes on my knees.

DONNA: That's the thing to do.

TEACHER: But I still lost control of myself. I was so freaked out, I didn't know my seat was wet until they pulled me out of the cage.

DONNA: There's no shame in it, Honey. Astronauts are always messing in their pants. The men who went to the moon? The whole time they were up there they were shuffling around in dirty diapers. When they came back down and they opened up the capsule? Whoo, step back!

TEACHER: It's all still very primitive, isn't it?

DONNA: Naw, it's much better now. The moon landing, they didn't know what they were doing. They got up there with duct tape and prayers. These days they've sent enough of them up, they pretty much have it down.

TEACHER: Should I be praying?

DONNA: You're asking me? Please, I pray every time I get in an elevator.

TEACHER: Do the astronauts pray?

DONNA: I always pray for them. I've never lost one yet.

TEACHER: I prayed to be chosen to go up.

DONNA: Well, there you go.

Desdemona: A Play About a Handkerchief

BY PAULA VOGEL

SCENE 11

In this comic but astute rendition of Shakespeare's *Othello,* Paula Vogel presents us with a very different kind of Desdemona from the one we've come to know. This Desdemona, though described as "Upper class. Very," is no saccharine, wrongly accused wife. This Desdemona has had sex with many men in many situations, including making some extra money at the "establishment" of her friend Bianca.

Othello the Moor, general of the Venetian army, has brought his new bride with him on his military expedition to Cyprus, far from their home in Venice. As in Shakespeare's play, his jealousy is aroused when Desdemona loses a handkerchief that he gave her (she doesn't know that it was found and secreted away by her bawdy maid, Emilia, who then gave it to her husband, the nasty Iago).

Desdemona tells Emilia everything and promises to help Iago get a promotion in Othello's army. Emilia, who is described as speaking in a broad Irish brogue, detests Iago but wants him to get a better-paying position so she will be left with more money when he dies. All scenes in the play take place in a "back room of the palace on Cyprus."

(EMILIA *eats her lunch.* DESDEMONA *plays in a desultory fashion with a toy. Then, frightened:*)

DESDEMONA: Emilia—have you ever deceived your husband Iago?

EMILIA: (*with a derisive snort*) That's a good one. Of course not, miss—I'm an honest woman.

DESDEMONA: What does honesty have to do with adultery? Every honest man I know is an adulterer . . . (*pause*) Have you ever thought about it?

EMILIA: What is there to be thinkin' about? It's enough trouble once each Saturday night, than to be lookin' for it. I'd never cheat, never, not for all the world I wouldn't.

DESDEMONA: The world's a huge thing for so small a vice.

EMILIA: Not my world, thank you—mine's tidy and neat and I aim to keep it that way.

DESDEMONA: Oh, the world! Our world's narrow and small, I'll grant you—but there are other worlds—worlds that we married women never get to see.

EMILIA: Amen—and don't need to see, I should add.

DESDEMONA: If you've never seen the world, how would you know? Women are clad in purdah, we decent, respectable matrons, from the cradle to the altar to the shroud . . . bridled with linen, blinded with lace. . . . These very walls are purdah.

EMILIA: I don't know what this thing called "purr-dah" means, but if it stands for dressing up nice, I'm all for it . . .

DESDEMONA: I remember the first time I saw my husband and I caught a glimpse of his skin, and oh, how I thrilled. I thought—aha—a man of a different color. From another world and planet. I thought—if I marry this strange dark man, I can leave this narrow little Venice with its whispering piazzas behind—I can escape and see other worlds. (*pause*) But under that exotic facade was a porcelain white Venetian.

EMILIA: There's nothing wrong with Venice; I don't understand why Madam's all fired up to catch Cyprus Syph and exotic claps.

DESDEMONA: Of course you don't understand. But I think

Bianca does. She's a free woman—a new woman, who can make her own living in the world—who scorns marriage for the lie that it is.

EMILIA: I don't know where Madam's getting this new woman hog-wash, but no matter how you dress up a cow, she's still got udders. Bianca's the eldest one of six girls, with teeth so horsy she could clean 'em with a hoof pick, and so simple she has to ply the trade she does! That's what your Miss Bianca is!

DESDEMONA: Bianca is nothing of the sort. She and I share something common in our blood—that desire to know the world. I lie in the blackness of the room at her establishment . . . on sheets that are stained and torn by countless nights. And the men come into that pitch-black room—men of different sizes and smells and shapes, with smooth skin—with rough skin, with scarred skin. And they spill their seed into me. Emilia—seed from a thousand lands, passed down through generations of ancestors, with genealogies that cover the surface of the globe. And I simply lie still there in the darkness, taking them all into me: I close my eyes and in the dark of my mind—oh, how I travel!

Independence

BY LEE BLESSING

Kess, in her early thirties, is a university professor in Milwaukee. She has been summoned home to Independence, Missouri, by her sister Jo because Jo claims their mother Evelyn tried to kill her by knocking her down (in her fall, Jo, who is twenty-five and pregnant, chipped a bone in her neck). Evelyn's mental health has been deteriorating for years and she has become increasingly violent.

The last time Kess was home, and the last time she saw or spoke to her mother, was four years ago when she arranged for Evelyn's confinement in the Mental Health Institute for a number of months. This time she would like to find a way to help Jo break out of her mother's clutches and build her own life. Among Kess's reasons for staying away is Evelyn's open disdain for Kess's lesbian relationship with her partner Susan.

The scene takes place in the living room of the family home (Jo still lives home, as does her nineteen-year-old sister Sherry). Evelyn, surprised at seeing Kess, asks Jo to make some tea for them, leaving them alone to talk.

EVELYN: Have a seat.

KESS: In a minute.

EVELYN: *(sitting near KESS's bag)* I will. I've been standing for hours. Out at the MHI. I work in the craft center, you know.

KESS: I heard.

EVELYN: I thought you'd be interested, since you were the one who brought me out there in the first place. Of course, now I'm helping other people, instead of being helped. They all like the projects I think up. Just simple things, really. Wood and yarn and paint and things. (*EVELYN opens KESS's bag and rummages inside.*) How long are you staying? Did you bring a lot with you?

KESS: What are you doing?

EVELYN: Looking at your things. (*holding up a book*) What's this book? It's awfully thick.

KESS: It's a study of imagery in seventeenth-century Scottish Border Ballads.

EVELYN: What do you use it for? Do you read it?

KESS: I'm writing a book of my own.

EVELYN: Really? What's your book called?

KESS: "Imagery in Seventeenth-Century Scottish Border Ballads."

EVELYN: Isn't that the same thing?

KESS: It's my view.

EVELYN: (*laughs, continues rummaging*) I'll never understand it.

KESS: Mom, why are you going through my things?

EVELYN: I haven't seen you. I'm trying to get an idea of who you are. How you've changed, I mean.

KESS: (*retrieving her bag, moving it away from her*) I haven't.

EVELYN: You came back. How long are you staying?

KESS: Jo and I are still talking that one over.

EVELYN: I hope you stay a long time. It's exciting to have all you girls together again. It's a rare treat.

KESS: Jo said you tried to kill her.

EVELYN: Why don't you sit down?

KESS: I'll sit down when I want to sit down.

EVELYN: Are you afraid to sit down? (*A beat. KESS sits in a chair.*) You always used to sit there. (*KESS immediately rises.*) It's so hard to know what to start talking about after four years, isn't it? Are you still a homosexual?

KESS: (*a beat*) Yes, Mother. I am still a homosexual.

EVELYN: I suppose that'll make it hard for you to give Jo much advice about this Don Orbeck fellow. She's awfully confused right now. She wanted to marry him, but I think I've pointed out the disadvantages of *that*.

KESS: What are they?

EVELYN: Oh—well, everyone counsels against getting married because of an inadvertent pregnancy. I mean, look at my own life. I married Henry Briggs just because we were expecting you, and that didn't work out so wonderfully, did it?

KESS: I guess not.

EVELYN: What is it about the women in this family? We get near a man, and the next thing we know we're pregnant. You're probably right to stay away from men.

KESS: Mom . . .

EVELYN: Are you sure you don't want to sit? I feel like I'm staring up at a big building.

KESS: I'll stand.

EVELYN: I hope you won't do any homosexual things while you're in town. I mean, it's your life, but . . .

KESS: *(moving toward the kitchen)* I wonder if Jo needs help?

EVELYN: Oh, she's gone down to the bakery for some rolls.

KESS: She has?

EVELYN: She always does when she makes tea. It's one of our little sins.

KESS: *(sighs, perches on the back of a chair)* Oh.

EVELYN: It's been so long since we've talked. I admit, I wished you dead there for a couple of years, but I'm over that now.

KESS: Mom . . .

EVELYN: Jo's almost fully recovered, too. From her neck, I mean. So, I guess you'd say we're all doing very well at the . . .

KESS: Mom, can I say something?

EVELYN: Of course. We're having a talk.

KESS: As I was driving down here, I was talking to myself—I was saying, "Mom's had four years. We both have. Four years of not seeing each other, not talking, not even writing. Maybe things are entirely different by now. Maybe we'll actually find that we've forgotten how we used to talk to each other. Maybe we'll invent a whole new way."

EVELYN: You talk to yourself in the car?

KESS: Why do we get into conversations like this?! Can't you just say, "Hello, Kess—it's nice to see you again"?

EVELYN: No.

KESS: Why not?

EVELYN: Because it isn't.

KESS: *(a beat)* Why not?

EVELYN: Isn't it obvious? You left this family long ago. You never visited, you never told us anything about your life . . .

KESS: I was trying to establish something for myself.

EVELYN: And then, four years ago, out of the blue, you came down here and decided I needed medical help.

KESS: You did.

EVELYN: In your opinion.

KESS: I found you sitting on the floor behind a chair, wrapped in a blanket.

EVELYN: And you gave me a hug. I remember; it was very sweet. Then you took me out to the MHI, and . . .

KESS: What did you want me to do? Take you up to Minneapolis with me? You wouldn't go. Quit my job? Move down here?

EVELYN: That could have been a start.

KESS: I'm a professional! I have a career. It takes all my time and energy—all my love to do it well. I'm not a hack teacher somewhere. I'm extremely good at what I do.

EVELYN: I know, dear. You're a specialist.

KESS: You were only in there three months.

EVELYN: How much love would you like, Kess?

KESS: What?

EVELYN: Isn't that what we're talking about? Really? You're not here for Jo. You're here for love. You want some of my love.

KESS: That would be nice.

EVELYN: Well then, it occurs to me we may only be dickering

about the amount. You're a specialist; maybe you don't need a lot of love from me. Maybe you only need a tiny bit. I think I could provide that.

KESS: Why did you try to kill Jo?

EVELYN: I didn't. I hit her.

KESS: She thinks you tried to . . .

EVELYN: You show me one mother who hasn't hit a child.

KESS: *(a beat)* Well. I'm going to be here for a little while. I think Jo and Sherry could use whatever comfort and protection that would afford.

EVELYN: They do not need protection . . .

KESS: I think they do. I think they need that, and love.

EVELYN: You are just like Henry Briggs, you know that? Only here when you want to create new tragedies.

KESS: Mom . . .

EVELYN: You have all his false appeal and his seeming logic. But just like Henry, you become part of this family only when it suits you, and . . .

KESS: Mother . . .

EVELYN: And one day you will leave for good. Won't you? Won't you?

KESS: Why did you hit Jo?

EVELYN: I never hit Jo! *(rising)* I remember when a mother and daughter could converse like human beings about these things. You ask anybody in Independence about me. They'll say Evelyn Briggs is the sanest, most well-loved one among us. I am wonderful with those patients. I don't know what Jo may have told you, but it's . . .

KESS: *(overlapping from "may")* Jo has only been . . .

EVELYN: But it's not true! I am perfectly capable of functioning in a warm and loving universe. Which is what I try constantly to create!

Nightswim

BY JULIA JORDAN

It is midnight and all is quiet outside Christina's house. Rose is in the front yard looking up at Christina's dark window. Rose and Christina are seventeen years old.

....

ROSIE: *(whispers loudly)* Christina. Christina! (CHRISTINA, *dressed for bed in a ratty old T-shirt and underwear, comes to the window. She has not been sleeping.)*
CHRISTINA: What?
ROSIE: Come out and play.
CHRISTINA: We're too old to play.
ROSIE: Wanna do something?
CHRISTINA: What?
ROSIE: I don't know, something.
CHRISTINA: Like what?
ROSIE: Wanna go climb the railroad bridge? Cross the river?
CHRISTINA: We're too old to climb the railroad bridge.
ROSIE: Go skinny-dipping in the old man's pool?
CHRISTINA: He's always watching.
ROSIE: So?
CHRISTINA: It's undignified.
ROSIE: We'll go to the lake.
CHRISTINA: The police will catch us.

ROSIE: They haven't all summer.

CHRISTINA: We haven't gone all summer.

ROSIE: So they won't expect us.

CHRISTINA: It's cold.

ROSIE: That'll make the water feel warm, like swimming in velvet.

CHRISTINA: There's no lifeguard.

ROSIE: So we can swim naked.

CHRISTINA: What if we drown like the Berridges' boy? Our bodies would get caught under the weeping willow in the water. No one would find us for weeks.

ROSIE: We won't go anywhere near that tree.

CHRISTINA: But there's no lifeguard.

ROSIE: You forgot how to swim?

CHRISTINA: No.

ROSIE: Let's go.

CHRISTINA: I'm tired.

ROSIE: Skinny-dipping is like resting itself.

CHRISTINA: What if that rapist with the mustache and the beady eyes is out there?

ROSIE: He's in jail.

CHRISTINA: There could be another one. Beady-eyed rapists are a dime a dozen. A copycat crazy.

ROSIE: Black water, black night. He won't even see us.

CHRISTINA: Our skin glows like 60-watt bulbs at night.

ROSIE: The water will cover us.

CHRISTINA: He'll come in after us.

ROSIE: Rapists can't swim so good.

CHRISTINA: He'll get us on the beach.

ROSIE: You can run, can't you?

CHRISTINA: He has a fast car.

ROSIE: You can hide, can't you?

CHRISTINA: He carries a flashlight. He senses fear. He'll find me.

ROSIE: You can fight, can't you?

CHRISTINA: He's bigger than me.

ROSIE: You can scream, can't you?

CHRISTINA: No one will hear me.

ROSIE: I'll hear you. Two against one.

CHRISTINA: What if there are two of him? Or three? Or a gang of crazies hiding under the weeping willow tree waiting for us.

ROSIE: We won't go anywhere near that tree.

CHRISTINA: What if there are two?

ROSIE: What if there are none?

CHRISTINA: I can't.

ROSIE: You're scared?

CHRISTINA: Yes.

ROSIE: Admit it.

CHRISTINA: I do.

ROSIE: Say it.

CHRISTINA: I'm scared.

ROSIE: Don't be.

CHRISTINA: Why not?

ROSIE: 'Cause it's a beautiful night for a swim.

CHRISTINA: It is?

ROSIE: The water will be like swimming in black velvet because the air is cool. The lake will be all ours because everyone is locked up in sleep. We will swim naked because there is no lifeguard. And there won't be any crazies because I have a feeling. *(beat)* It's a beautiful night for a swim.

CHRISTINA: The police.

ROSIE: It won't be the same ones.

CHRISTINA: What if it is?

ROSIE: They change their beats.

CHRISTINA: What if they haven't?

ROSIE: That was last summer.

CHRISTINA: I saw them, a picture of them, in the paper today.

ROSIE: I saw it, too.

CHRISTINA: They saved a mother's little girl. CPR. She called them heroes.

ROSIE: It's good they saved her girl.

CHRISTINA: Heroes.

ROSIE: They're heroes.

CHRISTINA: Heroes can do anything they want, you know. They give them the key to the city and stuff like that. They could catch us swimming naked and take our clothes and make us leave the water all naked and shine their flashlights on us and hold our clothes above their heads and laugh and say, "Jump." You'll cry.

ROSIE: I will not cry.

CHRISTINA: I won't know what to do. I'll jump and they'll laugh and I won't know what to do. I'll jump.

ROSIE: I promise you, on my honor, I will not cry.

CHRISTINA: What will you do if those heroes come?

ROSIE: I will hide under the weeping willow branches that grace the lake.

CHRISTINA: You said we wouldn't go anywhere near that tree.

ROSIE: I'll swim to the middle of the lake and tread water until they leave.

CHRISTINA: Your legs will tire. You'll drown like the Berridges' boy.

ROSIE: I'm a strong swimmer.

CHRISTINA: They'll come in after you.

ROSIE: They won't get their uniforms wet. It'd tarnish their medals.

CHRISTINA: They could take off their uniforms.

ROSIE: Then they wouldn't be cops.

CHRISTINA: They could take off their medals.

ROSIE: Then they wouldn't be heroes.

CHRISTINA: They could take our clothes and drive away in their police car. Sirens and lights and them laughing.

ROSIE: We'll drive home naked.

CHRISTINA: Our moms will catch us.

ROSIE: They've seen us naked before.

CHRISTINA: What if it's our Dads?

ROSIE: That won't happen.

CHRISTINA: What if it does? Naked? *(beat)*

ROSIE: *(in a father's voice)* "NO MORE SKINNY-DIPPING

BEHIND OUR BACKS—SNEAKING AROUND—DOING WHATEVER YOU PLEASE—FOR YOU, YOUNG LADY."

CHRISTINA: Those are your favorite jeans they'd be driving off with. You'd never get them back.

ROSIE: I don't care.

CHRISTINA: Took you two years to break them in.

ROSIE: I'll hide them in a tree.

CHRISTINA: There's only the weeping willow.

ROSIE: I know.

CHRISTINA: They'll find our clothes again and they'll know they've got two naked girls again. And one will shine his flashlight on you and one will shine his flashlight on me. And the water that maybe was like swimming in black velvet when we were alone and moving will be cold when we're still and wondering what to do. And they will order us out and we will be naked and shivering and your tan skin will turn white and frightened. They'll see right into us. Your eyes will fix on them and you won't look at me. You won't tell me what to do and I'll be so cold. They'll say, "Come on out now, girls." And the water will fall away from your body with only hands and wrists, white elbows and arms to cover you. Your arms look breakable. And I'll follow you watching the water run down your back. The flashlights will glare down our faces, down our legs. They'll shine their flashlights one for each of us. They'll smile at us trying to cover ourselves. They'll hold our clothes above their heads and smile at us naked and say, "Jump." And you'll cry and I'll cry and I'll jump.

ROSIE: We'll walk out of that lake like we've got nothing to be ashamed of and we'll look them right in the eye.

CHRISTINA: We won't cry?

ROSIE: We will not cry.

CHRISTINA: When they hold our clothes above their heads and won't give them back and say "Jump"?

ROSIE: We will not cry. You will not jump.

CHRISTINA: When they say with grins on their faces and our clothes in their hands, when they say . . .

ROSIE: (*cutting* CHRISTINA *off*) "Lucky for you."

CHRISTINA: "Lucky for you it was just cops that found you and not some crazy sicko."

ROSIE: "Murderous Peeping Tom."

CHRISTINA: "Rapist."

ROSIE: "What are you two thinking about swimming at this hour with no lifeguard?"

CHRISTINA: "What if a storm came up all of a sudden and lightning struck the lake?"

ROSIE: "Why, you could be electrocuted!"

CHRISTINA: "What are you thinking about swimming with no clothes on?"

ROSIE: "You could catch a chill and die of pneumonia!"

CHRISTINA: "It's cold at night with no sun!"

ROSIE: And when they say. "Run along home now, girls."

CHRISTINA: "Before we call your parents."

ROSIE: We'll just stare at them, but we won't say a word.

CHRISTINA: We won't?

ROSIE: We won't stoop to their talk, talking nonsense. We'll just press them with our knowing eyes and they'll know that we know better.

CHRISTINA: We know all about skinny-dipping at midnight.

ROSIE: Warm, black water, black sky, no flashlights to trash the darkness, one moon, some stars, and a weeping willow tree. A perfectly beautiful night for a swim.

CHRISTINA: Standing there naked we will not cry.

ROSIE: We will not.

CHRISTINA: I can't

ROSIE: Why?

CHRISTINA: The floorboards creak, they'll wake up.

ROSIE: Tiptoe.

CHRISTINA: My parents have radar.

ROSIE: Climb out the window.

CHRISTINA: There's nothing to climb.

ROSIE: Jump.

CHRISTINA: It's a long way down.

ROSIE: Bend your knees when you land.

CHRISTINA: Catch me.

ROSIE: You're too old for catching.

CHRISTINA: (*CHRISTINA climbs into the window frame.*) Just jump and bend my knees?

ROSIE: I don't like to swim alone.

CHRISTINA: It is a beautiful night for a swim.

ROSIE: C'MON JUMP.

(*CHRISTINA jumps. Lights out.*)

Scenes for Two Men

Lobby Hero

BY KENNETH LONERGAN

ACT I, SCENE 2

Jeff is a security guard working the night shift in the lobby of an apartment building. William, his black supervisor, is a stickler for doing everything right, for following rules and living an honest, clean life. It is a philosophy that has paid off for him (he became the youngest captain in the history of the security firm), and he is proud of how different he is from his irresponsible brother, who was arrested earlier in the day. But tonight, as William enters the lobby on his usual rounds, something is clearly bothering him.

It has been an odd night for Jeff, who is a bit of an oddball and misfit—and not a stickler for following rules. Just before William arrived, Jeff spent time talking to an attractive young female officer who was waiting in the lobby for her partner, a seasoned cop who she has fallen in love with. Jeff wound up telling her that her partner was actually visiting a prostitute in the building. William arrives just after the two police officers have left.

(JEFF *picks up his book but he can't concentrate and throws it down. He does nothing for a while.* WILLIAM *enters onto the street and comes into the lobby.*)

JEFF: Hey, William. How you doin'?

WILLIAM: Hello, Jeff. How's it going?

JEFF: Pretty good. The police were just here, but they didn't ask about you, and I signed them right in. It was that cop Bill and his partner. He said tell William Bill says hi.

WILLIAM: Was that all?

JEFF: That was all.

WILLIAM: *(sitting down)* OK . . .

JEFF: Oh, yeah, and I told Manuel to clean up the desk.

WILLIAM: *(takes out cigarettes)* What?

JEFF: I said, I told Manuel to clean up the desk—to straighten up the desk drawers—

WILLIAM: Oh yeah, yeah, thank you.

JEFF: I really laid into him, too, because this desk is disgusting. I mean, when you open this drawer it should be *spotless.* I told him I want to be able to eat my *breakfast* outta this drawer tomorrow morning. I told him you were ready to kill somebody about these drawers. I really did.

WILLIAM: OK, Jeff. Thanks.

JEFF: You're welcome. Taken care of. *(long pause)* You're not very chatty tonight . . .

WILLIAM: What?

JEFF: I said you're not very chatty tonight. You're not really holding up your end of the conversation very well.

WILLIAM: Sorry, Jeff, I've got a lot on my mind.

JEFF: That's OK. We don't have to talk about anything. I'm just glad to see your smiling face.

WILLIAM: Same here, Jeff. You just keep talking. If I hear anything worth responding to I'll just jump in.

JEFF: OK. *(pause)* How's your brother doing?

WILLIAM: I don't know. I haven't spoken to him.

JEFF: Did you find out what he did? Oh no, you knew what he did, you just didn't want to tell *me* about it. I forgot. That is completely fine. I don't mean to sound so inquisitive. I'm sorry. *(pause)* So did you see where the mayor says he's gonna shut down all the—

WILLIAM: *(on "shut")* All right, let me ask you something, Jeff.

Suppose somebody who's supposed to be near and dear to you was accused of doing some kind of terrible crime, and was trying to use you as an alibi. What would you do, for example, if it was a false alibi? That is to say, you weren't with the person when they said that you were?

JEFF: I don't know. I guess it would depend on who they were and what . . .

WILLIAM: Yeah, see, we already part company. I like to tell the truth.

JEFF: Well, so do I—

WILLIAM: What are you talking about, man? I didn't even get through the details of the hypothetical situation and you're already gearing up to perjure yourself.

JEFF: No I'm not. I was just—I mean if it was my *mother* or something—

WILLIAM: Right, because that's what everybody expects, right? But that's where I part company with ninety-five percent of the human race. So I'm a freak. But I wouldn't do it.

JEFF: Are you talking—I assume you're talking about your brother?

WILLIAM: It doesn't matter who I'm talking about.

JEFF: So but what did he do?

WILLIAM: I don't know what he did, man, because he hasn't been tried in a court of law.

JEFF: What are you, some kind of Robotron? What did they *accuse* him of?

(*Pause.*)

WILLIAM: They say—they arrested him and two friends for allegedly going into a hospital last night to steal pharmaceutical drugs, and some nurse apparently saw them and they attacked her—

JEFF: Oh my God . . .

WILLIAM: . . . and they beat her up with a pipe or something like that and now she's dead.

JEFF: Oh my *God* . . .

WILLIAM: . . . And according to my brother's girlfriend, my brother told the police I was with him at the time at some movie.

JEFF: Wow.

WILLIAM: Yeah, gave her a whole made-up schedule what we were supposedly doing last night for me to memorize: what movie, who called who, what time we ate, who ate what, you wouldn't believe it. See, he can't handle getting a job or applying himself to go to school, but he has the wherewithal to come up with *that* shit on the spur of the moment when he's in the jailhouse under arrest for murder at two o'clock in the morning.

JEFF: Wow.

WILLIAM: "Wow."

JEFF: Well, would—I mean, God, I mean—do you—

WILLIAM: And it's not like . . . See, his girlfriend called me tonight, and apparently two of my brother's friends—these *real* criminals, mind—were identified by some doctor, and the cops picked them up and they named my brother as the third guy. But the doctor didn't really get a good look at him, so they're trying to dig up something substantial that would link him to the scene. And meanwhile my brother says he was at home alone, with no alibi, and so would I say he was at the movies with me last night?

JEFF: Jesus Christ.

WILLIAM: See, I don't think *he'd* ever do anything that fuckin' heinous, but he's definitely done a lot of other shit. And I know these guys he's always with, and . . . You know, I want to be objective about it, to some degree. I want to . . . I can't just be saying, "Well, seeing how he's my brother, it is therefore impossible for him to have done this ghastly thing." You know what I mean?

JEFF: Yeah . . .

WILLIAM: I just wish I had more information. But who am I gonna talk to? His girlfriend? She just parrots everything he says, she's got no will of her own. And what's *he* gonna tell me? That he's guilty? He knows what I'll do then.

JEFF: Yeah . . . Wow.

WILLIAM: And I am not the type of person who sympathizes with the criminal element in this kind of situation. Not at all. But the fact remains that there's a lot of people in jail who don't belong there, a lot of black people in jail who don't belong there, and a lot of cops and prosecutors and what have you who just as soon throw somebody in jail as nobody. And I hate to say it, but my brother is tailor-made for the part, and if he's being railroaded in some way, I don't know what right I may have to my private reservations. So it's an interesting dilemma. It's interesting. But I'll tell you something, Jeff, and you can quote me on this right now: If he had anything to do with killing that woman I'd sooner put a bullet through his head myself than lift a finger to help him. Because that is inhuman. Inhuman. Even if he was just standing *by* . . . Some innocent person . . . And all she did was show up at work that night? *(pause)* But we're hoping it's all some terrible misunderstanding, right?

JEFF: Right. Right.

WILLIAM: So what would *you* do there, Jeff?

JEFF: Me? Oh, well, the first thing I would do is I would definitely try to find out if my brother was with those guys or not. Because that could really inform the whole situation right there.

(Pause.)

WILLIAM: Well no fuckin' shit, Jeff, how in the world do you expect me to do that?

JEFF:
Don't get mad at me, you asked me what I would do!

All right, all right!

All right!

WILLIAM: Well what the fuck do you expect me to do? "Find out if he was there or not."

Hot *dog*, I never would have thought of *that*.

WILLIAM: If I could just find *that* out the rest of this shit might just fall right into place!

JEFF:
Well can't you go see him?
Can't you talk to him? You'll
be able to tell whether or not
he's lying—

WILLIAM: No I can't go see
him, Goddamn it, he's locked
up in fuckin' Riker's Island! I
can't go see him 'til after the
arraignment!

OK, what about his girlfriend?
Maybe you should go see
her—

I already talked to her, Jeff!
Look, look, I don't actually expect you to solve this for me,
let's just forget I brought it up.

JEFF: I'm sorry. This kind of problem is not exactly within my
forté.

WILLIAM: Which is what?

(*Pause.*)

JEFF:
OK, you don't have to get
nasty, I'm only tryin' to be—

WILLIAM: What is your forté,
man?

What is your forté?

(*Pause.*)

JEFF: I don't have one. Losing money.

WILLIAM: All right, never mind, Jeff. Thanks anyway.

JEFF: Do you know if the nurse was white or black?

WILLIAM: No.

JEFF:
Because that could—

WILLIAM: What difference
does that make?

JEFF: It's just if she's white there's probably gonna be a big stink
about it in the papers, and if she's black they probably won't play it
up as much.

WILLIAM: Well, I don't know what color she was . . . I just better figure out what I'm gonna do before the cops catch up with me,

because I'm not gonna get two chances to do this right. (*He starts to go.*)

JEFF: Is there anything you want me to tell the cops if they show up?

WILLIAM: (*stops*) What?

JEFF: If the cops come by and ask me if I've seen you?

WILLIAM: Tell them you saw me.

JEFF: What if they ask me if you talked about your brother? What should I tell 'em?

WILLIAM: Maybe it'd be better if you didn't mention any of that till I figure out what I'm doing.

JEFF: Well—I don't feel comfortable *lying* to them.

WILLIAM: OK. Well . . . In that case, just—

JEFF: No I was just—I'm just kidding.

WILLIAM: Oh.

JEFF: Sorry.

(*Pause.*)

WILLIAM: What the fuck do you find funny about this, man?

JEFF: Nothing. I'm really sorry. I really apologize.

WILLIAM: All right. I should get going.

Our Lady of 121st Street

BY STEPHEN ADLY GUIRGIS

ACT I, SCENE I

Sister Rose has died. During her long life she touched many people from the New York City minority community where she taught children and helped the poor. Many of these have gathered for her funeral—but her body has disappeared from its casket. It is late morning at the funeral home and Balthazar (a detective) and Vic are standing in front of the empty casket.

In the scene, Balthazar tells Vic about a father's reaction to news of his son's murder. Later in the play, Balthazar reveals that he was the father in the story—that he had a hangover that morning and let his son go out and play alone, and that the pain of the loss is still with him.

....

(*Late morning. Ortiz Funeral Home. Main viewing room.* BALTHAZAR *and* VIC *stand in front of an empty casket.*)

VIC: What kinda fuckin' world is this?!
BALTHAZAR: Mmm.
VIC: I mean, am I alone here?!
BALTHAZAR: "Alone," "not alone"—
VIC: What did she ever do anyway, huh?! What did Rose ever do

till the day she died but be a fuckin' living saint on this earth to deserve this, this sacrilege!

BALTHAZAR: Sister Rose was a good woman—

VIC:—There are limits—I don't give a shit! Maybe you grew up in a godless jungle, but I remember when the world was not this! And this? This is not the world!

BALTHAZAR: OK.

VIC: Her fuckin'· father, he should rot in hell! That's first off! Demons should shit in his mouth daily, the Irish punk! Don't take much guts to beat on a woman, ya get me?

BALTHAZAR: I wasn't aware of her history—

VIC:—Why you think she became a nun anyway, beautiful girl like that? All this "needle exchange," "alcoholic drunk tank" she had runnin' up here? "Gangs" this, "stop the violence" that? All that thankless shit she did? Was it because she was a good person? Sure. But if ya look underneath it all, it's two things: She donned the habit because she was terrified of intimacy, and all them programs was a way to atone for the sins of her fuckin' piece-of-dirt Shanty-Irish Mick-fuck father!

BALTHAZAR:—Hey, what's your name?

VIC: My name?

BALTHAZAR: Yeah, friend, tell me your name.

VIC: It's Victor. Why?

BALTHAZAR: You wanna drink, Vic? A little nip? Take the edge off?

VIC: I prefer to keep my edge on, pal. (*BALTHAZAR drinks from a half-pint bottle.*)

BALTHAZAR: Gotta ask you about your pants, Vic.

VIC: My pants?

BALTHAZAR: You are aware that you're not wearing pants?

VIC: Of course I'm aware—they stole 'em!

BALTHAZAR: Where'd you sleep last night, Vic?

VIC: I slept here last night, and my name is Victor, not Vic.

BALTHAZAR: That's quite uncommon, isn't it? A mourner sleeping over at a wake?—

VIC: What are you, a cop?

BALTHAZAR: No. Vic, I'm a farmer. I came here to sell some eggs.

VIC: You accusing me of something?!

BALTHAZAR: I'm sorry. I'm not accusing, sir, just, I get a call, I come here, there's a man ranting in his underwear, a missing corpse, no sign of forced entry—and it's not the corpse of Ned the Wino or Bobo the Clown that's been stolen, it's our Sister Rose, sir. Sister Rose.

VIC: Look, I came over in the mornin' yesterday, it was a fuckin' madhouse in here, OK?! Crackhead junkies, politicians, reporters, screaming babies, I had ta leave. I came back at closin', tossed the funeral guy a coupla hundred bucks . . . I wanted, I needed a little time, alright?!

BALTHAZAR: OK.

VIC: I knew her my whole life since we were six for Christ's sake.

BALTHAZAR: I understand.

VIC: These fuckin' people, yesterday? Some of them showin' up in dirty jeans and T-shirts?! Eating pizza?! Little kids with video games makin' loud electrical noises?! I mean, "What goes on here," no?! . . . I saw one mothahfuckah kneelin' in front of Rose's casket, he's prayin', then his fuckin' cell phone goes off and he . . . he fuckin' answers it! Has a goddamn conversation in Spanish, and not a short one . . . Talkin' loud too, "Mira, mira, mira"—kneelin' over her fuckin' casket! I mean, what the fuck is that, mister?! Can you tell me?! 'Cuz I'm at a loss over here—

BALTHAZAR: Grief takes different forms.

VIC: That ain't grief! I don't know what the fuck that is, but it ain't grief!

BALTHAZAR: . . . I once knew a guy—hey now, listen ta me.

VIC: I'm here.

BALTHAZAR: True story: . . . I once knew a guy, a coupla detectives went to his apartment to inform him that his son had been raped and murdered in the playground up on 137th—

VIC:—Jesus—

BALTHAZAR: You know what his reaction was? And keep in mind this is a man who loved his son dearly, OK? . . . His reaction was: He wouldn't leave the house to I.D. the body until after the Knick game was over . . . It was "the playoffs," he said . . . They watched the whole fourth quarter together in silence . . . He served them ham sandwiches with warm beer . . . And this was a man who lived . . . for his son (*BALTHAZAR takes another swig from his bottle.*) . . . I am going to close this casket now. You are going to go outside and speak to my partner. He will secure you a new pair of pants. Where you live, Vic? Brooklyn? Queens?

VIC: Staten Island.

BALTHAZAR: We'll have a squad car drive you home.

VIC: I'm here for the duration.

BALTHAZAR: OK. Crime Scene needs to work through this room now, Vic. When they're done, the room will be open again. OK?

VIC: Fine.

BALTHAZAR: My partner's outside in front of a black and grey Ford. Ya can't miss him, he's Chinese and he walks with a pronounced limp.

VIC: For the record, I had nuthin' to do with this.

BALTHAZAR: I don't think that you did.

VIC: Just make sure you catch the mothahfuckah.

BALTHAZAR: Sister Rose was my teacher. I liked her very much.

VIC: . . . Ya know, if Rudy were still in office, this woulda never happened—I'm sure of it! He wouldn't of took this lyin' down for two seconds.

BALTHAZAR: . . . My partner—he's right outside.

VIC: Right . . . Say . . . Did they ever catch that guy?

BALTHAZAR: What guy?

VIC: The guy who murdered the kid.

BALTHAZAR: No . . . No, not yet.

VIC: What, uh, what ever happened to the guy with the ham sandwiches?

BALTHAZAR: . . . The guy with the ham sandwiches?

VIC: Yeah . . .

BALTHAZAR: Why? You want one?

VIC: One what?

BALTHAZAR: A ham sandwich.

VIC: Do I . . . ?

BALTHAZAR: It's a joke, Vic. I'm joking.

VIC: Not funny. Not funny at all.

The Value of Names

BY JEFFREY SWEET

Benny Silverman, in his late sixties, is a successful TV comic actor. He once had a successful Hollywood career but was blacklisted in the 1950s and out of work for many years after he refused to cooperate with the House Committee on UnAmerican Activities in their search for communists in Hollywood. His closest friend, Leo Gershen, did cooperate. Leo named names of people he knew who were communists, including Benny. The two men never spoke again.

Leo continued to have a successful career as a director and now, thirty years later, is about to direct Benny's daughter Norma in a play, if she agrees to work with him. Leo comes uninvited to Benny's plush house "high up in the Hollywood Hills" to see if a reconciliation with Benny is possible, and, if necessary, to convince Norma not to turn down the role.

The scene takes place on the patio. The two men quickly launch into some tart repartee, leading Norma to go off to let them work it out or fight it out on their own. Benny and Leo review much that has happened in their lives and Leo insists that he has nothing to apologize for.

....

BENNY: Sounds like you've got this all thought out.
LEO: It's not like I haven't had the time.

BENNY: Just one problem, Leo. When you called me up that night, you didn't call me because you thought you were right. You called me because you felt lousy about what you were going to do.

LEO: Benny, I never claimed to feel good about it.

BENNY: But you did it.

LEO: Only a fool fights the drop.

BENNY: You want to translate?

LEO: You've seen enough cowboy movies. If the bad guys have got the drop on you, it's crazy to draw on them. You're only going to get gunned down. Can't fight if you're dead.

BENNY: So now we're cowboys?

LEO: Thank you for taking what I have to say seriously.

BENNY: Seriously, OK: Leo, not only did you not fight the drop, you helped the bad guys gun down some good guys. What would the kids in the balcony say if Roy Rogers shot Gabby Hayes?

LEO: Bad guys, good guys . . .

BENNY: It's your analogy.

LEO: I said nothing about good guys.

BENNY: Oh, I see: there were no good guys?

LEO: Present company excepted, of course.

BENNY: No good guys. Well, that makes it nice and convenient, doesn't it? If everybody's equally scummy, then the highest virtue is survival. That must make you pretty goddamn virtuous. You should write a book about your philosophy, Leo. Really. I've got the title for you: *Charles Darwin Goes to the Theatre*.

LEO: Being a victim doesn't automatically entitle you to a white hat, Benny. It's that old liberal impulse—romanticize the persecuted.

BENNY: What the hell would you know about liberal impulses?

LEO: Hey, I've got my share of them.

BENNY: You—a liberal? Don't make me laugh.

LEO: I sure wouldn't want to do that, Benny—make you laugh.

BENNY: Maybe you're a checkbook liberal. You send in contributions to those ads with pictures of kids starving in South America, a couple bucks to the A.C.L.U. . . . .

LEO: More than a couple of bucks, but never mind . . .

BENNY: More than a couple? Well, hey, that changes my opinion completely.

LEO: I'll tell you where I part company with a lot of them, though. I won't romanticize. Just because someone's a martyr doesn't make him wise and good and pure. Sure, I sent in money to Joan Little's defense fund, but that doesn't mean I'd trust her to babysit my grandchildren.

BENNY: Joan Little was on trial for killing someone, for Christ's sake. The guys the Committee went after—only thing they did was make the mistake of believing in something unpopular. And the ones who wouldn't buckle under to the Committee—out with the garbage.

LEO: Which is exactly what they did to each other when they were members of the Party. Those bastards were always browbeating each other, excommunicating each other for not embracing "the correct revolutionary line." Do you remember when the Party endorsed Henry Wallace for President? Lenny Steinkempf got up in a meeting, said he thought it was a crappy idea. So what did the Party do? They threw him the fuck out. And after *they* threw him out, his *wife* Elaine, being a loyal Party member, *she* threw him out. As far as I was concerned, facing the Committee was an exercise in *deja vu*. Believe me, Nixon, and Mundt could have taken lessons from some of those old Commies. I wasn't about to put my dick on the block for any of those guys. Why should I keep faith with them when they couldn't keep faith with themselves?

BENNY: The point wasn't to keep faith with *them*. Leo, don't you remember anything about how or why we put together the New Labor Players?

LEO: Oh, for Christ's sake!

BENNY: For Christ's sake what?

LEO: *(laughing)* Benny, you aren't seriously going to hit me with the New Labor Players?

BENNY: And why not?

LEO: All that agitprop bullshit, the slogans, screaming our lungs raw . . .

BENNY: Worthless?

LEO: Not worthless, exactly . . .

BENNY: Then *what*, exactly?

LEO: All we ever did was play to people who felt exactly like we did. Invigorating—sure. Fun—absolutely. And a great way to meet girls. But don't try to tell me we ever accomplished any great social good. I doubt that we ever changed anybody's mind about anything.

BENNY: That's how you measure it?

LEO: You measure it differently?

BENNY: Seems to me there's some value in letting people know—because they laughed or maybe cheered at the same time as a bunch of other people—letting them know they aren't alone. That there are other people who feel like they do.

LEO: Maybe we should have broken out some pom-poms while we were at at.

BENNY: Pom-poms?

LEO: Hey, if you're going to cheerlead, you should have pom-poms. "Give me a P, give me an R, give me an O, give me an L!"

BENNY: Leo . . .

LEO: "Whattaya got? Proletariat! Whattaya got? Class struggle! Whattaya got? Dialectical materialism! Rah, rah, rah!"

BENNY: Some terrific joke, Leo. Very funny.

LEO: What's funny is you telling me this stuff.

BENNY: What's funny about that?

LEO: You think I don't know my own spiel when I hear it?

BENNY: Your spiel?

LEO: Of course my spiel. "Class consciousness is the first step. Through theatre we give dramatic form to our lives and hopes and so create our identity and the identity of our community." You like it? I've got another three or four hours of this. Rousing stuff, hunh?

BENNY: Yeah, I thought so.

LEO: Oh, I convinced myself pretty good, too. But I'm not a twenty-two-year-old kid anymore, and neither are you. And I'm not going to let you get away with pretending that "Capitalist Heaven" and the rest of it was any great golden age of drama. Face it, Benny, it was amateur night.

BENNY: I'm not talking about how sophisticated or how professional. Leo, what I'm saying is that when we started, all right, we may not have had much polish or technical expertise, but we did have a sense of purpose. There was a *reason* I started acting. There was a *reason* Mort Kessler started writing. There was a *reason* you started directing. And then came a point you gave up your reason so you could keep on directing.

LEO: Maybe directing *was* my reason.

BENNY: What—directing anything?

LEO: Of course not.

BENNY: You say of course not, but I don't take it for granted that there are things you wouldn't direct. Before the Committee—yes. But after?

LEO: So all of a sudden I'm a whore. Of course, it isn't whoring to do some dumb-ass sit-com. What was it called—*Rich and Happy?*

BENNY: *Rich But Happy.*

LEO: I stand corrected. Truly edifying, uplifting stuff. My God, in the old days, if somebody had told you that's what you'd end up doing! *Rich But Happy.* I mean, back then just the *title* would have made you gag!

BENNY: I had to live.

LEO: So did I, Benny. So did I.

BENNY: But if I did crap—and God knows I'm not holding up *Rich But Happy* as an example of high culture—but if I did crap, I didn't destroy other people to do it.

LEO: I know where this is heading: If a guy's politics aren't approved, aren't correct, then he can't be any good as an artist. I bet you're one of those people who think God took away Frank Sinatra's voice as a punishment for voting Republican.

BENNY: I'm not talking party affiliation . . .

LEO: I know what you're talking about: In order to be an artist, you've got to be a certified good guy.

BENNY: Being a *mensch* enters into it, yes.

LEO: And if he isn't, you feel cheated. Short-changed. Well, if art by bastards upsets you so much, you should drop everything right now, go into your library and toss out anything you have by Robert Frost. Now there was a world-class shit! And how about Ezra Pound! And let's not bring up Wagner!

BENNY: I don't have any Wagner in my house.

LEO: No? Well, now *there's* a brave stand! My hat's off to you, Benny! Keep those doors guarded. Be vigilant! Hey, you can't be *too* careful. I mean, you never know when somebody might try to sneak the fucking *Ring Cycle* into your house without your knowing it, right?

BENNY: This I'm enjoying—you linking arms with Wagner!

LEO: Tell me something, if you found out that Charles Dickens fucked ten-year-old boys, would that make him any less of a writer?

BENNY: Well, it sure as hell would make a difference in how I read *Oliver Twist*.

LEO: Whatever you or anybody else thinks about me as a person, I did good work, Benny. Not just before. After, too.

BENNY: I wouldn't know about after. I didn't see most of it.

LEO: Well, you missed some good stuff. If you don't want to take my word for it, you can take it from the critics. You can look on my fucking mantle in New York at the prizes and the plaques . . .

BENNY: I'm sure they would blind me.

LEO: They mean something, Benny, even if it's fashionable to sneer at them. They mean that a lot of people thought that the work was good.

BENNY: And that's important to you.

LEO: Yes, it is.

BENNY: You like having the good opinion of others.

LEO: Is that a crime?

BENNY: No, I don't think it's a crime. I like it, too. I'm just sorry to have to tell you that you haven't got *my* good opinion, Leo.

LEO: And I'm sorry to have to tell you I don't give a damn.

BENNY: Then why are you here?

LEO: Because I don't want your goddamn daughter walking out of my goddamn play.

BENNY: Fine, you told her that. So why are you still here?

LEO: Because I'm a masochistic idiot!

BENNY: What, you expected me to throw my arms open?

LEO: No.

BENNY: Then what?

LEO: Damn it, Benny—thirty years! It's been more than thirty years! We're going to start *dying* soon! *(a beat)* While there's still a chance. *(For a moment, there is little in this world that BENNY wants more than to respond to LEO.)*

Mojo

BY JEZ BUTTERWORTH

ACT I, SCENE I

The year is 1958. Sweets and Potts, two thugs in their early twenties, are waiting anxiously in an upstairs room at the Atlantic, a low-end club in the Soho district of London. In a nearby room a very important meeting is taking place between Ezra their boss and the owner of the club, Mr. Ross (a local mogul with lots of money), and Silver Johnny (a sexy young rock singer who has become a sensation at the club and who Potts claims to have discovered).

Sweets and Potts believe that if the meeting goes well, Ross will sign a lucrative deal with Ezra to back Silver Johnny, and Ezra will reward them for their efforts with a sizable piece of the action. As the scene begins, Sweets and Potts are sitting at a table with a pot of tea and three "pretty" cups.

....

SWEETS: Is that brewed?

POTTS: Four minutes.

SWEETS: You want a pill?

POTTS: My piss is black.

SWEETS: It's the white ones. Don't eat no more of the white ones. *(pause)* So where is he sitting?

POTTS: Who?

SWEETS: Mr. Ross.

POTTS: He's on the couch.

SWEETS: Right.

POTTS: Mr. Ross is on the couch.

SWEETS: Good. How is he?

POTTS: What?

SWEETS: Good mood, bad mood, quiet, jolly, upfront, off-hand. Paint me a picture.

POTTS: Tan suit. No tie. Penny Loafers. No tassel.

SWEETS: Uh-huh. Right. Does he look flush?

POTTS: He's Mr. Ross.

SWEETS: Absolutely.

POTTS: He's a flush man.

SWEETS: Naturally.

POTTS: Ten guinea Baltimore Loafers. Suit sweat a year for you couldn't buy. Shirt undone. Tanned like a darkie. Yes he looks flush.

SWEETS: Ten guinea Baltimore's? Fuck me briefly.

POTTS: Penny. No tassel.

SWEETS: They're talking about it aren't they . . . *(pause)* Okay. Okay. So where's Ezra?

POTTS: Ezra's at the desk, but he's not in his chair. He's round here to one side.

SWEETS: The Mr. Ross side or the miles away side?

POTTS: Round here to the side on the poochy stool.

SWEETS: Poochy stool. Good.

POTTS: Sit behind the desk it's like I'm the man. Like I'm trying to big you out. Sit round the side on the poochy stool, Hey Presto, we're all a circle.

SWEETS: Okay. Okay. So where's the kid?

POTTS: Couch.

SWEETS: Couch. Good.

POTTS: On the couch with Mr. Ross.

SWEETS: Exactly. Let him see the merchandise. *(They sit there, waiting for the tea to brew.)* You know Beryl? She goes to me tonight, she goes "When Silver Johnny sings the song my pussy-hair stands up."

POTTS: Relax.

SWEETS: I know. I know. Her pussyhair.

POTTS: We just sit here.

SWEETS: I know. Her fucking mange. Her fur. It stands up.

POTTS: I see these girls. It's voodoo. Shaking it like they hate it. Like they hate themselves for it.

SWEETS: In the alley. "Get it out," she says. "Get it out I'll play a tune on it . . ."

POTTS: One day he's asking his mum can he cross the road the next he's got grown women queuing up to suck his winkle.

SWEETS: Seventeen. Child.

POTTS: These girls. They shit when he sings.

SWEETS: Exactly. *(beat)* What?

POTTS: Mickey knows. They shit.

SWEETS: They what?

POTTS: It's a sex act. It's sexual.

SWEETS: Hold it. Hold it. Stop. Wait. *(beat)* They shit?

POTTS: All over.

SWEETS: *(beat)* What does that mean?

POTTS: Means they have no control in front of a shiny-suited child. Sad fucking world. The end. I'm going to use this as a rule for life: "Anything makes polite young ladies come their cocoa in public is worth taking a look at."

SWEETS: Good rule.

POTTS: Great rule.

SWEETS: There's got to be rules and that's a rule.

POTTS: Okay. Good. Sweets. Listen. *(beat)* When he announces it—

SWEETS: Hey—

POTTS: When Ezra—

SWEETS: Hey. Hey—

POTTS: If he takes you aside . . . (I know. I know. But listen.)—

SWEETS: Could be me could be you. Could be me could be you.

POTTS: Exactly. I'm planning. I'm . . . listen. He takes you aside

tells you takes me aside, it's not important. For me there's no difference.

SWEETS: It's exactly the same thing. Me or you. Exactly.

POTTS: Exactly. Good. The important thing is whichever way it
comes, when he announces it, when it happens, act "surprised and
happy."

SWEETS: Surprised and good. Good.

POTTS: Happy and good. Good. The end. That's four minutes.
(*POTTS stands and picks up the tea tray.*) What?

SWEETS: Absolutely. What? Nothing.

POTTS: I'll be straight back.

SWEETS: Right. Good luck.

POTTS: Relax.

SWEETS: I am relaxed. I'm talking. (*POTTS takes the tea into the
back room. He closes the door. SWEETS lights a cigarette. POTTS returns.*) So?

POTTS: So what?

SWEETS: So what happened?

POTTS: Nothing.

SWEETS: Right.

POTTS: They're drinking the tea.

SWEETS: Right. Good. What about the Campari? Has the kid
drunk his Campari?

POTTS: He's sipping it.

SWEETS: Good.

POTTS: It's casual.

SWEETS: Good sign.

POTTS: You know? Loose.

SWEETS: Excellent. Excellent sign.

POTTS: Ezra's still on the poochy stool. But he's moved it. He's
tugged it over in snug next to Sam.

SWEETS: Hold it. Hold it. Stop. Who?

POTTS: What?

SWEETS: You said Sam.

POTTS: Indeed.

SWEETS: Who's Sam?

POTTS: Mr. Ross.

SWEETS: Oh.

POTTS: Sam is Mr. Ross.

SWEETS: Oh right.

POTTS: Sam Ross. That's his name.

SWEETS: Since when?

POTTS: Everyone calls him Sam. His mum named him Sam.

SWEETS: Lah-di-dah.

POTTS: Listen. Sam Ross is here next to Ezra he's got his legs crossed and he's letting his Loafer hang off his foot like this. It's bobbing there.

SWEETS: Don't.

POTTS: Right next to Ezra's leg.

SWEETS: Stop.

POTTS: Eyes wide like this. Both of 'em. Like long lost puppies.

SWEETS: Fuck me. They're talking about it aren't they. What's the kid doing?

POTTS: Nothing. Sitting in between looking pretty.

SWEETS: Good.

POTTS: He ain't saying nothing. Just sitting there looking foxy.

SWEETS: Good. The kid's doing good.

POTTS: He knows why he's there. He's paid to warble and look pretty. He ain't paid to give it large in the back room.

SWEETS: Has he got the jacket on?

POTTS: Who?

SWEETS: The kid. Has he got the Silver Jacket on?

POTTS: He's took it off. It's on the table.

SWEETS: Hang on. Hang on. He's took it off?

POTTS: It's on the table.

SWEETS: Hang on. Hang on. What the fuck is he doing?

POTTS: What?

SWEETS: What the fuck is going on?

POTTS: What's up?

SWEETS: He's supposed to wear the Silver Jacket. He's Silver Johnny. Silver Johnny, Silver Jacket.

POTTS: Sweets—

SWEETS: Silver Johnny, Silver suit. That's the whole point.

POTTS: I know.

SWEETS: Ezra buys the Silver Jacket he should wear it.

POTTS: It's hot in there.

SWEETS: I don't give a fuck if it's hot. Mr. Ross deserves the full benefit. He's not called Shirtsleeves Johnny is he. He was called Shirtsleeves Johnny it would be perfect.

POTTS: It's laid back. It's a jackets off atmosphere. He's right to take the jacket off. It's good.

SWEETS: I'm not happy. *(pause)* Has he got the trousers on?

POTTS: What?

SWEETS: Has he got the silver trousers on?

POTTS: Of course he fucking has.

SWEETS: Well that's something.

POTTS: Fuck do you think they're doing in there? He's gonna sit there in just his pants?

SWEETS: I know. I'm just excited.

POTTS: He's got his trousers on.

SWEETS: I know. Relax.

POTTS: You relax.

SWEETS: I am relaxed. I'm talking.

POTTS: Exactly. *(pause)* Ezra done this. *(POTTS winks.)*

SWEETS: At you?

POTTS: Ezra don't forget. I mean who fucking discovered the kid? I did.

SWEETS: Right.

POTTS: Fact. One solid gold forgotten fact. Ask Mickey. Up Camden. Luigi's.

SWEETS: Luigi who fucks dogs.

POTTS: Yes. No. Luigi with the daughter. Parkway. With the Italian flag up behind the. The thing behind the . . .

SWEETS: With the daughter. Does the liver and onions.

POTTS: That's him. I'm up doing all the Camden jukes. Three weeks running Luigi's light on his pennies. Every machine in Parkway is pulling in eight nine quid a week, Luigi's it's one bag, two, three quid if you're lucky. So I say stop having a chuckle, inky pinky blah blah blah you're gonna get a kidney punched out.

SWEETS: Only fucking language they speak.

POTTS: So he's gone, listen, he's gone "No one's playing the juke."

SWEETS: Yeah right.

POTTS: He says. Nobody's playing it.

SWEETS: Like we're in outer Russia.

POTTS: Like it's the moon. Outer Russia. Exactly. He says they're doing it themself. He says they've got a kid comes in here, gets up in the corner, does it himself. The fucking shake rattle roll himself. I mean. Camden kids?

SWEETS: Micks.

POTTS: Do me a favour.

SWEETS: Micks and Paddies.

POTTS: Do me a good clean turn.

SWEETS: Micks and Paddies and Wops who fuck dogs.

POTTS: He says "Come back tonight, you'll see." So I come back tonight. I take Ezra, Mickey we're gonna scalp him take the rig back he's told us a fib. (*pause*) Lo and behold.

SWEETS: No.

POTTS: In the corner, all the moves. Doing "Sixty Minute Man." Everyone watching. In the corner. A child. (*pause*) That's what happened. I'm not whining. I'm not bleating. Am I supposed to get back in the van start doing sums? "I want xyz. Twenty, thirty, forty percent."

SWEETS: You're not some fuckin' vulture.

POTTS: I'm not some fucking doorboy. I want what's due. I want what's fucking mine.

Bluff

BY JEFFREY SWEET

Emily and Neal are living together in New York City. Her stepfather, Gene, is a salesman of dental supplies and has come from California to New York on business. Earlier in the day Emily introduced Gene to Neal when he visited them in their apartment. Tonight they are all rendezvousing at the bar in Gene's hotel before he takes them out for dinner.

Emily has pulled away from her family. She hasn't seen her mother, who is an alcoholic, for two years and she has had a love-hate relationship with Gene ever since he came into her life after her father died in an accident. Neal and Emily met when he came to the defense of a man in a gay-bashing incident and, despite Emily's emotional distance, he fell in love with her and soon moved into her apartment.

Neal, who is a lawyer, arrives at the bar before Emily. He orders some drinks and brings them over to Gene's table.

....

GENE: You should have let me take that. I could have put it on my expense thing.

NEAL: Hey, I'm flush. I robbed some widows and orphans today. How's the trip going?

GENE: Oh, fine. Everybody goes to the dentist, you know. I heard about how you two met. Pretty gutsy, going to bat for some fag.

NEAL: You know, there's a possibility we could get along.

GENE: If I didn't use words like "fag"?

NEAL: It would help.

GENE: I'm just—

NEAL: You're fucking with me.

GENE: Yes, you're right. I am. I am fucking with you. Or as the Germans would say, "I am with you fucking." Did you know they put their verbs at the ends of their sentences? The Germans?

NEAL: That's new information to me.

GENE: So I've been given to understand. "I am with you fucking."

NEAL: Is it that you want to find out what pisses me off?

GENE: Will you my apology accept?

NEAL: Will you up your ass it shove?

GENE: You want some totally unsolicited advice? Neal?

NEAL: What?

GENE: Don't do it.

NEAL: Don't—?

GENE: Get married. No, let me revise that: don't get married to *her*.

NEAL: I'm not good enough for her? She's not good enough for me?

GENE: "Good enough" has nothing to do with it. You're both— if you'll pardon my salesman's angle—you're both quality goods. Smart, not bad looking and other items of value. But you don't want to do this. My opinion.

NEAL: Unsolicited.

GENE: Unsolicited.

NEAL: I don't think she's interested in marriage anyway. Not right now.

GENE: Then it's—what is that word you lawyers like to use?— moot?

NEAL: Probably.

GENE: I just thought, if this idea were floating around in the realm of the possible—

NEAL: OK, I don't get it. Before, you were talking—you were giving her grief about us living together without benefit of clergy.

GENE: No, that wasn't me. That was me speaking on behalf of Emily's mother. Her mother isn't happy about this, and part of my job is to transmit these feelings to her. Her mother's feelings.

NEAL: I see.

GENE: So I did that. I communicated this to Emily. I can report back that I delivered the message. That I discharged my duty in good conscience.

NEAL: And this advice you're offering me, this is also in good conscience?

GENE: This is me speaking for me. I don't have to agree with her mother. And also, you've got a mouth and you think I'm a jerk, but I kind of like you.

NEAL: So what you're saying is in my interest?

GENE: She's very angry.

NEAL: We're talking about Emily again?

GENE: You've got eyes. This is news to you? Angry. Always has been. Long as I've known her anyway. I mean, I understand. Her father gets stolen from her when she's a kid, the guy her mother remembers as this mythic person—his perfect, handsome photo on the wall, a shrine. She thinks the life—Emily thinks, but her mother, too—the perfect life she could have had—perfect family, maybe her mother wouldn't have started drinking if it hadn't been for the grief, if it hadn't been for the accident of some truck driver falling asleep at the wheel on the same highway as her father. It's not fair. Emily and her mother lose this golden guy and get—me. You ever see a picture of her father?

NEAL: No.

GENE: I look *nothing* like him. His photo, like the picture of a promising rookie on a baseball card. I am no compensation at all. I am a joke. And I come into their home and I don't go away. I tried to get her mother to move somewhere else, we could start in a new place, a house that didn't still smell of him, she wouldn't do it. Wouldn't leave. I pressed as hard as I could, but I could tell it was a deal-breaker. And I didn't want that deal to break. I wanted to marry her. Every bit and piece of me wanted to marry her mother. It may be hard for you to believe, given the way she is now—

NEAL: I've never met her.

GENE: That's right, of course.

NEAL: Maybe a word or two on the phone when she calls—

GENE: Well, she really was something. She was drinking too much when I met her, but I could understand that. The loss of this guy she was so nuts about. I thought that that would pass. And I seemed to have a good effect on her. She cut way back. In the early days with me, hardly touched the stuff. That's some feeling, you know.

NEAL: A compliment?

GENE: To think you're having a good effect on someone. You can see that someone's better because you're there. You could fall in love with someone for being better because you're there.

(A beat.)

Well, that didn't last. But what does? Oh shit, listen to me. I'm sorry. I *am* a jerk. All right, I've said it. I've given you my very valuable opinion. It's up to you to make the choice for yourself. I mean, far be it for me to—

NEAL: Do you give this pep talk to all of Emily's boyfriends?

GENE: I only met a couple of the others.

NEAL: And did you say this to them?

GENE: No. But they weren't in any danger.

NEAL: Danger?

GENE: They weren't living with her. There wasn't any serious chance of anything happening beyond, how do I say it—?

NEAL: Screwing without a license?

GENE: You know how on a carton of milk, they stamp the expiration date? "December 12" or whatever. These guys, you could see the expiration date. I didn't feel I had to do anything. Time would take care of it.

NEAL: But me, you feel you have to do something.

GENE: I'm not even really saying not do it.

NEAL: No?

GENE: Just make sure you know what you're getting into first.

(*Laughs.*)

There's a nice specific piece of advice, right? You can really put that plan into action. But you're going to do what you feel like, so fuck me anyway—

As Is

BY WILLIAM M. HOFFMAN

Rich and Saul were lovers, living together in Saul's "fashionable loft space" in New York City (it is the 1980s). Rich moved out six months ago and has a new lover, so Saul has asked him to return to the loft to divide up their belongings. In truth, Saul—who is terrified of the growing AIDS epidemic devastating gay men—still loves Rich and hopes he can find a way to get him to return. Unbeknownst to Saul, Rich has learned that he has an early stage of AIDS.

....

(Lights come up on two casually dressed men in their thirties seated in the living area.)

    RICH: You take Henry.
    SAUL: Cut him in half.
    RICH: You can keep him.
    SAUL: What are we going to do about him?
    RICH: I said he's yours.
    SAUL: You found him.
    RICH: I don't want him.
    SAUL: Chet doesn't like cats?
    RICH: I knew this would happen. Don't start in.
    SAUL: We gotta get things settled.

RICH: Then let's. How 'bout if we simplify things: sell everything and split the cash.

SAUL: Even the cobalt glass?

RICH: Yes.

SAUL: And Aunt Billie's hooked rug? Say, how's she doing?

RICH: She's on medication. Sell the rug.

SAUL: I will not sell the manikin heads. I don't care what you say.

RICH: Then take them.

SAUL: And the chromium lamp? I love that lamp.

RICH: Take it.

SAUL: And the Barcelona chair?

RICH: The Barcelona chair is *mine*! *(beat)* Fuck it. Take it. Take
everything. I won't be Jewish about it. *(He rises to go.)*

SAUL: Why didn't you warn me we were going to play Christians
and Jews today? I would have worn my yellow star.

RICH: I've gotta go. *(RICH is leaving.)*

SAUL: Where're you going?

RICH: I'm not feeling so hot. Let's make it another day.

SAUL: *(blocking his way)* Sit down.

RICH: *(pushing his hand away)* Don't push me.

SAUL: Sorry. I don't like this any more than you, but we gotta do
it. It's been six months. *(lightening things up)* A divorce is not final
until the property settlement.

RICH: Saul . . . ? *(He's about to say something important.)*

SAUL: What, Rich? *(He waits expectantly.)* What?

RICH: Never mind.

SAUL: What? . . . What? . . . You always do that!

RICH: I want the chair.

SAUL: You can have the fucking Barcelona chair if Chet wants it
so bad! . . . What about the paintings? Do you want to sell the Paul
Cadmus?

RICH: Yes.

SAUL: You love the Cadmus. *(silence)* And who's going to buy
the Burgess drawings? Did you hear that Kenny died?

RICH: We'll donate them to the Metropolitan.

SAUL: Just what they always wanted: the world's largest collection of Magic Marker hustler portraits. (*RICH nods.*)

RICH: They're yours.

SAUL: But you commissioned them. We'll split them up: I get the blonds and you get the blacks—or vice versa.

RICH: All yours.

SAUL: Then you get the Mickey Mouse collection.

RICH: Sell it.

SAUL: You don't sell collectibles. Not right now. What's with this money mania? Between the book and the catering, I thought you were doing well.

RICH: I want to build a swimming pool.

SAUL: You don't swim.

RICH: I want a Mercedes.

SAUL: You don't drive. It's Chet—he'll bankrupt you! (*beat*) I don't believe I said that . . . (*sincerely*) Your book is beautiful.

RICH: I never thanked you for the cover photograph.

SAUL: (*shrugging off the compliment*) How's it selling?

RICH: Not bad—for short stories. Everyone mentions your photo. Ed White said—

SAUL: Your book is terrific. Really.

RICH: I'm glad you like it.

SAUL: One minor thing.

RICH: What's that?

SAUL: I thought the dedication was a bit much.

RICH: Why are you doing this?

SAUL: Don't you think quoting Cavafy in Greek is a little coy?

RICH: Please!

SAUL: Why didn't you just say, "To Chet, whose beautiful buns inspired these tales"?

RICH: Jesus Christ!

SAUL: I'm sorry! (*silence*)

RICH: I sold the IBM stock. You were right about it. You have always been right about money. (*He hands SAUL a check.*) This includes the thousand I borrowed for the periodontist.

SAUL: You sure?

RICH: Take it.

SAUL: I'm not desperate for it.

RICH: It's yours.

SAUL: I don't want it.

RICH: Damn it!

SAUL: *(taking the check)* Okay.

RICH: That makes us even now.

SAUL: *(examining the check)* Clouds and trees.

RICH: Let's get on with this.

SAUL: Is he waiting for you downstairs? You could have told him to come up.

RICH: Shit. No! Can it. *(beat)* I won't be wanting the copper pots.

SAUL: Why not? When you and Chet move to your space you'll want to cook again.

RICH: I just don't want them! People change. *(silence)* I'm eating out a lot.

SAUL: Chet can't cook?

RICH: *(deciding not to respond with a bitchy comment)* You keep the rowing machine.

SAUL: Have you lost weight?

RICH: And the trampoline.

SAUL: There's some Black Forest cake in the fridge. *(SAUL goes toward the kitchen to get the cake.)*

RICH: Stop it.

SAUL: Stop what?

RICH: Just stop.

SAUL: I can't.

RICH: We're almost through.

SAUL: I have feelings.

RICH: You have only one feeling.

SAUL: He won't make you happy.

RICH: Here we go again. *(RICH gets up to go.)*

SAUL: Don't!

RICH: Keep everything.
SAUL: I'm not myself.
RICH: Nothing is worth this.
SAUL: I've been upset.
RICH: I mean it.
SAUL: Don't go. Please. (*RICH sits. Long pause.*)

The Chosen

ADAPTED BY AARON POSNER AND CHAIM
POTOK FROM THE NOVEL BY CHAIM POTOK

SCENE 4

Like many teenagers in Brooklyn, New York, in 1944, Danny Saunders loves to play baseball—and he is very good at it. But Danny is a Hasid Jew from a very religious sect who wears the traditional clothing and hairstyle of his community—even when he is playing baseball. Reuven Malter is a Jewish teenager who also plays baseball, but his family is less orthodox and he wears ordinary clothing. The boys go to different yeshivas (Jewish religious schools); both are serious students of the Talmud (the body of Jewish laws). Both are sons of rabbis and both play for their school's baseball team. That's how they met—in a baseball game between their schools in which Reuven pitched a ball to Danny who hit it right back into Reuven's face, putting him in the hospital with eye and face injuries.

As the scene begins, Danny has come to Reuven's hospital room and Reuven wakes with a start from a bad dream about the baseball game.

For scene study purposes, you may omit the line of the adult Reuven. As the play is structured, Reuven is actually reminiscing about his lifelong friendship with Danny, which began that fateful afternoon on the baseball field.

DANNY: Sorry if I woke you. The nurse told me it was all right for me to wait here.

YOUNG REUVEN: *(Overlapping. Amazed, disoriented, just waking up. . . .)* Wha . . . what are . . . ?

DANNY: How is your eye? Is it going to be all right?

YOUNG REUVEN: Umm . . . yeah . . . maybe. *(still waking up, turns off radio . . .)* No thanks to you. You could have blinded me, you know.

DANNY: Yes, I know.

YOUNG REUVEN: What do you want? Did you come here to gloat?

DANNY: No. To apologize. I'm sorry for what happened.

YOUNG REUVEN: "Sorry"? That's all?

DANNY: You want me to be miserable? I'm that, too.

YOUNG REUVEN: Good! You should be!

DANNY: I did not come here to fight with you. If you just want to fight, I'll go home.

YOUNG REUVEN: Fine, go home. *(DANNY does not move.)* Well go on, what're you waiting for, an engraved invitation?

DANNY: I came here to *talk* to you.

YOUNG REUVEN: Well, I don't want to listen. Get the hell out of here! Go home and feel miserable! *(Beat. Then DANNY starts to leave, then stops and comes back . . .)* What?!? What do you want?

DANNY: You study Talmud?

YOUNG REUVEN: What?

DANNY: You study Talmud, right?

YOUNG REUVEN: Of course.

DANNY: Yoma. Page 87b. If someone asks you for forgiveness you are supposed to grant it. I told you I am very sorry for what happened. And I'm asking you to forgive me.

YOUNG REUVEN: Yeah, well, that passage in Yoma says you have to ask more than once. Besides, you could have killed me. In Sanhedrin . . . somewhere . . . it says that if someone comes to kill you—

DANNY: You should kill them first. Sanhedrin, page 72a. But that has to do with a thief breaking into a house.

YOUNG REUVEN: (*impressed despite himself*) Yeah, well, I think it applies here.

DANNY: No it doesn't. The Talmud is very specific.

YOUNG REUVEN: No, Raba asks that, uh, that the reason, umm . . . that the law about breaking in—

DANNY: (*with perfect recall, amazing confidence and clarity*) "Raba asks, What's the reason for the law of breaking in. Everyone knows that a person will protect his property. So if a thief breaks in he'll have in mind that the owner will protect his property and he'll be telling himself if the owner tries to stop me, I'll kill him. Therefore the law is, if anyone comes to kill you, kill him first." (*explaining*) Rav asked Rabbi Hanina thirteen times to forgive him for insulting him. Rabbi Hanina refused. Rashi explains that Rav was very hard on himself in such matters, and kept asking Rabbi Hanina. But the law is you only have to ask three times. Rabbi Hanina dreamt he saw Rav suspended from a palm tree and . . .

YOUNG REUVEN: (*finally interrupting . . .*) All right, all right, all right, that's enough.

DANNY: I have a photographic memory. My father says it's a gift from God. I can do it with *Ivanhoe,* too. Do you want to hear?

YOUNG REUVEN: No, that's okay. I'm impressed.

DANNY: Good. I was trying to impress you. I want to talk to you.

YOUNG REUVEN: What about?

DANNY: The baseball game. I can't stop thinking about it.

YOUNG REUVEN: Yeah, neither can I.

DANNY: If I ever don't understand something, I think about it until I understand it. But I still don't understand this.

YOUNG REUVEN: Don't understand what?

DANNY: Why I wanted to kill you.

YOUNG REUVEN: (*utterly amazed*) What???

DANNY: I don't understand why I wanted to kill you. (*beat*) It's really bothering me.

YOUNG REUVEN: Well, I should hope so.

DANNY: Don't be cute, Malter. I really wanted to kill you.

YOUNG REUVEN: Why?

DANNY: I don't know. That's what I'm telling you. But I did.

Remember right before that last pitch you threw me, I smiled at you?

YOUNG REUVEN: I remember. Believe me.

DANNY: It was right then. At that moment it just hit me. I wanted to step over the plate and . . . and just open your head up with the baseball bat.

YOUNG REUVEN: *(amazed again)* Wha . . . ?

DANNY: And it wasn't your whole team or anything, just you. Like it was just you and me out there, and I just . . . I just wanted to—I don't know, to—get you.

YOUNG REUVEN: Well, it was a pretty hot game. And I wasn't exactly wild about you, either.

DANNY: I don't think you even know what I'm talking about.

YOUNG REUVEN: Now wait a minute—

DANNY: It wasn't the game. It was *you*. You really had me going there, Malter.

YOUNG REUVEN: Quit calling me Malter. You sound like a teacher or something.

DANNY: So what should I call you?

YOUNG REUVEN: If you have to call me anything, call me Reuven.

DANNY: Okay. And call me Danny.

YOUNG REUVEN: Okay.

REUVEN: It was surreal. I'd never heard a Hasid speak anything but Yiddish before, yet here was Danny Saunders, whom I thought I hated, dressed as a Hasid, speaking perfect English, chatting about how he wanted to kill me because of some curveballs I'd thrown him.

DANNY: You know, you're a pretty rough player.

YOUNG REUVEN: So are you. Why do you always hit like that?

DANNY: Like what?

YOUNG REUVEN: Straight back at the pitcher.

DANNY: I don't know. I don't try. It just happens that way. Maybe the way I hold the bat. But I've never hurt anyone before. You were supposed to duck.

YOUNG REUVEN: I had no chance to duck.

DANNY: Sure you did.

YOUNG REUVEN: There wasn't enough time.

DANNY: There was time for you to bring up your glove.

YOUNG REUVEN: Yeah, but . . . *(he is caught, considering this for the first time . . .)* Huh . . .

DANNY: *(putting it together for the first time . . .)* Maybe you didn't want to duck.

YOUNG REUVEN: *(realizing along with him)* Maybe I didn't.

DANNY: *(still putting it together a piece at a time)* Maybe you didn't want to because I was the one who hit it. Maybe you didn't want to duck any ball that I hit.

YOUNG REUVEN: Right . . .

DANNY: You had to stop it.

YOUNG REUVEN: I think that's right.

DANNY: Like I wanted to "stop" you.

YOUNG REUVEN: Yeah, I guess so.

DANNY: Well, you stopped it.

YOUNG REUVEN: Yeah. I stopped it all right. *(beat)*

DANNY: I better get going. I have school.

YOUNG REUVEN: Oh, by the way, who won the game?

DANNY: Oh. We did. Sorry.

YOUNG REUVEN: Maybe you should be a professional baseball player.

DANNY: I don't think my father would be too happy about that.

YOUNG REUVEN: He'd say it was a game for *goyim*, huh?

DANNY: I don't know what he would say. He doesn't talk to me very much.

YOUNG REUVEN: Come on. He's a rabbi and he doesn't talk much?

DANNY: Oh, he talks a lot, just not to me.

YOUNG REUVEN: I don't understand.

DANNY: He prefers silence. He once told me he wished that we all could talk in silence.

YOUNG REUVEN: Talk in silence?

DANNY: That's what he said.

YOUNG REUVEN: I don't get it.

DANNY: I don't either. *(beat)* I better go.

YOUNG REUVEN: Okay.

DANNY: I'll come again tomorrow . . . if it's okay with you.

YOUNG REUVEN: Sure. *(DANNY starts out as MALTER approaches from the other side.)* Danny?

DANNY: Yes?

YOUNG REUVEN: Thanks for coming.

DANNY: Thanks for listening.

Buying Time

BY MICHAEL WELLER

ACT I, SCENE I

An exuberant celebration is taking place in a hotel in Mesa, Arizona (it is the mid-1990s). The law firm of Donne and Russo (D & R) has won a big corruption case that led to the "forced resignation" of the governor of the state. The revelers have just carried their party from the hotel room to the ballroom where reporters have assembled to interview them. As Max, the lead attorney on the case, moves toward the door to follow the group, he is stopped by Ben who noticed that Max is less upbeat than would be expected.

Both Max and Ben have worked for years in the pro bono unit of the firm providing free legal services for civic causes, and both have maintained the idealism they had as young attorneys. But neither gets the big salaries that others in the firm, like the corporate attorneys, get. Moreover, despite their stunning victory, the pro bono unit is still in jeopardy of being pared down.

Before the others went off to the ballroom they gave Max a tee-shirt with the letters YENOM EROM printed on the front, which read backwards says MORE MONEY. Max put the tee-shirt on and is still wearing it.

BEN: Is the tee-shirt a fashion statement?

MAX: *(notes that he's wearing it)* Whoops.

(MAX removes it.)

BEN: *(watching MAX, puzzled)* Kind of a serioso speech, Lasker. Not our typical Merry Max.

MAX: Middle age, what can I tell ya? I had a pony tail when we started here, remember?

(Pause. They smile, then break into whoops.)

BEN: We *did* it, Max, oh man, I've had highs before but—the Governor of the state, for fuck's sake. We did it, we saved the firm!

MAX: We saved *what*?!

BEN: Pro bono. Rule 7.

MAX: Dream on, Mister T.

BEN: Come on, man, the corporate guys were bean-counting our time sheets up the wazoo on this one, if we'd lost against the governor, they'd've been all over us like a bad suit, "You litigators wasted two thousand hours on a political vendetta, that's our Christmas bonus, Rule 7 is killing this firm, blah-blah-blah." Instead; cover story, *American Lawyer; Time Magazine* feature, "Donne & Russo, lawyers with a vision . . ." Corporate can't bitch at that result.

MAX: Guess who's boycotting the party, Hopalong; half the corporate section.

BEN: *(beat)* Okay, it's not their victory, fuck 'em.

MAX: *(growing anger)* It's the whole firm's victory. We should all be together down there, damn it!

BEN: You're beautiful when you're angry.

MAX: I'm serious, Bennett. Ten years ago they wouldn't have dared pull something like this. Five, even.

BEN: Let 'em boycott, let 'em sulk, let 'em crawl back in a hole and write contracts and badmouth litigators 'til the moon turns blue, as long as they can't get their hands on pro bono. *(a toast)* To our Holy of Holies, Bylaw 7, the public good, *pro bono publicum!*

MAX: *(stops him)* I came to Mesa to get laid, d'I ever tell you?

True story, and not a word of this to Maia, cause we were already engaged. I had this job interview in Frisco, and an old girlfriend from law school calls, "Hey, Maxie, drive through Mesa on your way west, and we'll get it on."

BEN: "Get it on!" God, I love Colonial English!

MAX: So we're in bed getting biological, and she starts in about this place where she's a summer associate; D&R, some little weird-ass firm that *pays* you for pro bono work, up to 20 percent of billable hours, and it's in the fuckin' *bylaws*, Rule 7 it's called, and I'm going "this chick is stoned, what's she talking about, legal aid or something"—she's grabbing my hand, putting it places but I'm getting curious about this firm of hers, like "who pays for these free hours?" and she's going "Harder Max, faster," but I'm very interested now, like "How does it work, the rainmakers subsidize the freebies, and they're *okay* with this?" She's making these moany-gurgling noises but now I'm going nuts trying to work it out; I mean, are these guys for-real grown up attorneys, or are we talking Larry-the-Lawyer wannabees who passed their bar exam after five tries? So next morning I swing by the place to check it out, and hallelujah! Everything she said was true. It was legal paradise, man. I applied on the spot.

BEN: Question; Did you satisfy the lady that night?

MAX: Answer; Does the Pope wear condoms?

BEN: Next question. Why this story?

MAX: The new guys, they're different. Social action means nothing to them. *Pro bono's* some historical curiosity, a quaint collectable from the Golden Age of Law. All the youngbloods dream about is a Lamborghini with wraparound stereo, tilt-back seats and a blond shiksa wearing a perfume called "Portfolio."

BEN: That's better. For a minute I thought you'd checked your sense of humor at the door.

MAX: The Governor was our swan song, B-man.

BEN: *(very concerned)* Max, what is *with* you tonight?

MAX: D'you see his face when they read the verdict? He was smirking. He lost a skirmish, but he knows he'll win the war. We're the dinosaurs. The new guys are fast and glib and fearless, and we're in their way. Just to hold the line against 'em from now on . . . I don't have the energy. I'm tired, Bennett. Okay? I want time with Maia and the kids. I want my life back.

BEN: Don't let this be going where I think it is!

MAX: *(beat)* I bought into a one horse operation, Livingston Montana. Wills, land titles, DWI; routine stuff; oil change, spark plugs . . .

BEN: But you're the next Managing Partner, it's a given. The firm is *ours* now, we can take it anywhere we want.

MAX: If we'd lost, I'd hang in a while till things calmed down. But this victory buys you time; you want the firm, take it.

BEN: *(beat)* No, man. There's a trust here. Del let us run with this case for one reason only; he knew you'd be Managing Partner after him, and you could keep the corporate section in line. *(then:)* What'll change your mind? A year off with pay? A bigger Christmas bonus? The firm needs you, Max.

MAX: You still believe in all that good stuff, don't you; our last Passionate Pilgrim. I'll tell something, Benito; if anyone can save pro bono from the barbarians, it's you.

BEN: "If?"

MAX: *Big* big if.

BEN: *(fighting the loss)* You're a shitty lawyer, a shitty friend, I hope you die a slow death alone in a motel room, now give me back my fucking tee-shirt.

MAX: *(with a grin)* I'll miss you, too.

(MAX offers his hand. Suddenly it's an embrace.)

Night Maneuver

BY HOWARD KORDER

SCENE 3

Twenty-six year old Lou works as an inventory clerk in an auto supply store, lives in a rundown one-room apartment with a single light fixture and a bathroom down the hall, and is unhappy with his life. But he has plans. He's been saving money to buy drugs and make big money by selling them. Now he is anxiously awaiting the phone call from his "connection," the person he will buy the drugs from, who is supposed to come to the apartment for the sale.

Lou's eighteen-year-old brother Tim has been staying with him, sleeping on an air bed. Tim seems slow and naive, and Lou has been lecturing him on how to live and what to think, and advises him to follow in the footsteps of their older brother Monty. Tim is mysterious and does odd things. He's told Lou that he hangs out in the park and uses drugs with a strange friend named Petey, and he recently brought back some false teeth that he said he found in the park.

But Tim is not as innocent and gullible has he appears: It is clear that he has a sense that Lou has made up the stories about Monty; and he has mugged a guy and stolen his dress clothes, and, unbeknownst to Lou, he has gotten wind of the impending drug deal. The scene below takes place about 7:30 in the evening. Lou has just returned from work.

(Lights up. LOU enters, dressed in work overalls. He is carrying a small take-out bag, which he drops on the bed. He shuts the door. He opens the dresser drawer and removes the envelope.)

LOU: Oh yes yes yes. *(He opens the envelope and lays out the money on the bed according to denomination, snapping each bill crisply.)* Well, boys, pretty soon you'll be moving on. Don't think it hasn't been fun. *(He puts the bills back and places the envelope in the drawer. He sits down, opens the bag, and takes out a hamburger, fries, and soda. He shakes the bag. Several plastic ketchup packets fall out. He unwraps the hamburger and attempts to open the ketchup, struggling unsuccessfully with each packet in turn. Finally he squeezes one in his fist. It explodes, splattering ketchup across his overalls. Pause. He takes some clothes off the floor and starts undressing. He catches himself in the sink mirror, stripped down to his shorts, He stares for a moment, then flexes like a muscle man. He notices Tim's jacket lying on the stool and puts it on. He strikes a tough-guy pose in the mirror. The sink light flickers and goes out.)* Oh shit. *(stumbling)* Ow! *(He falls. Silence. The door opens. No light from the hallway.)* Who's there? Is that you? *(Silence.)* Sorry about this . . . fucking bulb blew. I got a trouble lamp around here somewhere . . . just let me find the dresser. You got the stuff? You got the stash, I got the cash, ha-ha. *(Silence.)* Is that you? *(Silence.)* Who's there? *(Silence.)* Is someone there? *(Silence. Three loud clicks.)* Look, is that you? Don't think I can't see you. I can see you. Where are you? *(Silence. LOU is by the sink. He knocks various utensils to the floor.)* Don't come any closer. I got a knife. *(The door shuts.)* I'm gonna turn on the light! *(The light from the hand lamp reveals LOU alone, holding a spatula. He throws it down.)* Shit. *(He moves to open the door, thinks better of it, and sits down on the bed to examine his toe. He wraps a pillowcase around his foot. He hears the sound of someone at the door. He switches off the lamp and flings the door open. There is a brief struggle. The lamp is switched on. Tim is holding it in one hand. With the other he has LOU forced face down on the bed with his arm twisted behind his back.)* Let go of me!

TIM: It's only me, Lou.

LOU: I'll kill you, you son-of-a-bitch!

TIM: It's Tim, Lou.

LOU: Who?

TIM: It's me. It's Tim. *(pause)*

LOU: I know that.

TIM: You okay?

LOU: Yeah; I'm fine . . . Tim. Do me big favor, huh, and get off me.

TIM: I was just trying to stop you from hurting yourself.

LOU: Don't kid me. I know what to do in a pinch. You jumped me in the dark. What are you fucking around for?

TIM: I'm sorry, Lou. I couldn't see. I didn't know who it was.

LOU: Not now. Before.

TIM: When?

LOU: Just before, just before now!

TIM: I just got here. *(pause)*

LOU: Did you see someone outside the door?

TIM: No. What happened? *(pause)*

LOU: Nothing. Some psycho. He found out who he was dealing with and took off. I handled him.

TIM: It's a good thing you were home.

LOU: If it hadn't of been dark you could never had got me.

TIM: I know I couldn't, Lou. *(pause)* Why are we sitting like this, Lou?

LOU: Fucking bulb blew.

TIM: You shouldn't leave it on all the time. Fluorescent light isn't good for you.

LOU: I know what's good for me. Take care of yourself.

TIM: It can stunt your growth. *(He goes to the sink.)* I don't think it's the bulb. It's probably just a loose socket.

LOU: What was that supposed to mean?

TIM: Huh?

LOU: About stunting my growth.

TIM: Nothing, Lou. Nothing at all. It was something I heard.

LOU: That kind of crack was totally uncalled for. You know I'm sensitive.

TIM: I wasn't making a crack.

LOU: Fuck you. (*Pause. The sink light comes on, revealing* TIM *dressed in sneakers and the suit from the bag. It is much too small. The bed is littered with French fries and wet with spilled soda.*)

TIM: See, the socket was loose.

LOU: (*seeing the bed*) Oh, great. Look at that. That was my fucking *dinner*.

TIM: There's a hamburger in this shoe here.

LOU: Gimme that. (*Tim hands it to him. Pause.*) What the fuck? (*He jiggles his shorts. Several fries drop out. Pause.*)

TIM: Is that my jacket, Lou?

LOU: (*realizing he is still wearing it*) I was cold.

TIM: I don't mind if you wear it. I don't need it right now. It's a little chilly out, and that's a nice warm jacket. Why don't you use it tonight?

LOU: (*taking off the jacket*) I don't need it. Why don't you hang up your clothes?

TIM: You'll need something warm when you go out, Lou. I got some thermal socks. You can wear those too. You can wear anything of mine that fits you. (*He unplugs the lamp and puts it away.*)

LOU: What?

TIM: As long as it fits you, Lou. I mean, us being different sizes and all.

LOU: You are treading on very thin ice right now.

TIM: What I say?

LOU: You know what you said. (*He begins dressing.*)

TIM: Well, I'm sorry. (*pause*) What do you think of this?

LOU: You mean that suit?

TIM: Yeah.

LOU: You want my honest opinion?

TIM: Uh-uh.

LOU: You look like a chimpanzee. Now do me a favor, get out of here and don't come back.

TIM: Is something bothering you, Lou?

LOU: No, I'm happy as a clam.

TIM: I thought . . . maybe something at work . . . I dunno. (*pause*)

LOU: What the fuck are you doing here?

TIM: I . . . I haven't decided yet, I already told you.

LOU: I'm not talking about your place in the universe. I mean now. What are you doing here *right now*?

TIM: Well, I'm not doing anything. I'm just sitting here with my brother and we're shooting the breeze.

LOU: We're not "shooting the breeze," Tim. You're gibbering like a moron and I have things to do. *(reaching into his shorts, pulls out another French fry)* I can't *believe* how greasy these things are.

TIM: Like we did last night, Lou.

LOU: Shut up about that, huh? I don't have time now.

TIM: You going somewhere?

LOU: Drop it, Tim.

TIM: You going out?

LOU: Don't *ask* me these questions.

TIM: You gonna meet Marie? I just wanna know, Lou. *(hurriedly)* In case something happens to you. Or to me. So we can help each other. If you were hurt. Or lost, if you were lost. Or me, if I was lost! I mean . . . and what if we were *both* lost, how about that, huh? *(pause)*

LOU: Tim, and I don't mean this in any personal kind of sense, but I think you're highly fucked up. What time is it? *(snapping his fingers)* Come on, Tim, wake up. What time is it? *(TIM does not answer.)* What now, you're gonna cry? I don't have time for that. *(Pause. Trying to stay calm.)* Let me explain something to you, okay? Let me tell you this, and then you gotta get out of here. Are you listening?

TIM: Yes.

LOU: I don't think you realize, Tim, the fucking *complexity* of reality as we know it. Life is not a comic book, you get shot in the balls dance around like a total asswipe nothing's the matter. *Believe* me it's not. Do you have any fucking conception of what I do every day when I walk out that door? Do you?

TIM: You go to the supply shop.

LOU: Yes, Tim, that's inspired, I go to the supply shop. I'm not *talking* about that for chrissake. I'm saying how do I take care of myself, do you know? Do you know anything? Any way possible, that's how. *Any fucking way.* It's open season on your sweet ass for every rampaging bimbo roaming the streets. I don't care *who* you are. Do you hear this? You make deals, Tim. You keep yourself covered all the time. You make your connections and you *keep* them. You don't go putting up billboards. It's the fucking commandos, Tim. You get down on your belly and *crawl.* *(pause)* Do it!

TIM: Huh?

LOU: Get down on your belly! *(He pushes TIM to the floor and sits on his back. He leans close to TIM's ear.)* You know what I see when I look out that window?

TIM: A wall.

LOU: Beyond that, Tim. Beyond the fucking wall.

TIM: The street. The city. I dunno.

LOU: Not the city. That's not a city, It's a motherfucking huge gaping saber-toothed *cunt* with traffic lights. Remember that.

TIM: Okay.

LOU: Now, you want to stay here with me, that's fine. You live here as long as you have to. That is a family issue, and I'm the first to respect it. I mean I got down on my hands and knees before that woman's deathbed, Tim. Down on my knees. It's a sacred memory and I'm not gonna fuck with that. But Tim, and I want you to listen to this very closely, I am telling you now that my life and your life . . . they don't have anything to do with each other. *(Pause. LOU rises, goes to the dresser, and removes several bills from the envelope.)* Look, here's five dollars.

TIM: Thanks.

LOU: Go do something, okay?

TIM: What should I do, Lou?

LOU: Whatever you want. Go see a movie.

TIM: There's a good one down at the Bainbridge.

LOU: Wonderful. *(handing him another dollar)* Here, buy yourself some popcorn.

TIM: You're being so nice to me.

LOU: Don't get sappy. Just go.

TIM: The only thing is, I can't eat the popcorn at the Bainbridge. They don't salt it right.

LOU: What?

TIM: The salt, Lou. It's always too much or too little. And the lady at the counter never listens if you bring it back.

LOU: So buy some fucking Jujyfruits, for chrissake! Here's another five. Take the psycho with you. Have a good time.

TIM: You mean Petey?

LOU: Whatever.

TIM: Thanks, Lou.

LOU: Don't look at a gift horse, Tim.

TIM: I won't.

LOU: (*trying to usher him out*) So go enjoy yourselves. With my blessings.

TIM: I already seen it. Last week, Me and Petey, we sat through it three times. (*pause*)

LOU: Are you fucking with me? 'Cause if you are . . . I'm telling you to get out of here. Understand? *Out.* NOW.

TIM: Why? (*pause*)

LOU: What did you say?

TIM: I asked you why. Lou.

LOU: Oh, man, I don't know *what* you're playing but you better cut it right now. I got something big going down here and I want you gone. (*pause*) Do hear what I'm saying? I WANT YOU OUT OF HERE. (*Pause. TIM does not move.*) I'm gonna count to five. And then you're gonna be real sorry. One . . . two . . . three . . . four . . . (*pause*) five . . . (*pause*) SIX . . .

TIM: (*pleasantly*) You looked funny holding that spatula, Lou. I could see it in the dark. That was a good one. I almost couldn't keep from laughing. You did it on purpose, didn't you? You knew it was me, right? (*pause*) You must of known it was me.

LOU: What is this? (*TIM takes the false teeth out of his pocket and clicks them three times. He laughs.*)

TIM: Surprise, surprise.

LOU: What are you doing here?

TIM: Waiting.

LOU: Do it someplace else. You don't know what's going on, Tim. You're gonna fuck me up. Go outside and come back in half an hour.

TIM: I didn't think you'd be here. You said you wouldn't.

LOU: I never said that.

TIM: You did. Last night.

LOU: I don't know what you're talking about. Get out of here. Go play in the park.

TIM: I can't do that. Someone'll see me there. I . . . someone'll see me.

LOU: Shit, I don't care! You *can't* stay here. If he sees you the deal is fucked.

TIM: I don't think so, Lou.

LOU: Yeah? Why not? *(pause)* WHY THE FUCK NOT? *(pause)* Aw . . . awwww, Tim. No. *(pause)* Aww, Tim. *(pause)* Tim, this a joke? Tell me what this is. *(pause)* You don't know about this. You don't know what you're doing. You can't cop this deal . . . how could you fuck me over this way, Tim? Hmm? You know what I had to do for this deal? How I broke my balls trying for this? I need it. To get out of the hole. I need it so bad . . . Tim? *(pause)* HOW COULD YOU DO THIS TO ME? I'M YOUR FUCKING BROTHER, YOU SHIT! DOESN'T THAT MEAN ANYTHING TO YOU? I give you my trust . . . everything I have I give you . . . and you STICK ME UP THE ASS. You fuck your your own *brother.* Didn't I teach you anything, you lie to me like this? *(TIM sits, takes out a wallet from the "secret pocket" and starts counting the money inside.)* Chocolate money, you cocksucker? Give me that! *(pause)* You think Monty would of liked you? Monty wouldn't even of *touched* you. You don't even come close to him. You're nothing but a fucking *punk.*

TIM: Please shut up about Monty, Lou.

LOU: He wouldn't even piss on you. He would beat you to a pulp. He wouldn't even notice you're there. When you were little, Tim? He would watch you, me and him. And he would *laugh* at you.

TIM: That's a lie.

LOU: How would you know?

TIM: Prove it.

LOU: I don't have to. I was there.

TIM: That's not true.

LOU: Our Little Mongoloid.

TIM: *(standing)* Stop it!

LOU: Are you gonna *hit* me, Tim? Is that what you're gonna do? You're so weak. You're a weak faggot. Why don't you hit me? You need your crazy boyfriend to show you how? *(pause)* Chicken shit! Get away from the phone, I'm calling the cops. That's stolen property you're holding there. *(TIM scoops up the phone.)* Give me that.

TIM: No.

LOU: Oh, I am going to rip you. Fucking smear you across the walls. Now get away from the phone.

TIM: No!

LOU: Give it to me. *Give* me the phone. *(He takes the hamburger off the dresser and flings it in TIM's face.)* GIVE IT TO ME! *(TIM wheels on LOU and strikes him wildly with the receiver. LOU tries to block his swings and falls to the floor. TIM stands over him, the phone held over his head to deliver a crushing blow. Pause. TIM tosses the phone aside. The dial falls off and rolls away. He turns from LOU and goes to the window, keeping his face hidden. Silence. Singing off-key.)* "Well, you can tell by the way I walk that I'm a ladies' man . . ." *(Pause. He prods the phone with his foot.)* Shit. You know how much the phone company's gonna charge to fix that? *(pause)* Man, you did a real number on my ribcage, Tim. I gotta hand it to you. What time is it? *(pause)* You're an asshole, you know that, don't you? This is not some dumbass nickel bag you're trying to cop. You get caught with this it's the slammer. Make long bye-bye. *(pause)* What time is it? *(pause)* Ah, what do I care. I'm doing okay. *(pause)* YOU DUMB FUCK!

TIM: I'm sorry if I hurt you.

LOU: Ho, tell me another one.

TIM: Okay. I'm not sorry.

LOU: You're not? You ingrateful vicious bastard.

TIM: I am! I'm sorry! I didn't want this to happen! It's not *working*. It's not working. Me. It's *me! I don't work right.* Ever.

LOU: You have that special gift, Tim. You touch something and it turns to garbage. That guy is a million miles away by now. Are you happy, Tim? You fucked us both. Why are you wearing that?

TIM: I wanted to look nice.

LOU: You idiot. *(pause)* What time is it? *(pause)* Oh, who cares. All this . . . *fuck* all this. I got no complaints. *(silence)*

TIM: Lou, if he comes . . . what should I do?

LOU: Oh, he's coming, sure. *(He hangs up the phone and puts it back on the dresser.)*

TIM: If you hadn't of been here I could have done it right. You said you wouldn't be. But . . . I guess that was a trick, right? You just tricked me. Like you always say. *(pause)* I wish I could figure these things out. Think them all the way through. So they would make sense. But I tried, Lou. I tried really hard and I thought . . . well, he called, you weren't in, and I thought . . . if I could make the connection . . . I could go away. By myself. And I wouldn't have to bother you any more. I'd go away, you wouldn't know where. Maybe . . . I'd become a bum. And I'd forget my name. It could happen. But someday you'd see me on the street. And I'll be all dressed up in a silver suit. With silver shoes and diamond rings. You'd see me and you'd say, look at that. Look at Tim! He's . . . dressed so nice. And he's got girls on his arms. Lots and lots of girls. And you'd think, well, I guess I was wrong. Tim did okay. He really did all right. And I was wrong. And I'd see you. Maybe we wouldn't know what to do first. But afterwards we'd talk and it would be okay. Everything would be okay. And it would be like it never happened. *(pause)*

LOU: You have no mind for details.

TIM: That guy, Lou? Last night? I think I hurt him. I hurt him real bad. And I think someone saw me. So they're probably looking for me. I'm pretty sure they are. And that's true. *(pause)* Monty wouldn't piss on me, would he, Lou?

LOU: Shut up about that.

TIM: But he would of liked me, right? Hey, remember when you guys—

LOU: DON'T MENTION THAT COCKSUCKER TO ME. You think he ever showed me what to do? You think he ever helped me? Nobody ever fucked me up as bad as him. Nobody.

TIM: *(moving towards him)* Lou . . .

LOU: *(flinching)* Don't touch me.

TIM: I wasn't gonna touch you.

LOU: Don't give me that. I know what you do. You were gonna put your hands all over me. Take your stuff and get out of here.

TIM: What?

LOU: You heard me. It's *finished*. I wash my hands.

TIM: No, Lou. Please.

LOU: Go live with your fucking psychotic boyfriend, you fucking queen! You're always talking about Petey, let *him* take care of you. I'm through.

TIM: I can't do that.

LOU: Why not?

TIM: Because . . . because he's not real. Because I made him up. *(pause)*

LOU: Oh, fucking Christ.

TIM: In my head, Lou. Just for fun. Like a story.

LOU: *(staring at him)* Man, you are gone. You are *out* there. Are you from Earth? Where are you, Tim?

TIM: *(quietly)* I don't know. *(pause)* You want me to leave?

LOU: Ah, shit. Why am I stuck with you, Tim? Would you mind telling me that? *(He collapses on the bed. Silence. Phone rings. TIM and LOU look at each other. LOU gives TIM a slight nod of assent. TIM picks up the phone.)* Who is it? Is it for me? *(TIM remains silent, listening.)* Is it him? Is the deal off? Don't say anything. Listen to me. If the deal is on . . . say nothing. We'll work it out. Have him come over. We'll work it out between us. I'm willing to split. You hear, Tim? *I'll split it with you.* We'll pool what you got with my stake and go in for twice as much. Then we'll split. A big killing. Is that okay? I'm not being hard on this, am I? I trust you. Forget just now. Look, if we can establish this connection we'll make it fifty-fifty from now on. Don't worry about cops. You just sit tight 'til it blows over. A week, a month. I'll take care of it. And then we're out of here, Tim. We're set, all the way down the line. All the way. *(pause)* What's he saying? Is the deal on? *(pause)* Is he saying anything? *(TIM hands LOU the phone.)* Hello? . . . What? . . . What are you saying? I can't hear you . . . what? . . . Look, I can't hear what you're saying, could you . . . what are you saying? . . . I can't hear you . . . *(Blackout.)*

Monologues for Women

Kissing Christine

BY JOHN PATRICK SHANLEY

Christine and Larry are on their first date. They met at a lecture and Larry asked her out to dinner at a Thai restaurant. They are eating soup and drinking beer at a low table, sitting on chairs without legs. Christine reveals that she has not been married but lived with a man whom she left when she became bored. She also reveals that she had a serious accident three years ago (she fell through a trap door in a deli and landed on her head) which paralyzed her for six months. Major reconstructive surgery gave her a new face and speech therapy gave her a new voice. In addition, as a result of her brain injury, her personality changed—she became nicer. Essentially, she is now a new person. Larry has just confessed he is married and apologizes for being "duplicitous." But instead of getting upset with him, Christine tells him that she feels "sorry for all men" because they "suffer like dumb beasts." He then asks her about her life as a single woman.

....

CHRISTINE: Being single is mysterious. It's silent. You live large parts of your life unobserved. There's no one there saying, That's the third time you've gone to the bathroom. Why do you laugh like that? Are you going to do anything, today? There's no one there saying, You look unhappy. What is it? I find for myself that when I live with someone, my life lacks depth. It has scope, it has activity. . . . I don't know what I'm trying to say. Single, married, both ways are hard. Sometimes you want to suffer and not be seen. Then it's better to be single. Sometimes you don't even suffer unless there's someone there seeing you. Then it's much better to be single. It's better to be married when it's better to be married. For a woman, it's great when you're checking into a hotel and you're Mrs. Whatever. A very solid feeling I can only imagine.

Picasso at the Lapin Agile

BY STEVE MARTIN

Suzanne is nineteen, attractive, "street smart and in charge"—and living in Paris in 1904. Two weeks ago she met an intense, twenty-three-year-old bohemian painter named Pablo Picasso. She fell for him, took him to her apartment and had sex with him. Later that evening he came back to her apartment, gave her a drawing and they had sex again. Before he left, he told her that he might see her one day in the bar Lapin Agile. She has now come to the bar but Picasso is not there. So she waits and chats with the patrons, one of whom asks her how she met Picasso.

To use as a monologue, leave out all but Suzanne's lines.

....

SUZANNE: I . . . it was about two weeks ago. I was walking down the street one afternoon and I turned up the stairs into my flat and I looked back and he was there framed in the doorway looking up at me. I couldn't see his face because the light came in from behind him and he was in shadow and he said "I am Picasso." And I said, "Well so what?" And then he said he wasn't sure yet but he thinks that it means something in the future to be Picasso. He said that occasionally there is a Picasso and he happens to be him. He said the twentieth century has to start somewhere and why not now. Then he said, "May I approach you?" and I said okay. He walked up-

stairs and picked up my wrist and turned it over and took his finger-
nail and scratched deeply on the back of my hand. In a second, in
red, the image of a dove appeared. Then I thought, why is it that
someone who wants me can hang around for months, and I even
like him but I'm not going to sleep with him, but someone else says
the right thing and I'm on my back, not knowing what hit me.

GERMAINE: Yeah, why is that?

FREDDY: Huh?

GERMAINE: Never mind.

SUZANNE: See, men are always talking about their things. Like
it's not them.

GASTON: What things?

SUZANNE: The things between their legs.

GASTON: Ah, yes. Louie.

FREDDY and EINSTEIN: Ah . . .

SUZANNE: See! It's not them; it's someone else. And it's true;
it's like some rudderless firework snaking across town. But women
have things too, they just work differently. They work from up here
(she taps her head). So when the guy comes on to me through up
here, he's practically there already, done. So the next thing I know
he's inside the apartment and I said, "What do you want?" and he
said he wanted my hair, he wanted my neck, my knees, my feet. He
wanted his eyes on my eyes, his chest on my chest. He wanted the
chairs in the room, the notepaper on the table; he wanted the paint
from the walls. He wanted to consume me until there was nothing
left. He said he wanted deliverance, and that I would be his savior.
And he was speaking Spanish, which didn't hurt, I'll tell you. Well at
that point, the word "no" became like a Polish village. *(They look at
her, waiting, then:)* Unpronounceable. *(proud)* I held out for seconds. Frankly I didn't enjoy it that much 'cause it was kinda quick.

How I Learned to Drive

BY PAULA VOGEL

The play follows the life of Li'l Bit (her nickname) from the age of ten, when her charming and loving Uncle Peck first began to teach her to drive—and touch her sexually—to the age of thirty-five, when she finds herself still haunted by her experiences with Peck. In the following monologue she is twenty-seven, has moved away from her home in Maryland, and is teaching in upstate New York. She meets a high-school boy on a bus and senses his interest in her.

....

LI'L BIT: I felt his "interest" quicken. Five steps ahead of the hopes in his head, I slowed down, waited, pretended surprise, acted at listening, all the while knowing we would get off the bus, he would just then seem to think to ask me to dinner, he would chivalrously insist on walking me home, he would continue to converse in the street until I would casually invite him up to my room—and—I was only into the second moment of conversation and I could see the whole evening before me.

And dramaturgically speaking, after the faltering and slightly comical "first act," there was the very briefest of intermissions, and an extremely capable and forceful and *sustained* second act. And after the second act climax and a gentle denouement—before the post-play discussion—I lay on my back in the dark and I thought about you, Uncle Peck. Oh. Oh—this is the allure. Being older. Being the first. Being the translator, the teacher, the epicure, the already jaded. This is how the giver gets taken.

Wit

BY MARGARET EDSON

After months in an experimental treatment program for her ovarian cancer, Vivian Bearing has just learned that the grueling treatment she has undergone has not been effective and that she is dying. Vivian is a tough-minded intellectual who has always disdained emotion. Her mind is still sharp, but now her pain is becoming unbearable and she cannot keep her emotions in check. She knows that if she takes enough painkillers to ease her suffering she will lose what she treasures most in herself: her brilliant clarity of thought.

She has just asked Susie, the nurse (who calls her "sweetheart" and has gotten her a Popsicle), for more painkiller and now she denigrates herself for becoming soppy and dependent.

....

VIVIAN: That certainly was a *maudlin* display. Popsicles? "Sweetheart"? I can't believe my life has become so . . . *corny*.

But it can't be helped. I don't see any other way. We are discussing life and death, and not in the abstract, either; we are discussing *my* life and *my* death, and my brain is dulling, and poor Susie's was never very sharp to begin with, and I can't conceive of any other . . . *tone*.

(*Quickly*) Now is not the time for verbal swordplay, for unlikely flights of imagination and wildly shifting perspectives, for metaphysical conceit, for wit.

And nothing would be worse than a detailed scholarly analysis. Erudition. Interpretation. Complication.

(Slowly) Now is a time for simplicity. Now is a time for, dare I say it, kindness.

(Searchingly) I thought being extremely smart would take care of it. But I see that I have been found out. Ooohhh.

I'm scared. Oh, God. I want . . . I want . . . No. I want to hide. I just want to curl up in a little ball. *(She dives under the covers.)*

(VIVIAN wakes in horrible pain. She is tense, agitated, fearful. Slowly she calms down and addresses the audience.)

VIVIAN: *(trying extremely hard)* I want to tell you how it feels. I want to explain it, to use *my* words. It's as if . . . I can't . . . There aren't . . . I'm like a student and this is the final exam and I don't know what to put down because I don't understand the question and I'm *running out of time*.

The time for extreme measures has come. I am in terrible pain. Susie says that I need to begin aggressive pain management if I am going to stand it.

"It": such a little word. In this case, I think "it" signifies "being alive."

I apologize in advance for what this palliative treatment modality does to the dramatic coherence of my play's last scene. It can't be helped. They have to do something. I'm in terrible pain.

Say it, Vivian. *It hurts like hell. It really does.*

Blown Sideways Through Life

BY CLAUDIA SHEAR

Claudia Shear tells the story of her life in this one-woman play. She's from Brooklyn and defiant, and she's looking to make sense of a life that keeps blowing her "sideways." Most of her stories are about her experiences at work. "Last counting," she says, "I've had 64 jobs. . . . Now, I'm not 236 years old so obviously some of them were of unusually short duration . . ."

Her first job was at Berkoffs Hardware store.

Berkoffs Hardware store on Coney Island Avenue—I was 12 years old. I'd gone in with fake working papers and told them it was illegal to have a sign that said "Boy Wanted." I got the job—cleaning toilets. But what I really did was moon around the stockroom waiting for Barney the stock boy to notice me. He was thick, he was hairy, he was stupid. He was 16. He had a shag haircut and I loved him.

To be so young you want to be older. I was 13½ and I got a job at an Italian fast food place in a mall. A full hour from my house I was anonymous. I was able to create the entire mnemonically perfect scenario necessary to . . . lie about my age. I hung out with girls in cars and froze my face so I wouldn't utter gasps of disbelief at the shocking bits of information so casually revealed to me. This was glamour, this was nights out in Manhattan, in loud discos, dancing the Hustle, with the required bored face that implied that "I go out all the time—I'm not even thinking about this." I would keep some of the money back that I gave my mother and buy wonderfully trashy clothes—wrap halter dresses and a red crepe pantsuit with a peplum and . . . these shoes. In the 1970s these shoes cost $100.00. My mother freaked out. Up on these shoes I was grown-up. I was somewhere else, I was someone else—I couldn't believe I was worthy to own these shoes, they were so cool. Do you think this is a prop? You're wrong—I ran for the bus in these shoes.

The promise of the shoes fulfilled. I became a makeup artist for Helena Rubinstein at Bloomingdales. I was 15. During the glory days of pure excess, of entire menageries set up on the main floor, phalanxes of dancing girls, bushes of roses, all for the first day of a new perfume. I would change out of my girl school uniform and transform into . . . an over-painted salesgirl. Behind the counter we stood, arrogant, aloof, in fashionable masks of concealer, base, foundation, blush, powder, eyeliner, brow pencil, contour shadow, shimmer highlighter, lip liner gloss—our bizarre and perfect faces turning slowly, our Etruscan smiles as we murmured "Everyone is using cream blush. Everyone." I was truly blase, I mean I knew girls that were in their twenties . . . and were from France.

Collected Stories

BY DONALD MARGULIES

ACT I, SCENE 3

Ruth Steiner, in her late fifties, is a famous short story writer who lives in Greenwich Village and teaches writing at NYU. Lisa Morrison, in her late twenties and one of her graduate students, idolizes her, has read all her stories, and has managed to become her assistant.

In this scene, Lisa has been her assistant for a year (it is August 1992) and she and Ruth are having Sunday brunch in Ruth's apartment. Lisa, who has grown more confident and assertive in their relationship, has cajoled Ruth into telling her about her affair with the famous poet Delmore Schwartz. Ruth met Schwartz at the White Horse Tavern back in the late fifties when she was twenty-two and he was twice her age and "gray and bloated and going to seed." Yet, she recalls, "There was still something magnificent about him."

To use as a monologue, omit the brief exchange between Ruth and Lisa.

....

RUTH: So, yes, the power was undeniable. (*a beat*) He was only 44 but there was something ancient about him, something terribly mortal and immortal at the same time, if that makes any sense. He seemed to possess so much wisdom and yet, even then, even that first sleeting night, he seemed doomed. *(a beat)* What sheltered Jewish girl from Detroit, what self-styled poet, what virgin, would *not* have succumbed? *(LISA shakes her head.)* And I was pretty then, too.

LISA: I'm sure; I know.

RUTH: You've seen pictures.

LISA: Yes!

RUTH: Well, pretty enough. Shapely, anyhow. I looked damn good in those tight, co-ed, Lana Turner sweaters. I was good company for a man like Delmore. Being my father's daughter had provided me with years of practice. I was a good listener but I also had a real mouth on me, which he'd point out frequently, with pleasure. I would tease him, provoke him, take outrageous positions just to get a rise out of him, which I always did. *(pause)* I stuck by him for over a year but he was descending rapidly by then. He was quite mad, you know. Oh, he had his moments, lucid, marvelous moments but, when they came, the rampages were fiercer and fiercer. He could be cruel, inconstant. His *aura* sustained me. *(a beat)* I'd go to his awful rented rooms while he was out, *you* know: sordid furnished rooms with a sink and a hot plate, and I'd wash the dishes that piled up for days and clean up his mess and mend his clothes and he'd come in . . . and never say a word of thanks. One day I let myself in and found *another* bright-eyed girl lovingly washing his socks in the sink. "Oh," she said, surprised to see me. I turned around and left and never came back. *(a beat)* You probably know the rest of the tale: how he was staying in one of those hotels when he died in '66; how his body lay unclaimed in the morgue for days.

Lobby Hero

BY KENNETH LONERGAN

ACT I, SCENE 2

Dawn is a young, pretty rookie cop. She is waiting in an apartment building lobby for her partner Bill, an experienced officer who has been her mentor and with whom she has had sex. Bill asked her to wait in the lobby while he paid a visit to his friend Jim. Jeff, the building security guard, who is attracted to Dawn and has been trying to engage her in conversation, reveals to her that Bill actually went up to see a prostitute. This news adds to what has already been a rough night for Dawn.

Earlier in the evening she had her first violent street confrontation when she and her partner tried to break up a fight between two men. One of the men lunged at her and she hit him hard (maybe too hard) with her night stick, putting him in the hospital. Dawn is visibly rattled by the evening's events and Jeff tries to comfort her by telling her he thinks it is great that she has become a cop and that her family must be proud of her. She replies:

To use as a monologue, omit Jeff's line.

....

DAWN: Oh, they think I'm nuts. (*pause*) Well, not exactly, I mean, my mother thinks I'm a little bit nuts, but I happen to think that she's nuts too, so there's no harm done there, right?

JEFF: You have a lot of brothers? I bet you have a lot of—

DAWN: *(on "bet")* But I guess generally they're proud . . . I was near the top of my class at the Academy . . . I just . . . I just fucked up with *this* prick, that's all. And now I'm *screwed*. Because I obviously really misjudged him, you know? And for all I know he's been shootin' his mouth off all over the Department. And it wouldn't have been so hard to avoid the whole thing in the first place. But these guys . . . I mean, they seen so much horrible shit, it's like they don't give a damn about anything. So you gotta walk around like you don't give a damn about anything either. But they know you still do. And they wanna like, stamp it out of you or something. And like, test you, all the time. And it's always like: "Hey—you're not men, you're not women: You're cops. Act like cops and you'll be treated like cops." Only then it turns out they got a pool going as to who's gonna fuck you first, OK? And that's fine. I can handle it. You *make* them respect you. But then somebody decent comes along, and goes out of his way to make life easier for you—and I didn't even *ask* him, because I didn't expect anything different—I didn't *want* anything different. And then, Oh my God, it's true love—except when he comes down in that elevator, just watch: because *I'm* gonna be the one who's gonna be supposed to act like I'm a cop!

The Lucky Spot

BY BETH HENLEY

ACT I, SCENE I

The setting is the Lucky Spot Dance Hall on Christmas Eve 1934, in Pigeon, Louisiana, during the depths of the Depression. Reed Hooker, who won the building in a card game, hopes that when he opens tonight the money will start rolling in. He doesn't know that his headstrong and truculent wife, Sue Jack, who has been in jail for three years, is home on Christmas parole (in a jealous rage, she pushed a woman Hooker was having sex with over the balcony to her death).

Hooker's current lover, Cassidy, a fifteen-year-old waif, is pregnant and wants Hooker to divorce Sue Jack and marry her. He said he would as soon as Sue Jack returns from prison. To hurry things, she secretly arranged Christmas parole for Sue Jack.

Sue Jack still loves Hooker and hopes that despite her ragged clothes and cropped hair—certainly not looking like a dance hall girl anymore—he will still find her attractive and want her back (she believes he was the one who arranged for the parole). But she has already caused him a serious problem. The dance hall girls hired for tonight's gala opening remembered her ill-tempered ways and quit as soon as they learned she was back.

Sue Jack had been talking to the one dancer who didn't quit and with Cassidy. Both have now gone off, leaving her alone in the dance hall. Hooker enters in a huff about the dance hall girls leaving, and he won't accept Sue Jack's apology. He calls her a "bad luck charm" and tells her to go.

To use as a monologue, omit Hooker's line.

....

SUE JACK: I'm not the same as I was, Reed. Go on and look at me. You see, I'm not the same. I'm not the same one who kept on hurting you by drinking, and brawling and gambling it all away. And I'm not the young, laughing girl you married with the rosy cheeks and pretty hands. I guess I'm not sure who I am. And, I tell you, it's been making me feel so strange. When I was in prison, the only belonging I had was this old photograph of myself that was taken just before I ran off from home. In it I'm wearing this straw hat decorated with violets and my hair's swept back in a braid and my eyes, they're just . . . shining . . . I used to take out that picture and look at it. I kept on pondering over it. I swear it confused me so much, wondering where she was—that girl in the picture. I could not imagine where she'd departed to—so unknowingly, so unexpectedly. *(a pause)* Look, I won't drink or yell or fight or shoot pool or bet the roosters or—

HOOKER: Yeah, yeah, and I guess I've heard all that till it's frayed at the edges.

SUE JACK: Please, I don't wanna lose any more. I'm through throwing everything away with both fists.

The Altruists

BY NICKY SILVER

Sydney is in the middle of a rant at Ethan. She is in her apartment, dressed "chicly in a pink Richard Tyler suit," addressing Ethan who is under the covers in bed, perhaps asleep, perhaps not. Sydney, a successful soap opera actress, is "thirty-four, high-strung, shallow, and utterly self-absorbed." She is tired of Ethan's derision and disdain because she is not involved in social causes like he is and doesn't wear tattered East Village clothing. She is also tired of his friends stealing her belongings, and of his drunkenness and affairs with other women. The only positives on her list are Ethan's looks and sexual prowess ("you have beautiful eyes and the stamina of a ten-year-old").

....

SYDNEY: Was I hurt when you threw my plants out the window!? I was. I cared for those plants! I loved them! I watered them and loved them since they were seeds! They were like my children! But they were, after all, just plants. And, as you pointed out, you didn't hit anyone, you didn't kill anyone when you hurled the pots, the terra-cotta pots from the fifteenth floor! And you were drunk or high on some substance, purchased, no doubt with money taken from MY purse! So I released. I HAVE BEEN HEROIC! Only a heroine, only a mythic figure, could overcome the scolds and the scandals—when you told everyone we knew, my friends, my family,

MY THERAPIST, whom you had no business talking to in the first place—when you told everyone in New York City that I gave you syphilis, when we both know, we know without a doubt that Maria Portnoy gave you syphilis during that demonstration—and you in turn gave it to me! THAT WAS NOT FUNNY! I made allowances because every now and then, once a week, once a month, once in a blue moon, you made love to me and I saw fireworks, I heard orchestras! You made love to me and I remembered the beginning, when we made love nonstop, like Olympians! I put up with everything, I entered your world of East Village, Alphabet City, anti-trend-trendies, of sit-ins and marches and protests, because it felt good to have you inside of me! But no more! NO MORE, ETHAN! I'M A PERSON! I HAVE FEELINGS! I HAVE A BREAKING POINT AND I HAVE REACHED IT! Maybe I expect too much. Maybe I do. Maybe I'm looking for perfection. No man's perfect— BUT SOME ARE BETTER! And I have had it! LAST NIGHT WAS IT! When you refused to hold me, when you muttered some other name in your sleep, when you tried to kill me, when you held a pillow over my face, in an ugly, violent attempt to snuff out my life, I REALIZED . . . THINGS ARE NOT GOING WELL!

The Nina Variations

BY STEVEN DIETZ

SCENE 39

In *The Nina Variations* Steven Dietz has reimagined the last scene in Anton Chekhov's *The Seagull*. In fact, he has reimagined it forty-three different ways.

Treplev loved Nina and dreamt of writing great plays for her to star in, but she ran off with another man who eventually abandoned her. Years later, she visits Treplev in his study (where he has been trying to write), the place where they shared so many youthful dreams. She tells him of her unhappy life and her minor acting career, then leaves when he implores her to stay with him. He then kills himself.

In this monologue, in one of Dietz' versions of the how the last encounter between Nina and Treplev *might* have gone, Nina tells Treplev (also called Konstantin) about a terrible dream she had.

....

NINA: I dreamt you killed yourself and no one would tell me. I asked them—I asked your mother and Masha and Dorn, everyone—and they all said you'd gone away. That you'd returned to the city. That you were working on a new play. Why would I dream that? (*She looks at him. He looks at her, but says nothing.*) And, in fact, when I returned to the city, I saw your name on a marquee. A new play of yours was to open. Your photo was in front of the theatre. And next to it, the title of your play: *Nina*. And I bought a ticket, and went in and sat down, and I watched the play. And there were *people in it*. And *things happened in it* . . . quietly, like small quakes within a life. And there was love. Buckets of love. And I rushed backstage and I cried as I embraced the actors. And I asked: "Where is the author? Where is Konstantin Gavrilovich?" And the actress who had played the title role—the woman who had been your Nina—took me aside into a small room. And she took my hand. Looked in my eyes. "The fact is . . ."—she said—"Konstantin Gavrilovich has killed himself." *(long silence)* Why would I dream that?

Lola

BY DONALD MARGULIES

Lola is a Jew from Poland who, as a young woman during World War II, managed to survive the Nazi's Auschwitz concentration camp. She is now a housewife, living in Brooklyn, New York, with grown children.

....

LOLA: I met my husband Liberation Day. I lost my *sister* Liberation Day. I don't know how she dies, but she does. On Liberation Day. A lot of people lost people Liberation Day. The mourning period was very short in those days—if you planned on surviving. No time for shiva. If there was time for shiva, oh God, we all would've died. There was so much of it: death. All over the place. And, my sister, who I'll tell you I happened to love very much, *very* much. I never saw her again. What could I do? By that time, Papa, Mama, my brother Izzy who was never too smart, they were all dead. Not *me*, and there was nothing I could do about it; right? What could I have done, this little pip-squeak? That's what I looked like when my husband met me. I was a real *meiskeit*. You know what that means in Jewish? Uh . . . uh . . . what you kids, my daughter, calls a real loser: "Oh, Ma, is that Sharon a real loser." *(a beat)* I looked a real *meiskeit* because I almost lost my life, that's why. Auschwitz wasn't Grossinger's, honey. Three meals a day? Forget it! Shuffleboard? Go on! You've read about it, I'm sure. Well, it was worse than that, believe me, and I got there like at the tail end. They stopped giving numbers by the time I got there. They must've run out of numbers. Like at the bakery. You notice I don't have numbers on my arm? Well, that's the reason: they ran out of 'em. (*a beat*) So, I was a *meiskeit*. I wasn't the beauty I am today. I had typhoid. My teeth were falling out. I was very skinny, as you could imagine. Knock-kneed. So, between the teeth missing and my knees knocking, I was not your typical bathing-suit beauty. But my husband, I don't know, somehow he saw something. You see, he comes up to me Liberation Day. Somebody points me out to him: "Go, look, that girl there, she's from Lodz." That's where I lived before the camps. Turns out my husband, he, too, lived in the Lodz ghetto. I didn't know him. But, wait, I'll tell you—he comes up to me, a good-looking guy, not too tall, I look him up and down: Hmm, I think to myself, Not bad. He says to me: "Excuse me, I hear you're from the Lodz ghetto." I nodded. I didn't want to keep my mouth open too much, this good-looking guy might see all my teeth that fell out, so I nodded uh-huh. "Tell me," he said, "I'm looking for someone. From Lodz. Can you tell me if you happen to know if she's alive? Her name is Lola. She is a beautiful girl with a magical smile and a sense of humor you could *plotz*. Tell me," he said, "do you know if she survived?" I asked him what street does this Lola live on in the ghetto. He told me. It was my street. And what address? He told me. It was my address. And what was the last name of her family? (*a beat*) "That's me!" I screamed, all of the spaces in my magical smile showing. "That's me! I am Lola!" And he carried me away, and, like the whole thing was a dream . . . I woke up: a housewife in Flatbush making gefilte fish for her family. A boy and a girl. Today, that boy has a daughter named for my sister, and the girl, the girl is a clinical psychologist.

Defying Gravity

BY JANE ANDERSON

SCENE 18

Donna, an African-American, is a bartender near the NASA training facility in Cocoa Beach. The bar has become a hangout for astronauts and Donna has gotten to know many of them, including those who died in the 1986 *Challenger* explosion.

This scene takes place shortly after the disaster. Donna has just had a tense exchange with a distraught, inebriated NASA mechanic who blames himself for the accident. She tried to reassure him that it was not his fault, but then sent him away when he accused her of keeping him up too late the night before lift-off (they had been having an affair). After he goes, she speaks to the audience.

....

DONNA: (*DONNA turns to the audience.*) A reporter came in here, wanted to know, what was the last thing the astronauts said to me. What did they *say* to me? Yes, he said, exactly what did each of them say to you that last night when they left the bar? (*a beat*) Goodnight Donna, Goodnight, Night. Goodnight Donna. Night, Donna. Goodnight.—was that seven? Oh right, one more, Good night. He actually wrote all of that down. Then he wanted to know if I remembered anything else they might have said, it didn't have to be that particular night, any little tidbits. I said, Honey, a tidbit is something you feed a dog. He then amended himself, asked, did any of them *confide* in me. Yes they did, I said, but confide comes from confidential and it will remain that way. I could see the hair in his ears start to vibrate with excitement, ooh, this lady has tidbits! How am I gonna get them out of her? He decided to distract me, he looks over at the picture I have of my astronauts. What's that? he says. It was such a dumb-ass question I didn't even bother to answer, just kept wiping the bar. You must have felt very close to all of them, he said. I just kept wiping. Then he leaned in towards me, real close, trying to get into some confidence with me, he says, do you think they *knew*? I just kept wiping and wiping the bar until he went away. *(a beat)* One of my astronauts noticed that I keep a bible behind the bar. And this individual sat with me late one night and we talked about the afterlife. This individual was experiencing a moment of fear. This individual had doubts. I told this individual what I believe to be the truth: that the one thing we know about death, is that we all got to do it. And when and where we do it is left in the hands of God. And those who do it go on to a much higher place than those who are left behind. Those who do it are released of their bonds. Those who do it will finally know the secrets of the universe. And isn't that after all why some fool would want to put themselves on top of a rocket in the first place?

The Young Man From Atlanta

BY HORTON FOOTE

SCENE 6

It is 1950 in Houston, Texas, a city on the rise, and Will and Lily Dale Kidder had been living a fine life. Will, sixty-four, a successful business man, worked for the same company for almost forty years, and Lily Dale, sixty, had her religion and her music. They had a new luxurious home and what they believed was a happy family. But then their thirty-seven-year-old son Bill, who lived in Atlanta, drowned during a business trip—and it might have been suicide, since he walked far out into a lake even though he couldn't swim (Will believes it was suicide; Lily Dale is clinging to the hope that it was an accident).

This tragedy was soon followed by Will losing his job and suffering a heart attack. Then Lily Dale gave away a large amount of money—much needed now, since Bill has been unable to raise money for a new business—to their son's roommate from Atlanta, a man ten years younger than their son, who they first met when he came to Bill's funeral, and who before long told Lily Dale that he was too grief-stricken to return to work and needed money to help his sick mother and other family members.

Will and Lily Dale now realize that they never really understood their son (including why he never seemed interested in dating girls), and that the young man's sad stories were probably lies. She feels guilty for having given the money away without consulting Will (although she confides to her maid that Will always said "it was my money to do with like I wanted"). She tries to explain to Will why she did it.

To use as a monologue, omit Will's line and link Lily Dale's speeches.

....

LILY DALE: I know. I know. I have never deceived you before, Daddy, except for one time. It was when you went to Chicago for a business trip and my cousin Mary Cunningham came to stay with me and she talked me into letting two men come over to the house. And you came back from Chicago unexpectedly and they ran out of the back door.

(*A pause.*)

That was twenty years ago. I don't know why I had to tell you that. It has bothered me all these years—not that I would have done anything wrong. . . .

(*A pause.*)

I get lonely, Will. You've always had your work, gone away so much of the time, and then Bill went off to school, and then of course I had my music, but when Bill died I couldn't go near the piano anymore and I decided I should dedicate myself to God, and then this young friend of Bill's comes and he was sweet to me, and I missed Bill so, and I would always talk to him about Bill. And I never told you this, but just before Alice Temple committed suicide I went to see her and she told me that Bill had committed suicide, that everyone said that, and it upset me so, and I didn't want to tell you because I was afraid it would upset you, so I called his sweet friend in Atlanta and he told me he did not because he had talked to him the night before and all he talked about was God.

WILL: That boy is a liar, Lily Dale.

LILY DALE: He may be, Will, but it did comfort me to hear him say it, and I needed comforting, Will. I've spent my days here crying since Bill died, and I wouldn't have done anything in the world to hurt you, Will, because you know how much I love you and how grateful I am for all you've given me, and I do believe in prayer, Will, and I'm going to pray that you get well and strong and you'll find a way to start your business.

Appearances

BY TINA HOWE

Ivy needs a dress for a party in her office tonight and she wants to "stand out." So she's come to the fitting room in a department store with a bunch of dresses to try on. She is described as an "inexperienced shopper in her thirties." After trying on a number of dresses she has narrowed her search to two, a white one and a maroon one, and in her confusion has managed to put both on at the same time. She asks Grace, "the woman who guards the fitting room," which one she should take.

To use as a monologue, omit Grace's lines.

....

IVY: So, which one do you think I should get? *(She starts taking off the maroon dress.)*

I was supposed to be back at the office ten minutes ago. I promised Panda Schultz I'd help set up the appetizers.

GRACE: Here, let me help you.

IVY: The editorial department is doing the food and the art department is doing the drinks. The party starts at 6:30 sharp. Panda and I have got to have the appetizers ready and out by 6:30! The whole place is in an uproar because this is our first office party since Alex London joined the company and everyone is crazy about him . . . men as well as women! When he walks into a room secretaries collapse and senior editors walk into glass partitions. It's ridiculous! We're like a bunch of hysterical teenagers swooning in a locker room . . . *(lowering her voice)* You see, aside from his "animal thing," Alex London has the most beautiful mouth you've ever seen! It's the sort of mouth people jump off bridges for . . . you know, the kind with a very plump lower lip that's divided into two little mounds that are shaped sort of like rose petals. . . . He isn't really all that good looking . . . medium height with greying hair, nondescript eyes, and a rather sallow complexion . . . he just has this phenomenal lower lip that drives everyone into a frenzy.

GRACE: *(putting IVY's dress over her arm)* You don't have to tell *me* about lower lips! Kenny has a dimpled one and it's all Donna can do not to bite it off every time she sees him. It's half the reason she's marrying him, if you ask me.

IVY: It's going to be impossible to be noticed, everyone's dressing to kill!

GRACE: *(holds the dress up to her)* The trouble is, you can't really get the full effect when they're on at the same time.

IVY: All I'm hoping for is just three or four seconds of being *seen!* He doesn't have to speak to me. All I want is to be held in his eyes for a moment, actually *see* my reflection caught in his pupils . . . He's my boss, for God's sake! We speak to each other every day, but I can't seem to materialize when he looks at me! It's very scary because I feel as if I'm on fire with my whole body in flames . . .

GRACE: *(holding the maroon dress up to herself)* If only there were somehow *two* of you . . .

IVY: *(starts taking off the white dress)* Sometimes when I think about him, I feel myself starting to glow. It's true! Once when I was on the crosstown bus, I thought I saw him out the window and my face began to burn. I shut my eyes, afraid I was starting to radiate, my arms and face glowing like some huge iridescent firefly.

Lives of the Great Waitresses

BY NINA SHENGOLD

In a "greasy spoon" restaurant, Kay is rolling flatware in napkins. She is a black woman in her forties. She is "born again." She talks to the audience.

....

KAY: You either got it, or you don't. If you don't, you won't ever. So don't even bother. Don't strain. Oh, there's things you can learn, sure. The fine points. The stance. "Heat that up for you?" "Toasted?" But honey—scratch that, make it hon—a truly great waitress is *born*.

You get what I mean? It's a feel thing. Deep under the bones of your bones. In your cells. Some reporter once asked Louis Armstrong what "swing" meant. Louis looked the guy dead in the eyeball and said, "If you gotta ask, you'll never know." *He* would've made a great waitress.

My very first diner, we had one. Flo Kelly. A goddess in Supphose. Flo was all waitress. She could fill two dozen shakers one-handed and never spill one grain of salt. She could carry eight Hungry Man specials lined up on her arm like a charm bracelet. Flo could serve pie à la mode so it looked like Mount Everest topping the clouds. She poured gravy like tropical rain. In Flo's maraschino-nailed fingers, the short-order carousel spun like the Wheel of Fortune, and never, not once, did a customer's coffee get cold.

Well, I mean to tell you, that diner was *hers*. If Jesus Himself Amen came in and sat down to supper, he would've tipped double. Then one Blue-Plate Special, right after the lunch rush, Flo hung up her hairnet, cashed in her checks, and went sunny-side up. And that's when the Lord took my order. I knew what I was. I was called.

(She steps closer.)

Look in my eyes. I know mysteries way beyond menus. I have felt the Lord's love pierce my heart like a skewer through gyros. I have seen Jesus weep ice-kold milk with a K.

(She holds out her hand.)

Heat that up for you? Hon?

Laughing Wild

BY CHRISTOPHER DURANG

A woman enters, sits in a chair, and talks to the audience about the frustrations and irritations in her life. She may get up from the chair "if the spirit moves her." The backdrop is nondescript—"pretty much of a limbo setting."

....

WOMAN: Oh, it's all such a mess. Look at this mess. My hair is a mess. My clothes are a mess.

I want to talk to you about life. It's just too difficult to be alive, isn't it, and to try to function? There are all these people to deal with. I tried to buy a can of tuna fish in the supermarket, and there was this *person* standing right in front of where I wanted to reach out to get the tuna fish, and I waited a while, to see if they'd move, and they didn't—they were looking at tuna fish too, but they were taking a real long time on it, reading the ingredients on each can like they were a book, a pretty boring book, if you ask me, but nobody has; so I waited a long while, and they didn't move, and I couldn't get to the tuna fish cans; and I thought about asking them to move, but then they seemed so stupid not to have *sensed* that I needed to get by them that I had this awful fear that it would do no good, no good at all, to ask them, they'd probably say something like, "We'll move when we're goddam ready, you nagging bitch," and then what would I do? And so then I started to cry out of frustration, quietly, so as not to disturb anyone, and still, even though I was softly sobbing, this stupid person didn't *grasp* that I needed to get by them to reach the goddam tuna fish, people are so insensitive, I just hate them, and so I reached over with my fist, and I brought it down real hard on his head and I screamed: "Would you kindly, move, asshole!!!"

And the person fell to the ground, and looked totally startled, and some child nearby started to cry, and I was still crying, and I couldn't imagine making use of the tuna fish now anyway, and so I shouted at the child to stop crying—I mean, it was drawing too much attention to me—and I ran out of the supermarket, and I thought, I'll take a taxi to the Metropolitan Museum of Art, I need to be surrounded with culture right now, not tuna fish.

Monologues for Men

Cobb

BY LEE BLESSING

In the play *Cobb,* the great baseball player Ty Cobb is represented at three points in his life: Peach is Cobb at about twenty, at the beginning of his baseball career; Ty is in his early forties as his career was ending; and Mr. Cobb is in his early seventies, dying of cancer. Each is, in a sense, a ghost of Cobb, talking about the past and arguing with the others about what Cobb's life really was about. Cobb was born in Georgia in 1886 (fans called him the Georgia Peach). He played professional baseball for twenty-four years, held many records, and died in 1961.

The playwright describes Peach as intense, athletic, and quick to anger. At one point, Peach tells the audience about his start in professional baseball.

To use as a monologue, omit Mr. Cobb's lines and Ty's second line.

....

PEACH: *(to audience, his mood unbroken)* When I first told my father I wanted to be a ballplayer, it was like tellin' him I wanted to be a vagrant.

MR. COBB: What are you talking about now?

PEACH: We argued over it for a long time. But then I had a chance to play for a team over in Alabama—semi-pro, they hardly paid you nothin'. And he let me go. All my life he'd been like a glass

mountain—you couldn't climb him. Always sayin' no, demandin'
more. And then there he was, suddenly. Sayin', "Go on—go to Alabama, try baseball." For him it must've been like sayin', "Go try a
life of crime."

TY: He said one more thing, too. He said, "Don't come home a
failure."

MR. COBB: That's not important.

TY: Hell, it ain't!

PEACH: He was dead before he knew if I was a failure or not.
He wasn't dead in me, though. You know, I might've been a .280 hit-
ter if he hadn't said that to me. It's easy enough—just let your concentration slip. As it was, I hit .367 for my career. Over 24 years, .367.

This Is Our Youth

BY KENNETH LONERGAN

ACT I

Dennis is twenty-one and living in his own apartment on New York City's Upper West Side (it is 1982). He is described as "grungy, handsome, very athletic, . . . quick, fanatical and bullying." His parents pay his rent to keep him from living at home and he makes his money by selling drugs. One of his customers: a nineteen-year-old misfit named Warren, shows up with his bags after his father threw him out of their home. Dennis agrees to let Warren stay, temporarily, but laces into him when he complains about Dennis' demand for the money owed him for past drug purchases.

....

DENNIS: Yeah, and I always smoke pot with you, all of you, *my* pot, all the time, like hundreds and hundreds of dollars' worth. So why shouldn't I make some money offa you? You fuckin' guys like *gripe* at me all the time, and I'm providing you schmucks with such a crucial service. Plus I'm developing valuable entrepreneurial skills for my *future. Plus* I'm like providing you with precious memories of your youth, for when you're fuckin' *old.* I'm like the basis of half your personality. All you do is imitate me. I turned you onto The *Honey*mooners, Frank *Zappa*, Ernst *Lubitch, boxer* shorts,—*Sushi.* I'm like a one-man *youth* culture for you pathetic assholes. You're gonna remember your youth as like a gray stoned haze punctuated by a series of beatings from your Dad, and like, *my* jokes. God *damn*. You know how much *pot* I've thrown out the *window* for you guys in the middle of the *night* when you're wandering around the street like *junkies* looking for half a *joint* so you can go to *sleep*, because you scraped all the *resin* out of your *pipes*? And you bitch about the fact that along the way I turn a little *profit*? You should thank God you ever *met* me, you little fuckin' hero-worshipping little *fag*.

Spike Heels

BY THERESA REBECK

ACT I, SCENE 2

Edward, a successful Boston lawyer and a cad with women, has dropped in for a brief visit to his friend Andrew before he goes out to dinner with his secretary, Georgie, who lives in the apartment above Andrew's. Edward doesn't notice that Andrew is angry at him (because Georgie told him about Edward's mistreatment of her) and, after a brief phone call to Georgie (who, unbeknownst to Andrew, has made up with Edward), he quickly makes himself at home and looks for something to drink.

To use as a monologue, omit Andrew's lines.

....

EDWARD: *(finds the bottle of scotch)* Is this *scotch*? Andrew, congratulations. You learned how to drink scotch.

(He exits to the kitchen, delivers part of his speech there, reenters pouring scotch and sits.)

ANDREW: Edward—
EDWARD: *(calling)* You would not believe the day I've had. I spent the entire afternoon in front of McGilla Gorilla trying to con-

vince her that three Jamaican dope peddlers with a collective list of priors as long as the Old Testament had been denied their rights. Some of these judges—I mean, I didn't write the fucking constitution. It wasn't my idea to give everybody rights. That was our founding fathers, remember? If she doesn't like it, she can complain to the goddam supreme court. The stupid cop violated their rights. He pulls them over—get this, the cop pulls them over because they ran a red light—and they all get into an argument, so he pulls a search and seizure and finds six pounds of marijuana in the trunk. Marijuana, okay, we're not even talking cocaine. And can you show me probable cause in an argument about whether the light was yellow or red? Can you do that for me, please? Four hours I'm arguing this shit. I mean, I got assigned this crummy case; someone give me a fucking break! I hate this pro bono shit. If I'm going to defend criminals I really prefer that they have lots and lots of money.

The Lisbon Traviata

BY TERRENCE McNALLY

ACT II

Mike and Stephen's relationship has been in freefall. They still live together in their New York City apartment (it is the late 1980s), but their sexual relationship has been over for a while, and now Mike wants Stephen to move out. Stephen, who works as an editor for a major publisher, is fussy, testy, and bitchy, and is constantly trying to elevate Mike's taste in music and movies (Stephen is obsessed with Maria Callas and is irked by Mike's disinterest in her and in opera in general). Mike is a physician who had been married but is now divorced—and he has a new lover, Paul.

Earlier in the scene, Stephen was catty with Paul and then badgered Mike to the point where Mike punched him and knocked him down, twice, leading Paul to make a hurried exit. Mike, at the end of his tether, tries to explain to Stephen why he can't continue their "arrangement." Stephen resists accepting what Mike is telling him.

To use as a monologue, omit Stephen's lines and Mike's "I have been."

....

MIKE: This is about me. I'm trying to tell you how I feel. I know how you feel. I don't think you hear me any more. You hear the words, but you don't hear what I'm saying.

STEPHEN: Try me.

MIKE: I have been.

STEPHEN: Try me!

MIKE: I'm tired, Stephen. I'm tired of saying I'm sorry all the time. I'm tired of tiptoeing through my life because it might interfere with yours. I'm tired of being told what opera to like, what book to read, what movie to go to. I'm tired of being your father, mother, big brother, best friend, your analyst, your cheerleader.

STEPHEN: You left out lover.

MIKE: I haven't been your lover since the first night I said to myself, "Who is this person lying at my side, this stranger, who hasn't heard or held me since the last time it pleased him?" That's the night I should have grabbed you by the shoulders and screamed, "I don't want this, Stephen. I don't need just another warm body next to mine. I'm much too needy to settle for so little. Look at me. Love me. Be with me." Now I've waited too long. You weren't even sleeping. You were reading. Your friend was on your cassette player on your side of the bed. Maria Callas. You had your back to me. I had my arm around you. I was stroking one of your tits. I asked you how you thought I should handle Sarah—she was coming up to New York and wanted to see me. It was the first time since the divorce and I was scared. I'd hurt her in a way I was ashamed of. I really needed you and you just shrugged and said, "You'll do the right thing" and turned the page. I didn't stop stroking your tit, but you weren't the same person anymore. Neither was I. I kept my arm around you only because I was suddenly so scared. I was as alone as I must have made Sarah feel. I was holding on for dear life.

Bluff

BY JEFFREY SWEET

Emily, who left her family in California and moved to New York, has learned that her stepfather Gene (who is in New York on business) tried to seduce a woman in a bar earlier this evening. The scene takes place in Emily's apartment where she tells Gene she intends to let her mother Georgia know what he has been up to (Georgia, who is an alcoholic, is back home in California; she married Gene after her first husband, Emily's father and the love of her life, died in an accident). Emily, who has always had ambivalent feelings toward Gene and has pulled away from her mother, has been struggling to figure out what she wants to do with her life. In Gene's monologue, he confronts her with the reality of what will happen to Georgia if she finds out about his infidelities and divorces him.

To use as a monologue, leave out Emily's and Georgia's lines. Georgia is not actually in Emily's apartment but appears as a theatrical device. Emily is there with Gene and her boyfriend Neal.

....

   GENE: Community property, etc. I go live in a studio apartment somewhere, and she—maybe she's able to afford holding onto the house, though I have my doubts.
   GEORGIA: I'd manage.

GENE: But there she is, wherever she is. You've liberated her from me. And what is she doing?

EMILY: Doing?

GEORGIA: Doing?

GENE: Tell me what you see happening from here.

(Addressing this in GEORGIA's direction, though he continues to talk to EMILY.)

Is she enrolling at the local college for a class in how to write a sonnet? Is she volunteering at the Friends of the Zoo, nursing a baby penguin? Or could she be strolling into the kitchen? Could she be opening the cabinet over the sink and pulling out a glass?

(Turning back to EMILY.)

And who's gonna tell her not to? Me? I'm decorating my new studio apartment. So who? You? You gonna find a sublet for this apartment, take a leave of absence from work, fly back to California? Monitor her vitamins? Or—no, I've got it—drag her out from L.A. and move her in with you?

EMILY: *(cornered)* She deserves better.

GENE: Well, she's not going to get it!

(A beat.)

And neither am I.

(A beat.)

You think because *you're* young enough to have choices—because, if you want to, you can change boyfriends with the seasons, or move to Seattle tomorrow. Or you can decide you've done your bit for that charity outfit, now you want to switch careers, maybe make some real money. Or you want to work for yourself, start a catering business or some damn thing, make a few other changes you think for the better. But you live long enough, sweetheart, you go past the point where you can make those kinds of changes. And all that's left for you is to keep things going. Or try to.

EMILY: That's all that's left? Maintaining?

GENE: What do you think I've been doing with your mom? Sometimes coming home to scrape her up off the floor. Once in a while I get a call, from Noli or whoever—drop everything and run to the hospital. Stand by her bedside, look in her eyes and know that I'm not who she really wishes was there. Even after all this time. And only now and then do I see a little of what I thought I was marrying. You call what I do cheating. Jesus, what do you call what she's done? Who do you think left who? You worry about my passing the clap onto her. Last I heard, there are certain conditions for doing so, and those conditions haven't been a part of our life together for years. Or do you imagine there's much of anything left for me to share a bed with? But no, go ahead, kiddo, you make that call and punish me good. Get me tossed out of paradise. And once you've had that self-righteous thrill, put on your cap and figure out what you're gonna do next. Cuz if you think she can hack it by herself— Odds are next trip you'd make back wouldn't be for Christmas, but for a funeral.

As Is

BY WILLIAM M. HOFFMAN

The play was written when AIDS was first devastating the gay community in the 1980s. It takes place in New York City. The setting for the scene is the living room of Saul's "fashionable loft space." Saul has asked his former lover Rich to return to the apartment ostensibly to divide up their belongings. Rich moved out six months ago and has a new lover. But Saul's real agenda is to find a way to get Rich to return to him. He still loves Rich and is terrified by the plague that is destroying the lives of so many friends. ("K.S." in the speech refers to Kaposi's Sarcoma, cancerous skin lesions that are a symptom of AIDS.)

Saul's desperation makes him sarcastic and self-pitying, both of which only alienate Rich even more. Rich has recently had a book of his short stories published (Saul did the photograph for the cover) and his finances have improved; earlier in the scene he gave Saul a check to repay money he owed him. Eventually, Rich looses patience with Saul's mockery of him and heads for the door, telling Saul he can keep everything in the apartment. Saul tries to keep him from going.

....

SAUL: Don't go. Please. (*RICH sits. Long pause.*) I visited Teddy today at St. Vincent's. It's very depressing . . . He's lying there in bed, out of it. He's been out of it since the time we saw him. He's not in any pain, snorting his imaginary cocaine, doing his poppers.

Sometimes he's washing his mother's floor, and he's speaking to her in Spanish. Sometimes he's having sex. You can see him having sex right in front of you. He doesn't even know you're there. *(Pause. Both men look down at their feet.)* Jimmy died, as you must have heard. I went out to San Francisco to be with him the last few weeks. You must have heard that, too. He was in a coma for a month. Everybody wanted to pull the plug, but they were afraid of legal complications. I held his hand. He couldn't talk, but I could see his eyelids flutter. I swear he knew I was with him. *(pause)* Harry has K.S., and Matt has trouble breathing. He went for tests today . . . I haven't slept well for weeks. Every morning I examine my body for swellings, marks. I'm terrified of every pimple, every rash, even though I've tested negative. If I cough I think of Teddy. I wish he would die. He *is* dead. He might as well be. Why can't he die? I feel the disease closing in on me. All my activities are life and death. Keep up my Blue Cross. Up my reps. Eat my vegetables.

Sometimes I'm so scared I go back on my resolutions: I drink too much, and I smoke a joint, and I find myself at the bars and clubs, where I stand around and watch. They remind me of accounts of Europe during the Black Plague: groping in the dark, dancing till you drop. The New Wave is the corpse look. I'm very frightened and I miss you. Say something, damn it.

Dylan

BY SIDNEY MICHAELS

ACT II

Dylan Thomas, the great Welsh poet, has returned to New York after giving poetry readings all over the United States. He has not
been feeling well, which, given his drinking, smoking, and dissolute
life style, doesn't surprise his doctor. Dylan was persuaded to make
the appointment by Meg Stuart, a woman with whom he has been
having an extramarital affair.

···

*(A spot on DYLAN alone that widens gradually to reveal him in a doc-
tor's office.)*

DYLAN: I'm me. I smoke too much. I drink too much. I never
like to go to bed. But when I go to bed, I never like to have to get up!
I sleep with women. I'm not much on men. Necrophilism—that's
with dead bodies—leaves me cold. I never watch the clock and it
doesn't pay much attention to me. I write poems and I read 'em out
loud. I lie, I cry, I laugh, I cheat, I steal when I can. I must have an
iron constitution as I've been abusing it for years to an extent
which'd kill a good horse in a matter of hours. I love people, rich
and poor people, dumb as well as smart people, people who like poetry and people who never heard of poetry. I'm life's most devoted,

most passionate, most shameless lover. I must be. And I like a good party and a good time and applause and lots of pats on my back and pots and hats full of jack which I then like to spend without stinting. Comforts make me comfortable; nails in my shoe, an ache in my tooth and grit in my eye do not. I have lived in a time when men have turned Jews into soap. I've been, I must tell you, ever since those days, a wee bit confused about the godly nature of the human creature. But I'm not as confused as anyone I ever met or heard of. Because I am me. And I know me. I've sung a few songs in thirty-nine years just for the pleasure of singing, but now I have come to a point in my life when I think I have something to say. I think it's something about having the guts to thumb your nose at the social shears that clip the wings of the human heart in our mushrooming, complex, cancerous age. I'm hot for fireworks in the dull of night. I want the factual, killing world should go back to fancy kissing for its livelihood. I'm about to write an opera with Stravinsky. A play on my own, my first, called *Under Milk Wood*. And I've been offered to play the lead in a play on Broadway. Things are looking up. But I'm spitting a lot of blood and blacking out more often than I'm used to, and I think I had a touch of the d.t.'s this past week as I've started seeing little things that aren't there—mice, for example. Miss Meg Stuart, my friend, suggested that I come to see you, Doctor, as it's entirely possible and not a little ironic, now that things are finally looking up—*(long pause)* that I'm dying.

Life During Wartime

BY KEITH REDDIN

ACT 2

Tommy, a young security systems salesman, made his first sale to Gale, a divorced mother of a teenage son. Gale is older than he is, but that doesn't keep them from falling deeply in love and planning to marry. After Tommy makes a few good sales, his boss tells him about the company's sideline: robbing the homes in which they've installed security systems. The boss offers Tommy a piece of the action and he replies that he needs some time to think about it. A short while later, Tommy learns that Gale and her son have been murdered as they walked in on a burglary in their home. In the next scene, Tommy is in a bar talking to Richie, a total stranger.

....

TOMMY: This one time, I brought over this bottle of champagne, we were celebrating . . . I don't know, I'd made two or three sales in a row and I was feeling hot, like I could do anything and we sat at the kitchen table, in her kitchen and we drank this champagne and . . . we drank it pretty fast it was so cold and it was good champagne, it was a bottle of really good champagne and we drank it fast and we got drunk and we were laughing, laughing at anything either of us said, and I was sort of sliding out of my chair and then I said the floor looks really good, why don't I just lie on the floor and I did,

I was lying on the kitchen tiles and they were cold and I said Gale join me on the kitchen floor and she did and we were both so drunk and laughing and the floor was sort of spinning as we lay on it, like we were lying in this boat on the waves and we lay on the floor and looked up at the ceiling of the kitchen and we held each other and I loved her so much and I said that, I said I love you so much and I wanted to stay on the kitchen floor for the rest of my life, holding her, holding this beautiful woman that I loved, but of course you can't. You can't lie on the tile for too long, because, . . . I'm sorry I forgot your name . . .

Cyrano de Bergerac

BY EDMOND ROSTAND,
TRANSLATED BY BRIAN HOOKER

ACT II

The year is 1640 and Cyrano de Bergerac—soldier, swordsman, and poet—has made powerful enemies in Paris. Because he shows no respect to the nobility, his life is in danger and he can't get his poetry published or his plays produced. He secretly loves his cousin Roxanne, but because he is ugly, with an uncommonly large nose, he can't believe that she could love him.

In this scene he is in "The Bakery of the Poets," a pastry shop where poets gather to share their writing. Earlier, he met Roxanne there and was devastated by her revelation that she loves a young cadet who has been assigned to Cyrano's military troop. Then a crowd gathered to celebrate Cyrano's swordsmanship (he defeated a slew of swordsmen who were waiting to ambush a man whom he had befriended). But Cyrano was rude to the nobles who came and tried to ingratiate themselves to him. After the nobles stormed out, Cyrano's close friend, Le Bret, upbraids him for undermining all his opportunities for success. Cyrano replies:

··

CYRANO: What would you have me do?
Seek for the patronage of some great man,
And like a creeping vine on a tall tree

Crawl upward, where I cannot stand alone?
No thank you! Dedicate, as others do,
Poems to pawnbrokers? Be a buffoon
In the vile hope of teasing out a smile
On some cold face? No thank you! Eat a toad
For breakfast every morning? Make my knees
Callous, and cultivate a supple spine,—
Wear out my belly grovelling in the dust?
No thank you! Scratch the back of any swine
That roots up gold for me? Tickle the horns
Of Mammon with my left hand, while my right
Too proud to know his partner's business,
Takes in the fee? No thank you! Use the fire
God gave me to burn incense all day long
Under the nose of wood and stone? No thank you!
Shall I go leaping into ladies' laps
And licking fingers?—or—to change the form—
Navigating with madrigals for oars,
My sails full of the sighs of dowagers?
No thank you! Publish verses at my own
Expense? No thank you! Be the patron saint
Of a small group of literary souls
Who dine together every Tuesday? No
I thank you! Shall I labor night and day
To build a reputation on one song,
And never write another? Shall I find
True genius only among Geniuses,
Palpitate over little paragraphs,
And struggle to insinuate my name
In the columns of the *Mercury*?
No thank you! Calculate, scheme, be afraid,
Love more to make a visit than a poem,
Seek introductions, favors, influences?—
No thank you! No, I thank you! And again
I thank you!—But . . .

> To sing, to laugh, to dream,

To walk in my own way and be alone,
Free, with an eye to see things as they are,
A voice that means manhood—to cock my hat
Where I choose—At a word, a *Yes*, a *No*,
To fight—or write. To travel any road
Under the sun, under the stars, nor doubt
If fame or fortune lie beyond the bourne—
Never to make a line I have not heard
In my own heart; yet, with all modesty
To say: "My soul, be satisfied with flowers,
With fruit, with weeds even; but gather them
In the one garden you may call your own."
So, when I win some triumph, by some chance,
Render no share to Caesar—in a word,
I am too proud to be a parasite,
And if my nature wants the germ that grows
Towering to heaven like the mountain pine,
Or like the oak, sheltering multitudes—
I stand, not high it may be—but alone!

Dinner with Friends

BY DONALD MARGULIES

ACT I, SCENE 3

Tom is leaving Beth after twelve years of marriage (and two children) and doesn't want her to tell their closest friends Gabe and Karen without him being present. Tonight, however, he learned from Beth that she spilled the beans during a dinner party at Gabe and Karen's home (Tom was supposed to be there but decided instead to visit his new girlfriend in Washington—but ended up returning home because his flight was cancelled due to an unexpected snowstorm).

After a raging argument with Beth (culminating in ferocious love making), Tom rushes over to Gabe and Karen's home to explain that he is not a cad and has good reasons for ending his marriage. Karen is unpersuaded and goes to bed, leaving Tom alone with Gabe. Gabe asks him if there have been other women in the past.

To use as a monologue, leave out Gabe's line.

....

TOM: No, Gabe, there were no other women. There *were* opportunities, though. I mean, when you're out of town as much as I am . . . You're lonely, you're far from home, it doesn't seem like you're living in real time. I'd be in a hotel bar and strike up a conversation with a female colleague, or some divorcée with big hair, and I'd make them laugh and they'd look pretty and I'd feel competent again, you know?, and think: Gee, maybe I *am* still clever and attractive after all. There'd be that electricity in the air, that kind of buzz I hadn't felt since college, remember?, when a single move, any move at all, and there'd be sex? But I'd get scared and say good night and go back to my room and call Beth out of guilt, or hope, and get some shit about something I neglected to do or did badly. Well, by the time I met Nancy—she made me feel good from the first time I talked to her on the phone. I hadn't even laid eyes on her yet—she booked all my travel.

GABE: Uh-huh.

TOM: She had this great laugh and this flirty sense of humor, and she said, "We've been talking for weeks, I want to meet you already!" And I began to think, Why the hell not? What am I saving myself for? This hypercritical woman waiting for me back home? Who looks at me with withering disappointment. All the time. This accusatory, How-could-you-be-so-thoughtless look. So, on one hand, there's this *delightful* woman who makes me feel worthwhile and there's this *other* woman, my *wife*, who makes me feel like shit. Who would *you* choose?

Flyovers

BY JEFFREY SWEET

SCENE 1

Oliver has returned to the small town of his youth for his high school's twenty-fifth-year reunion. He has accepted the invitation of Ted, a former classmate, to have drinks at his home. In high school Oliver was a studious nerd who got picked on and Ted was the meanest of his many tormentors. Now Oliver lives in New York and is a well-known TV film critic who also interviews movie stars. Ted, though, hasn't done so well. He remained in the town and is now unemployed because the plant he worked in closed. The two men are chatting on Ted's patio and Oliver tells him that one of their classmates, Renee Rowley, has become a successful businesswoman in New York as the owner of four strip clubs. Ted expresses bitterness about how much better others have done than he, and then launches into a diatribe against the way movie stars live their lives.

To use as a monologue leave out Oliver's lines and begin with Ted's line—"You like Bruce Willis?"—then skip to the speech that begins "I don't understand him."

....

TED: Sure. I see that. You like Bruce Willis?
OLIVER: He's done some good work.

TED: You ever meet him?

OLIVER: Did an interview once.

TED: I don't understand him. I mean, here he is married to Demi Moore. Between them, they have all the money in the world. And he still lets her take her clothes off so everyone can see. You tell me how that's different from Lorrie Axelrod, this guy I used to work with at the plant, carries a picture of his wife in his wallet. Lying naked on the pool table in his rec room. "Like to see what I got?" This expression on her face of, "Take the goddamn picture already, will you?" And he pulls this out, says, "This is mine. You can look, but you can't touch. *I'm* the only one gets to touch." Like I would want to, you know? You see her in the supermarket, trying to decide which brand of spaghetti sauce to buy. I have to keep myself from saying, "Lady, I've seen your bush."

OLIVER: Hmmmm.

TED: So how is he different from Bruce Willis? He goes to a premiere of his wife's latest movie. All these stars around them— Danny DeVito, Sharon Stone, Denzel Washington—the media, sitting there in a crowded theatre, and there's his wife, there's Demi—forty feet high. Some actor putting his hands all over her. End of the movie, lights come up, Bruce gives Demi a kiss, says, "Good work, honey."

OLIVER: Well, he's done it, too. Nude scenes.

TED: I think they do it *to* piss us off. Like Lorrie Axelrod. "You can look, but you can't touch." If you're a guy on the street in a raincoat and you flash, you get arrested. If you do it at that strip club of Renee's, you're this pathetic thing one step up from a hooker. But if you get paid seven million dollars and wave your stuff around, you can pretend you're an artist. And people wonder what's wrong with this country. Another?

Stray Cats

BY WARREN LEIGHT

This is one of a series of nine monologues by what the author calls "nine stray cats," guys who aren't quite fitting in, or who have been knocked about, or who can't find their way home. This one is called "An LA Agent Talks About Love."

....

(He's youthful, tanned and treadmilled between 25 and 50. He stands, Armani suited, at the bar of a subdued-lighting, see-and-be ignored LA grill. His cell phone, date book, Porsche sunglasses, and mini-tape recorder are within reach, like appetizers. He speaks to an unseen client.)

You want to wait at the bar? 'Cause if you don't want to wait at the bar, I'll go. Do you want to go? "No"? You're right. We're here. Whatever. *(He spots someone. Covers up his feelings, a bit. Still, has to note:)*

See that girl over there—the blonde? With the two producers? *(He points to a high-maintenance babe—designer clothes, jewelry, make-up, hair in place.)*

Nice. Right? *(waits for acknowledgment)*

I fucked her. *(He pauses for respect.)*

No, I did. I fucked her—and let me tell you, that type is cold. Cold as ice. They use you. She's done, you're finished. If you treat them nice, you're dead. Treat'm like *dirt*. Beautiful woman—like that, you can't let them know you think they're beautiful. They'll play you for all you're worth. I meet someone like that, bottom line, I play it cool. First time I met her—I ignored her. Hey, I meet women like you a bundle times a day. That's what they have to think. She checks me out. Finds out who I am, finds out what agency I'm with. I can help her career. Now a couple of weeks go by—there's a party coming up—small thing. I make sure she's invited. She comes to the party—looks great. *(picks up his handheld recorder, speaks into it)*

Suzie, make sure Hillary, the actress who came in last week, from the gym, gets an invite to Quentin's screening. *(stops, then remembers to add:)*

The *early* one. *(places the recorder back on the table)*

Where was I—the *party*. She looks great. Again, I pretend not to notice her. At the end of the evening—I go over, talk to her. Conversation gets going and then—I just stop. Right in the middle. Don't excuse myself. Nothing. Just turn and walk away, boom, something came up. I leave the party. I don't say good-bye. Two weeks go by. I see her at the Ivy. I tell her to give me a call sometime. Next day—she calls. Do I want to meet her for a drink? I say, "Maybe," call me later. Around five she calls. I tell her I'm busy with work. If she wants, she can go to The Formosa. Maybe I'll be there in an hour. 6:30 she calls me.

"I'm here."

"So—I'm still at work—I still have things to do—if you don't want to wait—don't bother."

"I'll wait."

"Maybe I'll see you in half an hour." An hour goes by. She calls again. Angry. I don't apologize.

"I'm still here. Will you be here soon?"

"Maybe."

Forty-five minutes later I walk in. She's pissed as hell. It's not my problem. I buy a drink. Take her back to her place—fuck her brains out. The way I do it—I force myself on her. We get inside her room, I put her on the couch and just start fucking her. Drives her wild.

She wants it like that. They all want to be forced—not raped. Nobody wants to be raped. I don't think anybody wants to be raped. But I force her, and she goes wild. You know what I mean—you ever do that? *(waits for acknowledgment)* They love it. Treat them like dirt. I fucked her brains out—then I left. Didn't spend the night. *Don't ever spend the night.* This is very important. Then I make my mistake—the next morning, I call her.

"Hi, this is Richie." Boom. She goes cold. She knows I want her—so she turns to ice. I blew it. Never saw her again. *(Feels this loss. Then:)* Now that girl over there—the real blonde. Same type—expensive. She's got a man in Florida who keeps her. Comes in once and a while. Otherwise, she's on her own. I did the same thing with her. Met her, ignored her, treated her like dirt. Took her to dinner. Fucked her brains out. Only this time, I knew better. The next day, I didn't call her. Never called her. Never spoke to her again. *(Finishes his Scotch. And/or puts out his cigarette.)* I got her right where I want her.

Fresh Horses

BY LARRY KETRON

ACT I

Sproles, who is described as a "fifth year senior" in college, was brought to Larkin's "shack" by their mutual friend Tipton. Larkin, who has dropped out of college to figure out what he wants to do with his life, is living in an abandoned railroad maintenance station in the rural South. Sproles is about to give Larkin some upsetting information about his girlfriend Jewel: she has lied about her age—she is sixteen, not nineteen—and she is married to a another man. Sproles is looking for a way to help Larkin keep the bad news he is about to receive in "perspective."

To use as a monologue omit Larkin's lines.

....

SPROLES: Because I know there's *other* issues. Look, I'm not stupid. I know there's smaller but still important questions. Take some carpenter. He learns to drive a nail, he learns what so-and-so joint is, he builds a house. He's moving along in the scheme of things. But he's got this wife, she's smoochin the mailman. And his son's in some school somewhere, retarded. Those problems are important to this half-ass carpenter. Just like you have problems important to you. I'd just like to see you keep them in perspective.

LARKIN: Well I'll see what I can do.

SPROLES: Now wait a minute, don't get defensive.

LARKIN: I'm not getting defensive.

SPROLES: I learned perspective early. I'll tell you how. When I was a boy we lived this, ah, real sloppy little white frame house, you weren't proud of it. You weren't proud of it even a little bit. And we used to pile in the car, my family, and go driving around to the ritzy parts of town to see the new homes and shit like these rich-ass, split-level, three-car garage, long, low, motherfucking or Colonial houses. Where all these rich-ass people bedded down after they prob'ly did something like play ping-pong in their den. And maybe somebody had a teen-age son and he had a basketball court out back that was all paved and level and lit up at night. And me and the whole family, we view this, these places and activities of the well-to-do. At first you're sort of thrilled by it all, then you find yourself in the throes of depression by it. So before we drove home, well, we didn't drive directly home. No. My dad would drive us around to the poorest part of the town and show us the shitiest shacks and dumps he could find. Where the trash lived. Where they lived in these terrible dumps and conditions. This was to bring us down to earth. This was to bring us down from fantasy land. Now we pull into our own dirt driveway, we don't feel, we feel pretty good. *Pretty* good. No, not great. But better than if we only had those rich-titted beautiful places in our minds' eyes.